CW01082109

HỒ CHÍ MINH
SELECTED WRITINGS
(1920 — 1969)

HỒ CHÍ MINH
SELECTED WRITINGS
1920 — 1969

University Press of the Pacific
Honolulu, Hawaii

Ho Chí Minh
Selected Writings
1920-1969

by Ho Chí Minh

ISBN 0-89875-337-6

Reprinted from the 1973 edition

University Press of the Pacific
Honolulu, Hawaii
http://www.universitypressofthepacific.com

This collection comprises the most important speeches and writings of President Ho Chi Minh for the period extending from 1920 to 1969. They are precious landmarks which make it possible to understand the Vietnamese revolution in its historical evolution as well as in its various aspects.

The reader should be warned, however, that our translation is but a very inadequate rendition of the lively, crisp, concise, often humour-tinged, in short the inimitable style of President Ho Chi Minh, who is one of the best writers and poets of Viet Nam.

Let the reader try to fill this gap with the help of his own imagination.

FOREIGN LANGUAGES PUBLISHING HOUSE

HANOI. 1973

Kmai song . . . .

" It was this story about this guy who likes this girl.
It always is this story [in song] about the guy
who likes this girl ~ but he thinks he's too
poor, too dirty and the girl's family won't accept
him and he has to be happy only with his dreaming
about this woman and that hopefully, in his
next life they can be together" Zac Holtzman
                    Dengue Fever "Sleepwalking through
                                        the Mekong".

CONTENTS

PART ONE (1920 – 1945)

PART TWO (1945 – 1954)

PART ONE

(1920 – 1945)

SPEECH AT THE TOURS CONGRESS*[1]

(December 1920)

Chairman : "Comrade Indochinese Delegate, you have the floor." (Applause.)

Indochinese Delegate **: "Today, instead of contributing, together with you, to world revolution as I should wish, I come here with deep sadness and profound grief, as a Socialist, to protest against the abhorrent crimes committed in my native land. (Very good!).

"You all know that French capitalism entered Indochina half a century ago. It conquered our country at bayonet point and in the name of capitalism. Since then we have not only been oppressed and exploited shamelessly, but also tortured and poisoned pitilessly. (I would stress this fact that we have been poisoned, with opium, alcohol, etc.) I cannot, in but a few minutes, reveal all the atrocities perpetrated by the predatory capitalists in Indochina. Prisons outnumber schools and are always overcrowded with detainees. Any native suspected of having socialist ideas is arrested and sometimes put to death without trial. So goes justice in Indochina for in that country there is one law for the Annamese and another for the Europeans or those holding European citizenship. The former do not enjoy the same safeguards as the latter. We have neither freedom of the press, freedom of speech,

* Excerpt from the shorthand transcript of the Congress. (Ed.)
** Nguyen Ai Quoc, later President Ho Chi Minh. (Ed.)

freedom of assembly, nor freedom of association. We have
no right to emigrate or travel abroad as tourists. We live
in utter ignorance because we have no right to study. In
Indochina the colonialists do all they can to poison us
with opium and besot us with alcohol. Thousands of
Annamese have been led to a slow death and thousands
of others massacred to protect interests that are not
theirs.

"Comrades, such is the treatment inflicted upon more
than twenty million Annamese, that is more than half
the population of France. And yet they are said to be
under French protection *(applause)*! The Socialist Party
must act effectively in favour of the oppressed natives."
(Cheers.)

Jean Longuet [2] : "I have spoken in favour of the
natives !"

Indochinese Delegate : "Right from the beginning of
my speech I have imposed the dictatorship of silence...
(Laughter.) The Party must carry out propaganda for
socialism in all colonial countries. We shall see in the
Socialist Party's joining the Third International the promise that from now on it will attach to the colonial
questions the importance they deserve. We are very glad
to learn that a Standing Delegation has been appointed
for North Africa and we should be very happy if in the
near future the Party sends one of its members to Indochina to study on the spot the relevant questions and
what should be done about them."

A delegate : "With Comrade Enver Pasha ?"

Indochinese Delegate : "Silence, the Parliamentarians !"
(Applause.)

Chairman : "Now all delegates must keep silent,
including the non-Parliamentarians !"

Indochinese Delegate : "In the name of the whole of mankind, in the name of all Socialists, both those of the left and those of the right, we say to you : 'Comrades save us !' " *(Applause.)*

Chairman : "Through the applause which greeted him, the Indochinese Delegate can realize that the entire Socialist Party side with him to oppose the crimes of the bourgeoisie."

Communism is traditionally anti - bourgeois because of its power to corrupt society. But why they do this hasn't been analysed properly. It isn't really because of the power over people's lives & the running of a country, but much more because of the way it is INFILTRATED by the occult & international Secretiveness. In this way the bourgeois are as much a victim as those they organise. It is the front line in any society and the most human.

INDOCHINA*

It is wrong to say that this country, inhabited by more than 20 million exploited people, is now ripe for revolution ; but even wronger. to say that it doesn't want a revolution and is satisfied with the regime, as claim our masters. The truth is that the Indochinese people have no means of education and action. They can have neither press, meetings, associations, nor travels. It is a veritable crime for one of them to be found in possession of foreign newspapers or periodicals with somewhat advanced opinions, or a French working-class publication. Alcohol and opium, as well as the subsidized colonial press in the pay of the authorities, complete the government's obscurantist undertaking. The guillotine and prisons do the rest.

Morally and physically poisoned, gagged and penned up, this human herd may be thought to be forever destined to the altar of the capitalist god, to have stopped living and thinking, to be of no use in social transformation. Not at all! *The Indochinese are not dead, they still live, they will live forever.* Systematic poisoning by colonial capitalism has not stamped out their vitality, even less their consciousness. The wind from working-class Russia, revolutionary China or militant India has cured them of intoxication. It is true that they don't get educated by books or speeches, but in another fashion.

---

* Extract from an article by Nguyen Ai Quoc, published in the Soviet review *The Communist*, № 14-1921. *(Ed.)*

Suffering, destitution and brutal oppression are their only educators, and while the Socialists are remiss about their education, the colonial and native (mandarin) bourgeoisie are paying it affectionate attention. The Indochinese are making tremendous progress and, occasion permitting, will show themselves to be worthy of their masters. Under a mask of passivity, they hide something that is seething, rumbling and will, when the time comes, explode formidably. It is up to the elite to hasten the coming of that moment. The tyranny of capitalism has prepared the ground : the only thing for socialism to do is to sow the seeds of emancipation.

MANIFESTO OF THE "INTERCOLONIAL UNION"³, THE ORGANIZATION OF THE NATIVES IN ALL COLONIES*

Brothers in all colonies! In 1914, facing a terrible catastrophe, the ruling authorities turned to you and called on you to contribute by your sacrifices to the salvation of a fatherland which was said to be yours although until then it had manifested itself to you only through domination.

To persuade you to do so, they did not fail to dangle before your eyes all the advantages that your collaboration would bring you. But now that the storm is over, you remain as you were, living under the regime reserved for the natives with its special courts, deprived of all the rights that make for human dignity such as freedom of association and assembly, freedom of the press, freedom of movement, even within your own countries. So much for the political side.

In the economic field, you remain subject to the unpopular and heavy poll-tax and corvées, to the salt-tax, to poisoning through forced consumption of alcohol and opium as in Indochina, or to night-watch duty as in Algeria to look after the properties of colonial sharks.

* Excerpt from *French Colonization on Trial*, written by Nguyen Ai Quoc sometime in 1921-1925. *(Ed)*

For equal work you are less paid than your European fellow-workers. In a word, you were promised the moon and the stars. Now you see that all was but deception.

What is to be done for your liberation ?

Applying Karl Marx's formula, we tell you that your emancipation can only come from your own efforts.

It is to help you in this task that the *Intercolonial Union* has been founded.

With the assistance of French comrades who sympathize with our cause, it seeks to rally all the native people of the colonies now living in France.

Means of action : In pursuance of this just work, the Intercolonial Union has decided to bring the question before public opinion by means of the press and by word of mouth (talks, meetings, use of the rostrums of deliberative assemblies through our elected friends) and all other available means.

Oppressed brothers in the metropolitan country ! Deceived by your bourgeoisie, you have served as tools for their conquest of our countries ; practising the same machiavellian policy, *your bourgeoisie now plan to make use of us to repress all your efforts for self-liberation.*

In face of capitalism and imperialism our interests are the same. Comrades, bear in mind Karl Marx's appeal :

"Workers of the world, unite !"

The Intercolonial Union

THE ANTI-FRENCH RESISTANCE*

Focal points

When the Great War ended the Vietnamese people like other peoples were deceived by Wilson's "generous" declarations on the right of peoples to self-determination.[4] A group of Vietnamese, which included myself, sent the following demands to the French Parliament and to all delegations to the Versailles Conference.

CLAIMS OF THE VIETNAMESE PEOPLE

Ever since the victory of the Allies, all the subjected peoples have entertained high hopes about an era of right and justice which should follow the formal and solemn pledges taken before the whole world by the various powers of the Entente in the struggle of Civilization against Barbarism.

While waiting for the realization of the principle of Nationalities through the effective recognition of the sacred right of the peoples to self-determination, the people of the former Empire of Annam, now French Indochina, proposed to the governments of the Entente in general and the French government in particular the following demands :

1. Amnesty for all Vietnamese political detainees ;

2. Reform of the Indochinese judicial system by giving the Vietnamese the same judicial safeguards as to the Europeans and completely and definitively abolishing the

---

* Excerpt from an article written by Nguyen Ai Quoc in the years 1921-1926. *(Ed.)*

special tribunals which are instruments of terror and oppression against the most honest part of the Vietnamese people ;

3. Freedom of the press and freedom of opinion ;

4. Freedom of association and freedom of assembly ;

5. Freedom to emigrate and travel abroad ;

6. Freedom of teaching and creation in all provinces of technical and vocational schools for natives ;

7. Replacement of the regime of decrees by that of laws ;

8. Presence in the French Parliament of a permanent delegation elected by the natives to keep it informed of their aspirations !

. . .

To these demands we added a tribute to the peoples and to feelings of humanity.

However, after a time of waiting and study, we realized that the "Wilson doctrine" was but a big fraud. The liberation of the proletariat is the necessary condition for national liberation. Both these liberations can only come from Communism and world revolution.

REPORT ON THE NATIONAL AND COLONIAL QUESTIONS AT THE FIFTH CONGRESS OF THE COMMUNIST INTERNATIONAL*[5]

Inc. dealing with the press isssue

Comrades, I only wish to supplement Comrade Manuilsky's[6] criticism of our policy on the colonial question. But before entering upon that subject, I deem it necessary to supply some figures which will help us to see its importance even more clearly.

Countries	METROPOLITAN COUNTRIES		COLONIES	
	Area (sq. km)	Population	Area (sq. km)	Population
Great Britain	151,000	45,500,000	34,910,000	403,600,000
France	536,000	39,000;000	10,250,000	55,600,000
The United States	9,420,000	100,000,000	1,850,000	12,000,000
Spain	504,500	20,700,000	371,600	853,000
Italy	286,600	38,500,000	1,460,000	1,623,000
Japan	418,000	57,070,000	288,000	21,249,000
Belgium	29,500	7,642,000	2,400,000	8,500,000
Portugal	92,000	5,545,000	2,062,000	8,738,000
Holland	83,000	6,700,000	2,046,000	48,030,000

Thus, nine countries with an aggregate population of 320,657,000 and a total area of 11,407,600 square kilometres, are exploiting colonies with a total population of

* Excerpt from the shorthand transcript of the Congress (held from June 17 to July 8, 1924). (Ed.)

560,193,000 and covering areas adding up to 55,637,000 square kilometres. The total area of the colonies is five times that of the metropolitan countries, whose total population amounts to less than three-fifths that of the colonies.

These figures are even more striking if the biggest imperialist countries are taken separately. The British colonies taken as a whole are eight and a half times more populous and about 252 times bigger than Great Britain. France occupies an area 19 times bigger than her own. The population of the French colonies exceeds that of France by 16,600,000.

Thus, it is not an exaggeration to say that so long as the French and British Communist Parties do not apply a really active policy with regard to the colonies, and do not come into contact with the colonial peoples, their vast programmes will remain ineffective, and this, because they go counter to Leninism. Let me explain what I mean. In his speech on Lenin and the national question Comrade Stalin said that the reformists and the leaders of the Second International dared not put the white and the coloured people on the same footing, that Lenin had rejected that inequality and smashed the obstacle separating the civilized slaves of imperialism from the uncivilized ones.

According to Lenin, the victory of the revolution in Western Europe depends on its close contact with the national-liberation movement against imperialism in the colonies and dependent countries; the national question, as Lenin taught us, forms a part of the general problem of proletarian revolution and proletarian dictatorship.

Later, Comrade Stalin condemned the counter-revolutionary viewpoint which held that the European proletariat could achieve success without a direct alliance with the liberation movement in the colonies.

However, if we base our theoretical examination on facts, we are entitled to say that our major proletarian parties, except the Russian Party, still hold to the above-mentioned viewpoint because they are doing nothing in this matter.

What have the bourgeoisie in the colonialist countries done in order to keep the colonial masses under their oppressive rule ? Everything. Besides using all the means given them by their State administrative machine, they have carried out an intense propaganda. They have crammed the heads of the people of the metropolitan countries with colonialist ideas through speeches, films, newspapers, exhibitions — to mention only the more important means — while dangling before their eyes pictures of the easy, honourable and rich life which is said to await them in the colonies.

As for our Communist Parties in Great Britain, Holland, Belgium and other countries whose bourgeoisie have invaded the colonies, what have they done ? What have they done since the day they assimilated Lenin's theses in order to educate the proletariat of their countries in the spirit of genuine proletarian internationalism and close contact with the toiling masses in the colonies ? What our Parties have done in this domain amounts to almost nothing. As for me, born in a French colony and a member of the French Communist Party, I am sorry to say that our Party has done very little for the colonies.

It is the task of the Communist press to acquaint our militants with colonial questions, to awaken the toiling masses in the colonies and win them over to the cause of Communism, but what have we done in this respect ? Nothing at all.

If we compare the space devoted to colonial questions by such bourgeois newspapers as *Le Temps*, *Le Figaro*, *l'Oeuvre* or by those of other tendencies such as *Le Populaire* or *La Liberté* with that reserved for the same questions in *l'Humanité,* the central organ of our Party, we must say that this comparison is not to our advantage.

The Ministry of Colonies has worked out a plan for transforming many African regions into large private plantations, and turning the people of these regions into veritable slaves attached to the new owners' lands ; and yet our newspapers have remained wholly silent. In the French West African colonies, unprecedented measures have been carried out to force people into the army and yet our newspapers have not reacted. The colonialist authorities in Indochina have acted like slave traders, and sold Tonkinese people to plantation-owners on the Pacific islands ; they have extended the duration of the natives' military service from two to four years ; ceded the greater part of the colony's land to the sharks of financial capitalism ; and raised by a further 30 per cent taxes that already exceeded the natives' ability to pay. And this while the natives were being driven to bankruptcy and dying of hunger in the wake of floods. And yet, our newspapers have kept silent. No wonder the natives are following such liberal democratic organizations as the *Ligue des droits de l'homme* and other similar organizations which take care of them or pretend to take care of them.

If we go a bit further, we shall see incredible things, which suggest that our Party disregards all that concerns the colonies. For instance : l'*Humanité* did not publish the appeal made by the Peasants' International to the peoples of the colonies, sent to it by the Communist International for publication.

Prior to the Lyons conference[7] it published all the theses except that on the colonial question. L'*Humanité* carried many articles on the successes achieved by the manipulating of chosen i cars

Senegalese boxer Siki, but did not raise its voice when the dockers at Dakar port, Siki's fellow-workers, were arrested in the middle of their work, hauled onto lorries, taken to jail then to the barracks to be forcibly put into uniforms and turned into "guardians of civilization". The central organ of our Party daily informed its readers of the feats of the pilot Oisy, who flew from Paris to Indochina. But when the colonial administration pillaged the people of "noble Annam", robbed them of their lands in favour of French speculators, and sent out bombers to bring to reason the pitilessly despoiled natives, it did not find it necessary to inform its readers of these facts.

Comrades, the French bourgeoisie, through its press, is perfectly aware that the national and colonial questions cannot be separated from each other. But in my opinion, our Party has not thoroughly understood this. The lesson of the Ruhr, where colonial troops had been sent out to "quiet" the starving German workers and had encircled the suspected French regiments; the example of the Army of the Orient in which colonial forces were issued machine guns to "raise the morale" of French troops worn out by the hard and protracted war; the events which occurred in 1917 at places in France where Russian troops were stationed;[8] the lesson of the strike of agricultural workers in the Pyrenees in which colonial troops were forced to play the shameful part of black-legs; and finally the presence of 207,000 colonial troops in France itself — all these facts have not made our Party think and realize the necessity of laying down a clear and firm policy on colonial questions. The Party has missed many good opportunities for propaganda. The new leading organs of the Party have acknowledged its passivity in this matter. This is a good sign, because once the leaders of the Party have realized and recognized this weak point in the Party's policy, there is hope that the Party will do its utmost to rectify its errors. I firmly believe that this congress will be a turning point and will induce the Party to correct its past shortcomings. Although Comrade Manuilsky was quite right in his remarks on the elections in Algeria, I must say, to be more objective, that our Party has indeed missed a good opportunity here but has retrieved its error by nominating colonial candidates in the elections for the Seine department. This is not much but it will do for a beginning. I am very happy to see that our Party is again inspired by the best intentions and enthusiasm — something new for us — and that it needs only to translate all this into practical deeds to arrive at a correct policy on the colonial question.

What practical deeds? It is not enough, as has been done so far, to work out long theses and pass high-sounding resolutions which are, after the Congress, sent to museums. What we need are concrete measures. I propose the following ones:

1. To publish regular articles on colonial questions in *l'Humanité* (at least two columns each week);

2. To increase propaganda and recruit Party members among the natives of the colonial countries where the Communist International has set up branches;

3. To send comrades from the colonial countries to study at the Eastern Toilers' University in Moscow;

4. To come to an agreement with the *Confédération générale des travailleurs unitaire* (United General Confederation of Labour) [9] on the organization of toilers from colonial countries working in France;

5. To make it a duty for Party members to pay greater attention to colonial questions.

In my opinion, these proposals are logical ones, and if the Communist International and the delegates of our

Party approve them, our delegation to the next Congress will be able to say that the united front of the French people and the colonial peoples has become a reality.

Comrades, as disciples of Lenin, we must concentrate all our forces and energies on the colonial question as well as on all other questions in order to implement his precious teachings.

Comrade Douglas (an English delegate)...

Comrade Smeran...

Comrade Nguyen Ai Quoc :

The French colonies occupy an area of 10,241,510 square kilometres with 55,571,000 inhabitants and are scattered over all four continents. In spite of the differences in race, climate, custom, tradition and economic and social development, there are two common points which can lead to their unity in struggle :

1. The economic situation : In all the French colonies, industry and commerce are little developed and the majority of the population are engaged in agriculture. Ninety-five per cent of the people are peasants.

2. In all the colonies, the native peoples are unremittingly exploited by French imperialist capital.

I have not enough time to make a thorough analysis of the situation of the peasants in each colony. Therefore, I shall use only a few typical examples to give an idea of the peasants' life in the colonies.

I shall begin with my own country, Indochina, which naturally I know best.

During the French conquest, military operations drove the peasants away from their villages. When they returned they found their lands occupied by colonists who had followed in the wake of the occupying troops and

Catholicism

who had shared among themselves the land that the native peasants had cultivated for generations. Thus, our peasants were turned into serfs forced to cultivate their own lands for foreign masters.

Many of those unfortunate people who could not endure the harsh conditions imposed by the occupiers, left their lands and wandered about the country. They were called "pirates" and hunted down by the French. *occult strategy*

The lands robbed in this way were allotted to planters, who had only to say a word in order to get concessions of sometimes more than 20,000-25,000 hectares.

These planters not only occupied lands without any payment but also obtained all that was necessary to exploit them, including manpower. The administration sent prisoners to work for them without pay, or ordered the villages to supply them with manpower.

Besides this wolfish administration, one should mention the Church. The Catholic Mission alone occupied one quarter of the areas *under cultivation* in Cochinchina. To lay hands on those lands it used unimaginable methods : bribery, fraud and coercion. Here are a few examples. Availing itself of crop failures it gave the peasants loans, with their rice-fields as security. The interest rates being too high, the peasants were unable to pay off their debts and their mortgaged fields went to the Mission. Using all kinds of underhand methods, the Church succeeded in laying hands on secret documents that could harm the authorities, and used these to blackmail them into granting it all it wanted. It entered into partnership with big financiers for the exploitation of the plantations granted free to them and the lands stolen from the peasants. Its henchmen held high positions in the colonial government. It fleeced its flock no less ruthlessly than the planters did. Another of its tricks was to get poor people to reclaim waste land with promises that it would be allotted to them. But as soon as the crops were about to be harvested, the Mission claimed ownership of the land and drove out those who had toiled to make it productive. Robbed by their "protectors" (religious or lay), our peasants were not even left in peace to work on their remaining tiny plots of land. The land registry service falsified the results of the cadastral survey so as to make the peasants pay more taxes. These were made heavier every year. Recently, after handing over thousands of hectares of land belonging to Annamese highlanders to speculators, the authorities sent bombers to fly over these regions so that the victims dared not even think of rebelling.

If the despoiled peasants, ruined and driven away, were again able to reclaim virgin land, the administration would seize it once it was put under cultivation and would oblige them to buy it back at prices fixed by the authorities. Those unable to pay would be driven out pitilessly.

Last year, the country was devastated by floods; yet, taxes on rice-fields increased 30 per cent.

In addition to those iniquitous taxes that have ruined them, our peasants still have to bear numerous burdens : corvées, poll-tax, salt-tax, forced buying of government bonds, forced contribution to fund-raising campaigns, etc.

French capitalists in Algeria, Tunisia and Morocco have carried out the same policy of robbery and exploitation. All the good irrigated land was occupied by the colonists. The natives were driven away to areas at the foot of mountains or to arid spots. Financial companies, profiteers and high functionaries divided the land of these colonies among themselves.

In 1914, through direct and indirect operations, the banks in Algeria and Tunisia reaped profits amounting to 12 258,000 francs from a capital of 25 million francs.

The Bank of Morocco with a capital of 15,400,000 francs, made 1,753,000 francs' profit in 1921.

The Franco-Algerian Company has occupied 324 000 hectares of the best land in the colony.

The Algerian Company has occupied 100,000 hectares.

A private company has been granted 50,000 hectares of forest, while the Capzer Phosphate and Railway Company has occupied 50,000 hectares of land with rich deposits, and in addition has secured priority rights over 20,000 hectares of land in the neighbourhood.

A former French deputy has occupied 1,125 hectares of land with rich mineral deposits, valued at 10 million francs and producing a yearly income of four million francs. The natives, the real owners of these mines, receive annually only one *centime* (1/100 of a franc) per hectare.

French colonial policy has replaced collective ownership by private ownership. It has also abolished small holdings to the advantage of big plantations. It has robbed the colonial peasantry of more than 5 million hectares of their best land.

In 15 years, the peasants of Kabylia were dispossessed of 192,090 hectares.

From 1913 onwards, each year Moroccan peasants have been ousted from 12,500 hectares of land under cultivation. Since France won the war "fought for the sake of justice" that figure has risen to 14,540 hectares.

At present, in Morocco, 1,070 French people occupy 500 000 hectares of land.

Like their Annamese brothers, the peasants in Africa lead an unbearably hard life, subjected to continuous corvées and heavy taxation. Their misery and sufferings

are beyond description. Reduced to eating wild vegetables and tainted cereals they fall a prey to typhoid
fever and tuberculosis. Even in good harvest years,
peasants are seen rummaging in rubbish heaps and disput-
ing scraps of food with dogs. In lean years fields and
roads are strewn with corpses.

Peasants' life in West Africa and French Equatorial
Africa is still more horrible. These colonies are in the
hands of about 40 companies. They control everything :
land, natural resources and even the natives' lives ; the
latter lack even the right to work for themselves. They
are compelled to work for the companies, all the time,
and only for the companies. To force them to work for
nothing, incredible means of coercion are used by the
companies. All lands and fields are confiscated. Only
those who agree to do the farming required by the companies are allowed to have some tiny plots of land.
People are affected with all kinds of diseases through
malnutrition and the death rate, especially among the
children, is very high.

Another method is to hold old people, women and children
hostage. They are penned up in crowded huts, ill-treated,
beaten up, starved and sometimes even murdered. In
some localities the number of hostages equals that of
the workers, in order to discourage the latter from running away. The natives are not allowed to till their own
land before finishing work on the plantations. Hence the
frequent famines and epidemics in the colonies.

The few tribes who have fled to the forest to escape
the planters' exploitation, live like animals, feeding on
roots and leaves, and die from malaria and the unwhole-
some climate. Meanwhile the white masters are devastating their fields and villages. Here is an excerpt from an
officer's diary which gives a clear, concise and gruesome
description of the way the colonial peasants are repressed :

"Raid on Kolowan village.

"Raid on the Fan tribe at Cuno. Villages and orchards destroyed.

"Raid on the Bekamis. Village burnt down; 3,000 banana-trees cut down.

"Raid on Kua village. Village destroyed. Plantations razed.

"Raid on Alcun. All houses burnt down, all farms destroyed.

"Raid on Esamfami village. Village destroyed. All hamlets along the Bom river burnt down."

The same system of pillage, extermination and destruction prevails in the African regions under Italian, Spanish, British and Portuguese rule.

In the Belgian Congo, the population fell from 25 million in 1891 to 8.5 million by 1911. The Herero and Camard tribes in the former German colonies in Africa were completely exterminated: 80,000 were killed under German rule and 15,000 during "pacification" in 1914. The population of the French Congo was 20,000 in 1894. It was only 9,700 in 1911. In one region there were 10,000 inhabitants in 1910. Eight years later there remained only 1,080. In another region with 40,000 black inhabitants, 20,000 people were killed within two years, and in the following six months 6,000 more were killed or disabled.

Densely populated and prosperous regions along rivers were turned into deserts within a mere 15 years. Ravaged oases and villages were strewn with bleached bones.

The plight of the survivors was atrocious. The peasants were robbed of their tiny plots of land, the artisans lost their crafts, and the herdsmen their cattle. The Matabeles were cattle-breeders: before the arrival of the British, they had 200,000 head of cattle. Two years later only 40,900 were left. The Hereros had 90,000 head of cattle.

Within 12 years the German colonists had robbed them of half that number. Similar cases are numerous in all the black countries which have come into contact with the whites' civilization.

In conclusion, let me quote these words of the African writer René Maran, author of *Batuala*: "Equatorial Africa was a densely populated area, rich in rubber and dotted with orchards and farms full of poultry and goats. Within seven years everything was destroyed. Villages were in ruin, gardens and farms laid waste, poultry and goats killed. The people were exhausted by continuous hard work for which they got no pay. They had neither strength nor time left to till their own fields. Disease and famine caused the death rate to increase. And yet they are the descendants of strong and healthy tribes full of combativeness and stamina. Here civilization has disappeared."

To complete this tragic picture, let me add that French capitalism has never hesitated to drive whole regions to misery and famine if this proves of advantage to it. In many colonial countries, e.g., the Reunion Islands, Algeria, Madagascar, etc., cereals have been replaced by other crops required by French industry. These crops bring more profits to the planters. Hence a rising cost of living and chronic famine.

In all the French colonies popular anger has followed in the wake of misery and famine. The native peasants are ripe for insurrection. In many colonies, they have indeed risen up but their rebellions have all been drowned in blood. The reason for their present passivity is the lack of organization and leaders. The Communist International must help them to re-organize, supply them with leading cadres and show them the road to revolution and liberation.

LENIN AND THE COLONIAL PEOPLES*

Lenin laid the basis for a new and truly revolutionary era in the colonies.

He was the first to denounce resolutely all the prejudices which still persisted in the minds of many European and American revolutionaries. Everyone knows the theses of the Communist International on the colonial question.

The colonial question has been brought to the fore in all congresses of the Communist International, the Trade Union International and the Communist Youth International.

Lenin was the first to realize and assess the full importance of drawing the colonial peoples into the revolutionary movement. He was the first to point out that, without the participation of the colonial peoples, the socialist revolution could not come about.

He found the necessary methods for effective work in the colonial countries and stressed the need to turn to account the national revolutionary movement in these countries.

The colonial delegates to the various congresses of the Communist International will always remember the concern that Lenin, their leader and comrade, displayed for the colonial countries. He showed deep insight into even the most complex and purely local conditions of work.

* Published in the Soviet review *Krasnui*, № 2-1925. *(Ed.)*.

Everyone of us now has had time to convince himself of the correctness of Lenin's judgments and the value of his teachings. Lenin's skilful methods enabled him to stir up the least enlightened and most backward colonial peoples. Lenin's strategy on this question has been applied by Communist Parties all over the world, and has won over the best and most active elements in the colonies to the communist movement.

Lenin's solution of the very complex question of nationalities in Soviet Russia is an excellent propaganda weapon for the colonies.

In the history of the colonial peoples weighed down with sufferings and deprived of their rights, Lenin is the creator of a new life, a beacon which shows oppressed mankind the road to liberation.

Sadly however behind the international success of Lenin & his gathering of mass support, lie the forces of Baal who commandeer it for the purposes of mass sacrifice again. A good argument therefore, for the isolationist policies of small territories.

APPEAL MADE ON THE OCCASION OF THE FOUNDING OF THE INDOCHINESE COMMUNIST PARTY

(February 18, 1930)

Workers, peasants, soldiers, youth and school students!
Oppressed and exploited fellow-countrymen!
Sisters and brothers! Comrades!

Imperialist contradictions were the cause of the 1914-1918 World War. After this horrible slaughter, the world was divided into two camps: one is the revolutionary camp which includes the oppressed colonial peoples and the exploited working class throughout the world. Its vanguard is the Soviet Union. The other is the counter-revolutionary camp of international capitalism and imperialism, whose general staff is the League of Nations.

That war resulted in untold loss of life and property for the peoples. French imperialism was the hardest hit. Therefore, in order to restore the forces of capitalism in France, the French imperialists have resorted to every perfidious scheme to intensify capitalist exploitation in Indochina. They have built new factories to exploit the workers by paying them starvation wages. They have plundered the peasants' land to establish plantations and drive them to destitution. They have levied new heavy taxes. They have forced our people to buy government bonds. In short, they have driven our people to utter misery. They have increased their military forces, firstly to strangle the Vietnamese revolution; secondly to prepare for a new imperialist war in the Pacific aimed at conquering new colonies; thirdly to suppress the Chinese revolution; and fourthly to attack the Soviet Union because she helps the oppressed nations and the exploited working class to wage revolution. World War Two will break out. When it does the French imperialists will certainly drive our people to an even more horrible slaughter. If we let them prepare for this war, oppose the Chinese revolution and attack the Soviet Union, if we allow them to stifle the Vietnamese revolution, this is tantamount to letting them wipe our race off the surface of the earth and drown our nation in the Pacific.

However, the French imperialists' barbarous oppression and ruthless exploitation have awakened our compatriots, who have all realized that revolution is the only road to survival and that without it they will die a slow death. This is why the revolutionary movement has grown stronger with each passing day: the workers refuse to work, the peasants demand land, the students go on strike, the traders stop doing business. Everywhere the masses have risen to oppose the French imperialists.

The revolution has made the French imperialists tremble with fear. On the one hand, they use the feudalists and comprador bourgeoisie to oppress and exploit our people. On the other, they terrorize, arrest, jail, deport and kill a great number of Vietnamese revolutionaries. If the French imperialists think that they can suppress the Vietnamese revolution by means of terror, they are grossly mistaken. For one thing, the Vietnamese revolution is not isolated but enjoys the assistance of the world proletariat in general and that of the French working class in particular. Secondly, it is precisely at the very time when the French imperialists are frenziedly carrying out terrorist acts that the Vietnamese Communists, formerly working separately, have united into a single party, the Indochinese Communist Party, to lead the revolutionary struggle of our entire people.

Workers, peasants, soldiers, youth, school students !

Oppressed and exploited fellow-countrymen !

The Indochinese Communist Party has been founded. It is the Party of the working class. It will help the proletariat lead the revolution waged for the sake of all oppressed and exploited people. From now on we must join the Party, help it and follow it in order to implement the following slogans : *princeples*

1. To overthrow French imperialism and Vietnamese feudalism and reactionary bourgeoisie ;

2. To make Indochina completely independent ;

3. To establish a worker-peasant-soldier government :

4. To confiscate the banks and other enterprises belonging to the imperialists and put them under the control of the worker-peasant-soldier government ;

5. To confiscate all the plantations and property belonging to the imperialists and the Vietnamese reactionary bourgeoisie and distribute them to the poor peasants.

6. To implement the 8-hour working day ;

7. To abolish the forced buying of government bonds, the poll-tax and all unjust taxes hitting the poor ;

8. To bring democratic freedoms to the masses ;

9. To dispense education to all the people ;

10. To realize equality between man and woman

THE PARTY'S LINE IN THE PERIOD OF THE DEMOCRATIC FRONT (1936 — 1939)[*10]

1. For the time being the Party should not put forward too exacting demands (national independence, parliament, etc.). To do so is to play into the Japanese fascists' hands.

It should only claim democratic rights, freedom of organization, freedom of assembly, freedom of the press and freedom of speech, general amnesty for all political detainees, and freedom for the Party to engage in legal activity.

2. To reach this goal, the Party must strive to organize a broad Democratic National Front.

This Front should embrace not only Indochinese but also progressive French people residing in Indochina, not only the toiling people but also the national bourgeoisie.

3. The Party must assume a tactful, flexible attitude towards the national bourgeoisie, strive to draw them into the Front and keep them there, urge them into action if possible, isolate them politically if necessary. At any rate, we must not leave them outside the Front, lest they should fall into the hands of the reaction and strengthen it.

4. With regard to the Trotskyites there can be no compromise, no concession. We must do everything possible to unmask them as agents of fascism and annihilate them politically.

---

* This is an excerpt from a report made by Nguyen Ai Quoc to the Communist International in July 1939. *(Ed.)*

5. To increase and consolidate its forces, to widen its influence and work effectively, the Indochinese Democratic Front must maintain close contact with the French Popular Front which also struggles for freedom and democracy and can give us great help.

6. The Party cannot demand that the Front recognize its leadership. It must instead show itself to be the Front's most loyal; active and sincere element. It is only through daily struggle and work, when the masses of the people have acknowledged the correct policies and leading capacity of the Party, that it can win the leading position.

7. In order to carry out this task the Party must uncompromisingly fight sectarianism and organize the systematic study of Marxism-Leninism in order to raise the cultural and political level of the Party members. It must help the non-Party cadres raise their standard. It must maintain close contact with the French Communist Party.

8. The Central Executive Committee must supervise the Party press to avoid technical and political mistakes (e.g. in publishing comrade R.'s biography, the *Labour* revealed where he had been and how he had come back, etc. It also published without comment his letter saying that Trotskyism is a product of personal vanity, etc.).

LETTER FROM ABROAD

(June 6, 1941)

Venerable elders!
Patriotic personalities!
Intellectuals, peasants, workers, traders and soldiers!
Dear fellow-countrymen!

Since France was defeated by Germany, its power has completely collapsed. Nevertheless, with regard to our people, the French rulers have become even more ruthless in carrying out their policy of exploitation, repression and massacre. They bleed us white and carry out a barbarous policy of all-out terrorism and massacre. In the foreign field, bowing their heads and bending their knees, they resign themselves to ceding part of our land to Siam and shamelessly surrendering our country to Japan. As a result our people are writhing under a double yoke of oppression. They serve not only as beasts of burden to the French bandits but also as slaves to the Japanese robbers. Alas! What sin have our people committed to be doomed to such a wretched fate? Plunged into such tragic suffering, are we to await death with folded arms?

No! Certainly not! The twenty-odd million descendants of the Lac and the Hong are resolved not to let themselves be kept in servitude. For nearly eighty years under the French pirates' iron heels we have unceasingly and selflessly struggled for national independence and freedom. The heroism of our predecessors, such as Phan Dinh Phung, Hoang Hoa Tham and Luong Ngoc Quyen and the glorious feats of the insurgents of Thai Nguyen, Yen Bai, Nghe An and Ha Tinh provinces will live for ever in our memory. The recent uprisings in the South and at Do Luong and Bac Son testify to the determination of our compatriots to follow the glorious example of their ancestors and to annihilate the enemy. If we were not successful, it was not because the French bandits were strong, but only because the situation was not yet ripe and our people throughout the country were not yet of one mind.

Now, the opportunity has come for our liberation. France itself is unable to help the French colonialists rule over our country. As for the Japanese, on the one hand, bogged down in China, on the other, hampered by the British and American forces, they certainly cannot use all their strength against us. If our entire people are solidly united we can certainly get the better of the best-trained armies of the French and the Japanese.

Fellow-countrymen! Rise up! Let us emulate the dauntless spirit of the Chinese people! Rise up without delay! Let us organize the Association for National Salvation to fight the French and the Japanese!

Dear fellow-countrymen! A few hundred years ago, in the reign of the Tran, when our country faced the great danger of invasion by Yuan armies the elders ardently called on their sons and daughters throughout the country to stand up as one man to kill the enemy. Finally they saved their people and their glorious memory will live for ever. Let our elders and patriotic personalities follow the illustrious example set by our forefathers.

Notables, soldiers, workers, peasants, traders, civil servants, youth and women who warmly love your country! At present national liberation stands above everything. Let us unite and overthrow the Japanese, the French and their lackeys in order to save our people from their present dire straits.

Dear fellow-countrymen!

National salvation is the common cause of our entire people. Every Vietnamese must take part in it. He who has money will contribute his money, he who has strength will contribute his strength, he who has talent will contribute his talent. For my part I pledge to follow in your steps and devote all my modest abilities to the service of the country and am ready for the supreme sacrifice.

Revolutionary fighters!

The hour has struck! Raise aloft the banner of insurrection and lead the people throughout the country to overthrow the Japanese and the French! The sacred call of the Fatherland is resounding in our ears; the ardent blood of our heroic predecessors is seething in our hearts! The fighting spirit of the people is mounting before our eyes! Let us unite and unify our action to overthrow the Japanese and the French.

The Vietnamese revolution will certainly triumph!

The world revolution will certainly triumph!

INSTRUCTIONS FOR THE SETTING UP OF THE ARMED PROPAGANDA BRIGADE FOR THE LIBERATION OF VIET NAM*[11]

(December 1944)

1. The name of the *Armed Propaganda Brigade for the Liberation of Viet Nam* shows that greater importance is attached to its political than to its military action. It is a propaganda unit. In the military field, the main principle for successful action is concentration of forces. Therefore in accordance with the new instructions of our organization, the most resolute and energetic cadres and men will be picked from the ranks of the guerilla units in the provinces of Bac Can, Lang Son and Cao Bang, and an important part of the available weapons concentrated in order to establish our main-force brigade.

Ours being a national resistance by the whole people we must mobilize and arm the whole people. While concentrating our forces to set up the brigade, we must maintain the local armed forces which must co-ordinate their operations and assist each other in all respects. For its part, the main-force brigade has the duty to guide the cadres of the local armed units, assist them in training, and supply them with weapons if possible, thus helping these units to develop unceasingly.

* Set up on December 22, 1944. *(Ed.)*

2. With regard to the local armed units, we must gather their cadres for training, send trained cadres to various localities, exchange experience, maintain liaison, and co-ordinate military operations.

3. Concerning tactics, we must apply guerilla warfare; maintain secrecy, quickness of action and initiative (now in the east now in the west, arriving unexpectedly and departing without leaving any traces).

The Armed Propaganda Brigade for the Liberation of Viet Nam is the first-born unit. It is hoped that other units will soon come into being.

Its initial size is modest but it faces brilliant prospects. It is the embryo of the Liberation Army and can expand from North to South, throughout Viet Nam.

V. positive

APPEAL FOR GENERAL INSURRECTION
(August 1945)

Dear fellow-countrymen !

Four years ago, I called on you to unite, for unity is strength and only strength will enable us to win back *independence and freedom.*

At present, the Japanese army has collapsed. The National Salvation Movement has spread to the whole country. The League for the Independence of Viet Nam (Viet Minh) has millions of members from all social strata: intellectuals. peasants, workers, businessmen, soldiers, and from all nationalities in the country : Viet, Tho, Nung, Muong, Man, and others. In its ranks our compatriots march side by side regardless of age, sex, religion and fortune.

Recently, the Viet Minh convened the Viet Nam People's National Congress [12] and appointed the *National Liberation Committee* to lead the entire people in the resolute struggle for national independence.

, This is a great advance in the history of the struggle waged for nearly a century by our people for their liberation.

This is a source of powerful encouragement for our compatriots and great joy for myself.

However, we cannot content ourselves with that. Our struggle will be a long and hard one. The Japanese defeat does not mean that we shall be liberated overnight. We still have to make further efforts and carry on the struggle. Only unity and struggle will bring us independence.

The Viet Minh is at present the basis for the unity and struggle of our people. Join the Viet Minh, support it, make it even greater and stronger!

At present, the *National Liberation Committee* is the equivalent of a provisional government. Let us rally around it and see to it that its policies and orders are carried out throughout the country!

This way, independence is certain to come to our people soon.

Dear fellow-countrymen!

The decisive hour has struck for the destiny of our people. Let all of us stand up and rely on our own strength to free ourselves.

Many oppressed peoples the world over are vying with each other in wresting back independence. We should not lag behind.

Forward! Forward! Under the banner of the Viet Minh, let us valiantly march forward!

PART TWO

(1945 — 1954)

In 1992, in the place where I was working, already fraught with terrible tensions, as the rest of the world was doing dreadful things to our country, a woman appeared. Very well dressed, neat, youthful & good-looking with a breezy freshness about her, she came to teach French. Very impressive in the staff-room, when worked with elsewhere, became extremely unco-operative, and very secretly rallied other people to that end. It made you look very bad & done in such a way that one couldn't prove anything. In the end she helped to get contracts terminated. Talking to the Vietnamese later on, they said they recognized her, had had terrible things done to them in the workplace, were made to look bad until they lost their jobs & became destitute. There was another young French woman on her team that looked like a witch. V. hyperactive & undermining she reinforced the work of the first woman.

Even more recently I learned that such people are agents, not originally from the country they claim to represent, but from the bowels of secret societies & occult world organizations. The ones described above were from Saudi Arabia, evil lines arising from the death of a princess famously executed in the 1960's. They were designed *to promote anarchy, destruction & the taking of territory. Also leading to mass sacrifice [Her remains were dismembered & disappeared from Saudi] The first step in destroying the majority of a population, is to take away their employment. There was a second incident of work harassment in Hong Kong; this time two men. Again shared*

DECLARATION OF INDEPENDENCE OF THE DEMOCRATIC REPUBLIC OF VIET NAM*

with, and recognised by, Vietnam The source, the U.S.

"All men are created equal. They are endowed by their Creator with certain unalienable Rights; among these are Life, Liberty and the pursuit of Happiness."

This immortal statement appeared in the Declaration of Independence of the United States of America in 1776. In a broader sense, it means: All the peoples on the earth are equal from birth, all the peoples have a right to live and to be happy and free.

The Declaration of the Rights of Man and the Citizen, made at the time of the French Revolution, in 1791, also states: "All men are born free and with equal rights, and must always remain free and have equal rights."

Those are undeniable truths.

Nevertheless, for more than eighty years, the French imperialists, abusing the standard of Liberty, Equality and Fraternity, have violated our Fatherland and oppressed our fellow-citizens. They have acted contrary to the ideals of humanity and justice.

Politically, they have deprived our people of every democratic liberty.

They have enforced inhuman laws; they have set up three different political regimes in the North, the Centre

* Read on September 2, 1945 by President Ho Chi Minh at a meeting of half a million people in Ba Dinh square (Hanoi).

and the South of Viet Nam in order to wreck our country's oneness and prevent our people from being united.

They have built more prisons than schools. They have mercilessly massacred our patriots. They have drowned our uprisings in seas of blood.

They have fettered public opinion and practised obscurantism.

They have weakened our race with opium and alcohol.

In the field of economics, they have sucked us dry, driven our people to destitution and devastated our land.

They have robbed us of our ricefields, our mines, our forests and our natural resources. They have monopolized the issue of bank-notes and the import and export trade.

They have invented numerous unjustifiable taxes and reduced our people, especially our peasantry, to extreme poverty.

They have made it impossible for our national bourgeoisie to prosper; they have mercilessly exploited our workers.

In the autumn of 1940, when the Japanese fascists invaded Indochina to establish new bases against the Allies, the French colonialists went down on their bended knees and opened the doors of our country to welcome the Japanese in.

Thus, from that date, our people were subjected to the double yoke of the French and the Japanese. Their sufferings and miseries increased. The result was that towards the end of last year and the beginning of this year, from Quang Tri province to the North, more than two million of our fellow-citizens died from starvation.

On the 9th of March this year, the French troops were disarmed by the Japanese. The French colonialists either fled or surrendered, showing that not only were they incapable of "protecting" us, but that, in a period of five years, they had twice sold our country to the Japanese.

Before the 9th of March, how often the Viet Minh had urged the French to ally themselves with it against the Japanese! But instead of agreeing to this proposal, the French colonialists only intensified their terrorist activities against the Viet Minh. After their defeat and before fleeing, they massacred the political prisoners detained at Yen Bai and Cao Bang.

In spite of all this, our fellow-citizens have always manifested a lenient and humane attitude towards the French. After the Japanese putsch of March 9, 1945, the Viet Minh helped many Frenchmen to cross the frontier, rescued others from Japanese jails and protected French lives and property. In fact, since the autumn of 1940, our country had ceased to be a French colony and had become a Japanese possession.

When the Japanese surrendered to the Allies, our entire people rose to gain power and founded the Democratic Republic of Viet Nam.

The truth is that we have wrested our independence from the Japanese, not from the French.

The French have fled, the Japanese have capitulated, Emperor Bao Dai has abdicated. Our people have broken the chains which have fettered them for nearly a century and have won independence for Viet Nam. At the same time they have overthrown the centuries-old monarchic regime and established a democratic republican regime.

We, the Provisional Government of the new Viet Nam, representing the entire Vietnamese people, hereby declare that from now on we break off all relations of a colonial character with France; cancel all treaties signed by France on Viet Nam, and abolish all privileges held by France in our country.

The entire Vietnamese people are of one mind in their determination to oppose all wicked schemes by the French colonialists.

We are convinced that the Allies, which at the Teheran [13] and San Francisco [14] Conferences upheld the principle of equality among the nations, cannot fail to recognize the right of the Vietnamese people to independence.

A people who have courageously opposed French enslavement for more than eighty years. a people who have resolutely sided with the Allies against the fascists during these last years, such a people must be free, such a people must be independent.

For these reasons, we, the Provisional Government of the Democratic Republic of Viet Nam, solemnly make this declaration to the world :

Viet Nam has the right to enjoy freedom and independence and in fact has become a free and independent country. The entire Vietnamese people are determined to mobilize all their physical and mental strength, to sacrifice their lives and property in order to safeguard their freedom and independence.

TO OUR FELLOW-COUNTRYMEN IN NAM BO

(September 26, 1945)

Dear fellow-countrymen in Nam Bo!

Our newly-won national independence is threatened
by foreign invasion. In the war against the Japanese, the
French colonialists either surrendered or fled; now that
the war has ended, they are coming back either secretly
or openly. Within a period of four years, they sold out
our country twice. Now they seek to re-impose their rule
on our people.

I believe, and so do our people throughout the country,
in your firm patriotism. Let us recall these proud words
of a great French revolutionary, "I'd rather die as a
free man than live as a slave."

Like you, I am sure that the Government and the
whole country will do their utmost to support the fighters
and people who are selflessly fighting to defend our
national independence.

I am sure, and so are all our people, that individuals
and nations the world over who cherish equality and
freedom all sympathize with us.

We are bound to win for we have the united force of our
entire people. We are bound to win because our struggle is a just one.

I just want to make this recommendation to you : as
regards the Frenchmen captured in the war, we must

watch them carefully, but also treat them with leniency. We must show the world, and the French people in particular, that our cause is a pure and just one, that we want only independence and freedom, that we are not moved by hatred and rancour.

We must show the world that we are a civilized people, more civilized than the murderers and aggressors.

Long live independent Viet Nam!

Long live our fellow-countrymen in Nam Bo!

TO THE PEOPLE'S COMMITTEES IN THE WHOLE COUNTRY (North, South, Centre) AND AT ALL LEVELS (Province, District and Village)

(October 1945)

Dear friends,

Our country was oppressed by the French for more than 80 years and by the Japanese for nearly five years. The misery we suffered was beyond description. Even now it is a heartbreaking thing to remember it. Our people's unity and the Government's wise guidance have allowed us to break the bonds of slavery and win back our independence and freedom.

Without the people, we shall have no strength; without the Government, no guidance. Therefore, the Government and the people must form a monolithic whole. We have now founded the Democratic Republic of Viet Nam. But without happiness and freedom for the people, independence would be meaningless.

Our Government has promised that it will strive to bring every citizen his share of happiness. Building our country and putting things in order will have to be done gradually and cannot be completed within a month or a year. But we must make a correct start. We must bear in mind that all Government organs, from the central to the village level, are the people's servants, that is to say they must work in the public interest, not oppress the people as government organs did under the French and Japanese rule.

What is of benefit to the people we must strive to do.

What is harmful to them we must strive to avoid.

We must love the people: they will love and respect us.

I know that many of you have correctly carried out the Government's policies and won the people's hearts. But others among you have committed very serious mistakes, the main ones being:

1. *Violation of legality* — Traitors whose guilt is clearly established must of course be punished, and no one can complain. But sometimes arrests are made and property confiscated out of personal enmity, causing discontent among the population.

2. *Abuse of power* — Abusing their positions as members of such and such committees, some people are doing as they please in defiance of public opinion, having no regard for the people and forgetting that they have been elected by the people to serve them, not to browbeat them.

3. *Corruption* — Good food, fine clothing, wasteful expenditure, frivolous amusement — where does the money for all this come from ?

Some may go so far as to divert public property to their own use, casting aside integrity and honesty. Mister Commissar rides in official cars, then his wife does, then even his children. Who is going to pay for these expenses ?

4. *Favouritism* — Some build their own group of followers, appoint their friends and relatives to positions for which they have no ability, shove aside people who are competent and honest but are not to their liking. They forget that this is a matter of public concern, not a private affair.

5. *Sowing of discord* — Some oppose one section of the people to another instead of urging mutual concession and concord. In some places, fields lie fallow and the peasants are complaining. Some cadres forget that at present they must work for the unity of the whole people, irrespective of age and fortune, in order to safeguard our independence and fight the common enemy.

6. *Arrogance* — As officials, some consider themselves to be sacrosanct, and look down upon the people. Their every gesture shows them to be "mandarin revolutionaries". They fail to realize that their arrogance will lose them the people's confidence, and harm the Government's prestige.

Mistakes are not to be feared, but they must be corrected when discovered. He who has not fallen into the above-mentioned errors should try to avoid them and make further progress. He who has committed such errors must endeavour to correct them. If he fails to do so, the Government will not condone his mistakes.

It is for the sake of the people's happiness and the national interest that I have made these comments. We must engrave upon our minds the words "justice" and "integrity".

I hope you will make progress.

APPEAL TO THE PEOPLE TO FIGHT FAMINE
(1945)

Owing to the barbarous policies of the French colonialists, who among other things requisitioned paddy and forced our peasants to grow jute instead of rice, over two million people starved to death in Bac Bo in the early part of this year. Then came floods and drought. Moreover, the war started by the French colonialists in Nam Bo has hampered the sending of rice from the South to the North.

Famine is even more dangerous than war. Thus, in six years of war, France lost one million people and Germany nearly three million, while in the North of our country, famine killed over two million of our compatriots in barely half a year. We cannot allow more of them to starve.

In war, all the forces of the country must be mobilized and organized to fight the enemy. In our struggle against famine, we must also mobilize and organize our entire people.

Now famine is looming. If we do not seek to fight it by every means, it will be on us in a few months' time.

The ways to fight famine are manifold: like banning the distillation of spirits from rice or maize, the making of pastry of all kinds, etc., in order to save cereals; channelling food from one region to another, the former thus acting as a "patron" to the latter; boosting the cultivation of tubers and vegetables, etc. In a word, we must do everything that helps alleviate the people's hunger at present and prevent famine for the coming season.

The struggle against famine, like other important tasks, requires determined and strenuous efforts, readiness for sacrifices, and oneness of mind from the entire people.

For instance, the ban on spirits and pastry for a few months will surely affect those engaged in these trades, but I am sure they will temporarily give up their personal interests to help save others from hunger. Nobody would have the heart to enjoy personal comforts while his compatriots are starving.

Our fight against famine as well as against foreign invasion will certainly succeed because our entire people are wholeheartedly engaged in it. The local Committees must carry out good propaganda and explanatory work to enable everyone to understand fully and execute the directives to this effect. They must find appropriate ways to fulfil their tasks without alienating the people. Their members must set an example in putting into practice the watchword: "Industry, Thrift, Selflessness, Justice."

APPEAL TO FIGHT ILLITERACY
(October 1945)

Citizens of Viet Nam!

Formerly, when they ruled over our country, the French colonialists carried out a policy of obscurantism. They limited the number of schools; they did not want us to get an education so that they could deceive and exploit us all the more easily.

Ninety-five per cent of the total population received no schooling, which means that nearly all Vietnamese were illiterate. How could we have progressed in such conditions?

Now that we have won back independence, one of the most urgent tasks at present is to raise the people's cultural level.

The Government has decided that before a year has passed, every Vietnamese will have learnt *quoc ngu*, the national romanized script. A Popular Education Department has been set up to that effect.

People of Viet Nam!

If you want to safeguard national independence,

If you want our nation to grow strong and our country prosperous,

Every one of you must know his rights and duties. He must possess knowledge so as to be able to participate in the building of the country. First of all he must learn to read and write *quoc ngu*.

Let the literates teach the illiterates ; let them take part in mass education.

Let the illiterates study hard. The husband will teach his wife, the elder brother his junior, the children their parents, the master his servants ; the rich will open classes for illiterates in their own houses.

The women should study even harder for up to now many obstacles have stood in their way. It is high time now for them to catch up with the men and be worthy of their status of citizens with full electoral rights.

I hope that young people of both sexes will eagerly participate in this work.

TO OUR FELLOW-COUNTRYMEN IN NAM BO BEFORE GOING TO FRANCE[15] FOR NEGOTIATIONS

(May 31, 1946)

Dear fellow-countrymen in Nam Bo,

The news of my going to France with a delegation for official negotiation has caused concern to our people, especially in Nam Bo. What does the future hold for Nam Bo ?

Please, don't worry. I pledge my word that Ho Chi Minh will never sell his country.

You in Nam Bo have been fighting self-sacrificingly for many months now to safeguard the territorial integrity of Viet Nam ; for this, our entire people are grateful to you.

You in Nam Bo are citizens of Viet Nam. Rivers may dry up, mountains may erode ; but this truth can never change.

*
* *

I advise you to unite closely and broadly. The five fingers are of unequal length but they are united in the hand.

The millions of our fellow-countrymen are not all alike ; but they are descended from the same ancestors.

We must therefore be generous and broad-minded and admit the fact that the offspring of the Lac and the Hong are all more or less patriotic. With regard to those who have gone astray, we must use friendly persuasion. Only in this way can we achieve unity, and broad unity will bring us a bright future.

Through this short message written before my departure, I wish to convey my cordial greetings to all of you, dear fellow-countrymen in Nam Bo.

Entirely positive

APPEAL FOR NATION-WIDE RESISTANCE
(December 20, 1946)

Compatriots all over the country!

As we desire peace we have made concessions. But the more concessions we make, the more the French colonialists press on, for they are bent on reconquering our country.

No! We would rather sacrifice all than lose our country. Never shall we be enslaved!

Compatriots! Stand up!

Men and women, old and young, regardless of religious creed, political affiliation and nationality, all Vietnamese must stand up to fight the French colonialists and save the Fatherland. Those who have rifles will use their rifles; those who have swords will use their swords; those who have no swords will use spades, hoes or sticks. Everyone must endeavour to oppose the colonialists and save his country!

Members of the army, the self-defence corps and the militia!

The hour for national salvation has struck! We must shed even our last drop of blood to safeguard our country.

Even if we must endure the greatest hardships in our war of resistance, with our determination to face all sacrifices, we are bound to win.

Long live independent and unified Viet Nam!

Long live the victorious Resistance!

TO THE VIETNAMESE PEOPLE, THE FRENCH PEOPLE AND THE PEOPLES OF THE ALLIED NATIONS

(December 21, 1946)

We, the Vietnamese Government and people, are determined to struggle for our country's independence and reunification, but we are also ready for friendly co-operation with the French people. That is why we signed the Preliminary Agreement of March 6, 1946, and the Modus Vivendi of September 14, 1946.

But the French reactionary colonialists lacked sincerity and regarded those agreements as scraps of paper.

In Nam Bo they continued to arrest and massacre Vietnamese patriots and to engage in provocations. They bullied honest Frenchmen who advocated sincerity, and set up a puppet government in order to divide our people.

In southern Trung Bo they continued to terrorize our compatriots, attack the Vietnamese army, and invade our territory.

In Bac Bo, they provoked clashes to occupy Bac Ninh, Bac Giang, Lang Son and many other localities. They blockaded the port of Haiphong, thus making it impossible for Vietnamese, Chinese, other foreigners and also French residents to carry out their businesses. They tried to strangle the Vietnamese people and wreck our national sovereignty. They used tanks, aircraft, heavy artillery and warships to massacre our compatriots, and occupied the port of Haiphong and other towns along the rivers.

That was not all. They put their naval, land and air forces on the alert and sent us ultimatum upon ultimatum. They massacred old people, women and children in the capital city of Hanoi itself.

On December 19, 1946, at 8 p.m. they attacked Hanoi, the capital of Viet Nam.

The French colonialists' aim to reconquer our country is obvious and undeniable.

The Vietnamese people are now facing these alternatives either to fold their arms and bow their heads and fall back into slavery, or to struggle to the end for freedom and independence.

No! The Vietnamese people will never again tolerate foreign domination.

No! The Vietnamese people will never again be enslaved. They would rather die than lose their independence and freedom.

French people!

We are your friends and want sincere co-operation with you within the French Union because we share a common ideal: freedom, equality and independence.

It is the reactionary French colonialists who have sullied France's honour and sought to divide us by provoking a war. As soon as France clearly understands our aspirations to independence and reunification and calls back the bellicose French colonialists, friendly relations and co-operation between the peoples of Viet Nam and France will be restored immediately.

French soldiers!

We have no grudge against each other. Only selfish interests have driven the reactionary colonialists to provoke clashes. Profits are for them, death for you, and decorations for the militarists. For you and your families, only suffering and destitution. Think the matter over.

Are you going to shed your blood and lay down your lives for the reactionaries ? Join us, you will be treated as friends.

Peoples of the Allied nations !

At a time when the democratic countries are striving to organize peace following the end of the World War the French reactionaries are trampling underfoot the Atlantic and San Francisco Charters. They are waging an aggressive war in Viet Nam for which they must bear full responsibility. The Vietnamese people ask you to intervene.

Fellow-countrymen !

The war of resistance will be a long and hard one. Whatever sacrifices we must endure and however long the war of resistance will last, we are determined to fight to the end, until Viet Nam is completely independent and reunified. We are 20 million against 100,000 colonialists. We are bound to win.

On behalf of the Government of the Democratic Republic of Viet Nam, I give the following orders to the Army, self-defence corps, militia and to the people of all three parts of Viet Nam :

1. If the French troops attack us, we must fight back hard with all available weapons. Let our entire people stand up to defend their Fatherland !

2. We must protect the lives and property of foreign residents and give the prisoners of war good treatment.

3. Those who collaborate with the enemy will be punished.

Those who help the resistance and participate in the defence of their country will be rewarded.

Fellow-countrymen !

The Fatherland is in danger, let all of us stand up !

Long live independent and reunified Viet Nam !

Long live the victorious war of resistance !

APPEAL ISSUED AFTER SIX MONTHS
OF RESISTANCE
(June 19, 1947)

Fellow citizens,

Fighters in the Army, Militia and Self-Defence Corps,
The reactionary French colonialists have mobilized scores of thousands of men in their ground, naval, and air forces and spent scores of millions of piastres daily for their military expenses. By using overwhelming forces in lightning attacks they hoped to occupy our country within a few months. They also hired a clique of stooges with the aim of undermining our resistance and dividing our people. But their schemes, both military and political, have utterly failed. Today the war of resistance has been going on in Nam Bo for two years, and in the whole country, for six months. Our forces are growing ever stronger, our successes ever more obvious. Why ?

a) *Because we are fighting a just war*
We only defend our own country. we only fight for the unity and independence of our Fatherland.

As for the French reactionary colonialists, they seek to occupy our country, enslave our people. Therefore, we are in the right : Justice will prevail.

b) *Because our compatriots are closely united*
Our entire people share a common resolve : never to fall back into slavery ; a common will : never to lose

their country ; a common aim : to win back unity and independence for the Fatherland.

Our oneness of mind stands like a bronze wall defending our Fatherland. However cruel and perfidious the enemy, running into this wall, he is sure to fail.

c) *Because our fighters are courageous*

We have but inferior weapons and little experience, but our fighters' determination and spirit of sacrifice have defeated the enemy's brutal force and they have scored glorious, resounding feats of arms.

d) *Because our strategy is correct*

The enemy wants to win a quick victory. If the war drags on, he will suffer increasing losses and will be defeated.

That is why we use the strategy of a protracted war of resistance in order to develop our forces and gather more experience. We use guerilla tactics to wear down the enemy forces until a general offensive wipes them out.

The enemy is like fire and we like water. Water will certainly get the better of fire.

Moreover, in the long war of resistance, each citizen is a combatant, each village, a fortress. The twenty million Vietnamese are bound to cut to pieces the few scores of thousands of reactionary colonialists.

e) *Because we have many friends*

The reactionary colonialists' aggressive war is unjust and hated by all. Our resistance for national salvation is a just cause and is therefore receiving support from many people. The majority of the French people want to live in peace and friendship with us.

The peoples of the colonies sympathize with us.

The Asian peoples support us. World opinion is favourable to us.

On the moral plane, the enemy has already failed completely and we have won total victory.

Fellow-citizens!

Combatants!

Our long war of resistance will have to go through many more difficult periods.

We must endure sacrifices and hardships and make great efforts. But we are ready to face sacrifices and sufferings and to exert ourselves for five, ten years in order to break the chains which have held us in slavery over the past eighty years, and regain unity and independence forever. On behalf of the Government,

I order all combatants to fight even more vigorously and emulate one another in attacking the enemy;

I call on all our people to strive to increase production, build up food reserves in secure areas, watch over the dykes, and assist the troops;

I urge all political, administrative and technical personnel to redouble their efforts to overcome difficulties, correct shortcomings and become model cadres.

We are of one heart and of one mind. We are bound to win.

Forward!

Smash the French reactionary colonialists!

The Vietnamese and French peoples are friends!

The long war of resistance will certainly end in victory!

Long live independent and reunified Viet Nam!

ANNIVERSARY OF THE FOUNDING OF THE VIET NAM LIBERATION ARMY

(December 22, 1947)

From the Liberation Army to the National Defence Army.

The first platoon of the Liberation Army was a little seed which has grown into an immense forest: the present National Defence Army. Watching its first steps a superficial observer might have considered it to be some childish amusement or the work of some "utopians" and scoffed at it: "How can this handful of youths, students and peasants, a motley crowd of *Tho, Nung, Trai* and *Kinh* armed with a few dilapidated rifles and a dozen scimitars, dare to call themselves an army and assume the responsibility for liberating the nation?"

But our Party, determined to build a Liberation Army, had entrusted this task to Comrade Vo Nguyen Giap.

The result proves that our Party's policy is correct. It is correct because it is based on this simple and practical truth: the Vietnamese people must be and will be liberated. To liberate the country, we must fight the Japanese and French fascists. To fight them, we need military forces. To get these forces, we must organize them. To this end, we must work out plans and resolutely implement them.

At the beginning, everything was lacking: food, weapons, clothing, medicines. Often our fighters went without food but they remained in high spirits.

From a few dozens their number soon increased to several hundred. Young men enlisted en masse. The people of Viet Bac gave the liberation units all-round assistance ; some even sold their buffaloes and ricefields to get money for the Army. People of other localities also helped. Thanks to this support and to their own combat successes, our units increased in number and strength. Not only liberated zones were founded but revolutionary bases were set up everywhere.

Their courage and strict discipline have won the liberation fighters deep affection from the people.

*

*   *

In the first stage, the task of the Liberation Army was to help make the August Revolution and establish the Democratic Republic. In the following stage, it left excellent cadres and glorious traditions to the National Defence Army.

Commemorating the founding of the Liberation Army in the midst of our war of resistance, we must bear in mind the following points :

1. The National Defence Army and the guerillas must maintain their iron discipline and morale, their determination to win and their other virtues: intelligence, courage, integrity and loyalty.

2. Formerly, starting from scratch and having to face two enemies — the Japanese and the French — we none the less succeeded in organizing a mighty force, the Liberation Army, to overthrow them. Now we are fighting only one adversary, the reactionary French colonialists, while having the Party, the National Assembly, the Government, the Front, the immense forces of the National Defence Army and the guerillas

together with the support of our twenty million fellow-countrymen and of world public opinion: so our war of resistance will certainly end in victory.

I take this opportunity to convey my thanks to our compatriots in Viet Bac who wholeheartedly assisted the Liberation Army formerly and are now doing their utmost to support the war of resistance. I also send my cordial greetings and the assurances of our determination to win to Liberation Army veterans who are now fighting in the ranks of the National Defence Army.

TO THE NATIONAL
CONGRESS OF MILITIAMEN
(April 1948)

On this occasion, I affectionately wish you good health, and ask you to convey my greetings to all our militiamen and guerillas. Here are a few suggestions about your work.

Generally speaking, militiamen and guerillas have rendered good services to the resistance. In many places, they have fought the enemy either in close co-ordination with the National Defence Army or on their own; they have displayed great energy and reaped good successes in combating spies and bandits, annihilating puppet administrative organs, destroying the enemy's communication lines, learning the national script, and increasing production.

Such villages as Dinh Bang and many others have earned a reputation of heroism because of their guerilla activities. Many fighters have distinguished themselves: Pham Van Trac, Le Binh, Nguyen Van Y, Do Van Thin, Dang Van Gieng, Pham Van Man..., and others. We must also congratulate those guerilla units made up of old folk and women who have bravely attacked the enemy.

These are *good points* which we should further develop.

But our militiamen and guerillas have also shortcomings which must be corrected at once. In many places the meaning of guerilla warfare has not been clearly and thoroughly grasped, hence an erroneous tendency to wage big battles, and attack strong fortified positions. Besides, the watchword of self-supply and self-sufficiency has not been put into practical effect, and the intensification of production not properly emphasized. There is still lack of close co-ordination with the National Defence Army and lack of initiative in attacking the enemy. Concerning organization and training, too much attention is paid to matters of form, too little to practical deeds. These shortcomings must be resolutely and rapidly corrected. We must:

1. Effectively organize and train militiamen and guerillas in *each village; take the village militiamen and guerillas as basis*, while consolidating the guerilla units released from production duty;

2. Drive home to each fighter where our strength lies, and inspire him with faith in this strength and in our rudimentary weapons;

3. Combine guerilla action very closely with operations by the National Defence Army;

4. Make each fighter fully conscious of his glorious duty;

5. Give them a clear grasp of guerilla tactics: to keep the initiative, to seek out and attack the enemy, to harass him and engage in sabotage work; and to keep gaining small successes which will add up to a big victory;

6. Realize self-supply and self-sufficiency by effectively increasing production;

7. Bring about these things through emulation. Let village vie with village, district with district, province with province, zone with zone.

I promise that the Government will reward the most outstanding fighters and units in this *emulation* drive.

With the clear and *practical* plan to be worked out by the Congress, with the enthusiasm of all militiamen and guerillas, with the help of our compatriots, I am sure that our militiamen and guerillas will fulfil their glorious task : to kill many enemy troops, to capture many guns, to achieve many feats of arms in order to speed up the victory of the long war of resistance, and the realization of national reunification and independence.

Cordial greetings. We shall win !

TO THE MEETING OF THE
CENTRAL COMMITTEE OF THE VIET MINH
(April 20, 1948)

Dear Comrades,

On account of my many occupations, I am sorry to be unable to attend this meeting of the Viet Minh Central Committee which opens today. I wish the delegates good health and the meeting good successes. Below I wish to remind the delegates of some of our experiences.

The successes gained by the Viet Minh are due to its correct policies :

a) Since the very beginning the Viet Minh's home policy has been to unite the whole people and win independence for the Fatherland. To reach this aim, the Viet Minh decided to fight both the Japanese and the French. As we were then only a handful, with hardly any weapons, and the Japanese and French were joining forces to repress the patriotic movement, this decision was considered a foolish one by some people. But the results showed that the Viet Minh's policy was correct.

b) The foreign policy of the Viet Minh was to side with the democratic camp.

While the German, Italian and Japanese fascists were ruling the roost and winning victory upon victory. and while the democratic countries were suffering bitter setbacks, such a policy was also considered a crazy one by some people. But at that time the Viet Minh already foresaw certain victory for the democratic Allies. The results also showed that the Viet Minh's policy was correct.

c) While the Japanese and the French were co-operating closely, the Viet Minh foresaw that they would betray each other, and that the first to do so would be the Japanese. Owing to this foresight, the Viet Minh prepared a plan to turn this opportunity to account. The results also showed that the Viet Minh's policy was correct.

d) When the August Revolution was victorious and power was seized, the Viet Minh decided to organize a broadly-based Government including all people of talent in the country, to take in hand State affairs. Some people then thought that it was not certain that the prominent personalities would gladly co-operate with the Viet Minh. But as the Viet Minh put the interests of the Fatherland and the people above everything, and showed complete devotion to the common cause and absolute selflessness, such personalities willingly joined the Government.

e) When it became necessary to develop even further the unity of the whole people, the Viet Minh in a timely way proposed the organization of the Lien Viet [16] and helped it develop rapidly and broadly, thereby contributing to its own development and consolidation.

f) The Viet Minh's policy was to safeguard peace. but when the war of resistance broke out, the Viet Minh gave all-out support to the Government's policy of protracted resistance. In this war of resistance, the Viet Minh foresees victory, certain victory. The past is a guarantee for the future.

In short, ever since the founding of the Viet Minh, experience has shown all its policies to be correct; these successes must be stressed and developed.

However, the Viet Minh has one shortcoming: its rapid development has not allowed it to give proper training to its cadres everywhere; that is why in many places cadres have not correctly applied the general policy. Some elements have even become corrupt.

At present, on the one hand, the Viet Minh must pay attention to the training of cadres from village level upwards. On the other hand, its cadres must carry out self-criticism in order to be equal to their hard and glorious task. Its members must set good examples in performing every task in the Resistance and the reconstruction of the country.

I hope that this meeting will work out practical plans to develop and consolidate the Viet Minh in this campaign of patriotic emulation.

Cordial greetings.

V. Significant

APPEAL FOR PATRIOTIC EMULATION
(June 11, 1948)

What is the aim of patriotic emulation?
> It is to fight famine and poverty,
> To fight ignorance, and
> To fight the foreign invaders.

The way to do this is to rely upon
> The people's forces, and
> The people's spirit,

In order to bring about

> Happiness for the people.

Thus, the duty of all Vietnamese whatever their occupations — intellectuals, peasants, workers, traders, soldiers — is to emulate one another, so as to

> *Work faster, better and more.*

Every Vietnamese, old and young, men and women, rich and poor, whatever his or her social position, must become a fighter struggling on the military, economic, political or cultural front, for the implementation of this watchword:

Resistance by the entire people and in every field.

In our patriotic emulation, we resist foreign aggression while at the same time rebuilding the country.

The first results of patriotic emulation will be the following :

The entire people will have enough food and clothing,

The entire people will have learnt to read and write,

The entire army will have enough food and armaments to wipe out the invaders, and

The whole nation will be completely re-unified and independent.

Thus we shall have obtained

> Independence for the nation;
> Freedom for the citizens; and
> Happiness for the people.

In order to attain these fine goals, I urge all to engage in emulation :

Let old folk encourage their children and grand children to participate enthusiastically in every endeavour ;

Let young pioneers study hard and help grown-up people ;

Let manufacturers and traders develop their enterprises ;

Let workers and peasants increase production ;

Let intellectuals and specialists create and invent ;

Let civil servants devotedly serve the people ; and

Let the army and the militia wipe out many enemy troops, and seize great quantities of weapons.

In short, let all emulate with each other ; let all partici- pate in the war of resistance and the reconstruction of the country. In this seething drive, patriotic emulation will strike deep roots and spread to every field and every stratum of the people, and will help us overcome all difficulties and thwart all enemy schemes in order to secure final victory.

With the dauntless spirit and the inexhaustible force of our people, with the patriotism and determination of our people and army, we can and will certainly win great successes in our patriotic emulation drive.

Fellow-countrymen!

Members of the armed forces!

Forward!

TO THE 6th CONGRESS OF PARTY CADRES
(January 18, 1949)

Present at this congress are delegates of the North, Centre and South and high-ranking Party cadres in the administration, army, economy and finance, Party apparatus, mass organizations, control organs, etc. This is very good.

The problems raised for discussion have been many but all have been directed to one goal: the victory of the Resistance, the building of a new democracy in preparation for an advance to socialism.

The course having been charted, let us follow it. We shall certainly reach our destination.

These are our tasks for this year:

1. To boost our military effort; to put the war of resistance, the armed struggle above everything else. All activities must aim at winning victory for the Resistance.

2. To put in order the administrative machinery at all levels, from village upwards. If re-arrangement is made from the base up, and vice versa, we shall naturally achieve success.

3. To produce much and to spend little. No unnecessary expenditure. Such is the content of all our economic and financial policies.

4. To re-organize the mass organizations. Our successes are due to the people. Yet at present many mass organizations are still very weak.

5. To perform the above tasks, we must first of all perfect our Party's organization. We must set forth the chief tasks and concentrate on them.

We can liken the Party to a power generator, and the above tasks to electric lights. The more powerful the generator, the brighter the lights.

Here are some urgent tasks for our Party:

a) We lack too many cadres. We must gradually train a sufficient number of them. To this end, the Party must help its members study and learn through their own efforts. For their part, the cadres must study hard.

Many of our comrades have good practical experience, but only an elementary education. The intellectual comrades have read a great deal but have only little practical experience and are not used to the Party's working methods.

So, it is necessary to raise the theoretical level of veteran cadres while teaching the intellectual cadres to do mass work.

b) There are two shortcomings in the present style of work in the Party:

— veteran cadres work the "handicraft" way;

— new cadres work the scientific way but they go too far and fail to adapt themselves to the conditions of the war of resistance.

We should correct our working methods, make them ever more rational and suit them to the present circumstances, and avoid formalism and mechanicalness.

c) Before the masses, we won't win their love and esteem by merely inscribing the word "Communist" on our foreheads.

The people only love and respect those with good conduct and morality. Those who want to guide the masses must set good examples for them. Many comrades have done so, but others have degenerated. Our Party must help them cleanse themselves.

When you call on people to practise thrift, you yourself must do it. Our comrades must acquire the four revolutionary virtues: industry, thrift, integrity and uprightness.

To make the revolution, one must first and foremost remould oneself.

d) Although we may come from different nationalities and classes, we follow the same doctrine, pursue the same goal, are bound together for life and death, and share weal and woe. That is why we must sincerely unite. To reach our destination, to organize ourselves is not enough: we must besides be sincere in our minds.

There are two ways to achieve ideological unity and inner cohesion: *criticism and self-criticism.*

Everyone, from the top down, must use them to achieve ever closer unity and greater progress.

e) To keep discipline:

Though comprising a large number of people, our Party goes to combat united as one man. This is due to discipline. Ours is an iron discipline — that is, a severe and conscious one.

We must strive to maintain this iron discipline of our Party.

*
* *

This conference is being held at a time when the world revolutionary movement is progressing rapidly. This is especially evident in the victory of the Chinese people and Party.

Our Party is the Indochinese Communist Party but we must also contribute to the liberation of Southeast Asia. It ranks next to the Chinese Communist Party in strength and was the first to come to power in Southeast Asia. This is said not for the sake of vanity but so that we should strive to fulfil our responsibility.

The world's people today number about 2,000 million ; the Communist parties have a total membership of over 20 million ; so there is one Communist for every hundred persons or so. In Indochina, according to current figures, this ratio is one to a hundred and twelve. This is a heartening fact. If everybody fully discharges his duties, our war of resistance will certainly gain quick victory and national construction swift success.

Long live the Indochinese Communist Party !

Long live the victory of World Revolution !

TO PEASANT CADRES
(November 1949)

Ours is an agricultural country.

More than nine-tenths of our people are peasants.

More than nine-tenths of our peasants are middle, poor and landless peasants.

The National Defence Army, the regional forces, the militia and guerilla units are mostly made up of peasants.

The production work to feed the army, the workers and the functionaries is carried out by the peasants.

The work of doing sabotage to check the enemy, repairing roads, ensuring communications and transport, is mostly done by the peasants.

In a word, the peasants constitute an immense force of the nation and a most loyal ally of the working class.

For the war of resistance and national construction to be successful, for genuine independence and reunification to be achieved, reliance should be placed on the peasant forces.

Our peasants make up a tremendous force, inspired by ardent patriotism, determination to struggle and readiness for sacrifices.

Political work among the peasants consists in :

— Tightly organizing them.

— Closely uniting them.

— Fully awakening their political consciousness.

— Leading them to struggle vigorously for their own interest and that of the Fatherland.

To carry out *political agitation* among the peasants means to stir them up; that is, to make them clearly understand the interests of the nation and those of their class, to get them to join the National Salvation Peasants' Association in great numbers in order to struggle for their own objectives and actively participate in the war of resistance and in national construction.

To achieve this end, peasant cadres must avoid subjectiveness, formalism and red tape.

Provincial cadres must go to districts and villages.

District cadres must go to villages and hamlets.

Cadres must go to the base to see and hear for themselves, talk to people, ponder over things and act accordingly.

They must conduct practical investigations, give assistance, exercise control, draw lessons and exchange experiences, with a view to helping the peasants and learning from them.

In the organs of power and in the leading bodies of the Peasants' Association, poor peasants and landless peasants must have an effective share.

If our cadres (peasant cadres and administrative cadres) strictly adhere to these principles, and this they should do at all costs, we shall surely reap fine results in all these fields:

— Emulation in production to stave off famine;

— Emulation in learning *quoc ngu* to liquidate illiteracy;

— Emulation in assisting the army, and fostering the militia and guerilla forces to annihilate the foreign aggressors.

TO THE TRADE-UNION CONGRESS

(February 23, 1950)

On the occasion of the holding of your congress, I cordially wish you all good health and fine and practical successes. In the national war of resistance, our working class has made an important contribution and recorded glorious achievements; naturally, from now on, it must redouble its efforts. In my opinion, the congress should tackle the following main tasks:

— To organize and train all workers in the liberated zones and in the areas still under enemy control,

— To lead the workers to engage in the patriotic emulation drive, and to prepare for the general counter-offensive;

— To organize intellectual and manual workers;

— To assist and guide the peasants in every respect;

— To keep close contact with the working class the world over, first and foremost, with the Chinese and French workers.

Our working class must be the leader in the war of resistance, in national construction, and in the building of a new democracy. Therefore, all workers, men and women, must strive to learn and progress and set good examples in every field so as to fulfil the glorious task of their class.

Cordial greetings! We shall win!

1st mention

ANSWERS TO THE PRESS
ON U.S. INTERVENTION IN INDOCHINA*
(July 25, 1950)

QUESTION : *Mr. President, what is the present state of the U.S. imperialists' interventionist policy in Indochina ?*

ANSWER : The US imperialists have long since openly intervened in Indochina. It is with their money and weapons and on their instructions that the French colonialists have been waging war in Viet Nam, Cambodia and Laos.

However, the US imperialists are seeking more and more to oust the French colonialists and gain complete control over Indochina. They intervene ever more directly and actively in every field — military, political and economic. For this reason contradictions have multiplied between them and the French colonialists.

QUESTION : *Mr. President, what influence does this intervention exert on the Indochinese people ?*

ANSWER : The US imperialists supply their henchmen with armaments to massacre the Indochinese people.

They dump their goods in Indochina to prevent the development of local small industries.

They disseminate a depraved culture to poison the youth in areas under their temporary control.

* Published in *Cuu quoc,* organ of the Viet Minh, July 25, 1950. *(Ed.)*

They practise a policy of corruption, cajolery and division. They take bad elements into their service and work out joint schemes to conquer our country.

QUESTION : *What shall we do against them ?*

ANSWER : To gain independence, the Indochinese peoples must completely defeat the French colonialists, their enemy number one. At the same time, we must oppose the US interventionists. The deeper their interference, the closer our solidarity and the more vigorous our struggle.

We must expose their plots before all our people, especially those living in areas under their temporary control.

We must unmask all those who serve as running dogs for the US imperialists in their attempts to blandish, deceive and divide our people.

Close solidarity between the peoples of ·Viet Nam, Cambodia and Laos constitutes a force capable of defeating the French colonialists and the US interventionists. The US imperialists have failed in China, they will fail in Indochina.

We are running into many difficulties but we are bound to win.

ON THE FIFTH ANNIVERSARY OF THE AUGUST REVOLUTION AND NATIONAL DAY

(September 2, 1950)

Fellow-countrymen at home and abroad,
Members of the National Defence Army, regional forces, militia and guerilla units,
Cadres of the administration and mass organizations,
Young people and children!

Today we celebrate the fifth anniversary of the August Revolution and National Independence Day. Our Resistance has also lasted five years.

Let us briefly review the situation in the course of these five years so as to define our forthcoming tasks.

Prior to the August Revolution we were confronted with *two direct enemies*, Japanese imperialism and French colonialism, and an indirect enemy, the reactionary Chinese Kuomintang. That means that our enemies had immense forces.

Prior to the August Revolution, power was not in our hands and we had no regular army; the national front was still small and worked underground. That means that our forces were most deficient.

However, thanks to our skill in turning to account the international situation and in *uniting and mobilizing our people*, we were able to turn our weakness into strength, defeat the three enemies, bring the Revolution to victory and gain national independence.

*

No sooner had our country regained her independence than the French colonialists attacked us.

Relying on their powerful army, well officered and armed with modern weapons, they intended to wage a *lightning war* and win a *quick victory*.

With only freshly organized troops and rudimentary weapons, we decided to *carry out a long war of resistance*.

Facts have proved that *our strategy has got the better of the enemy's.*

Since the outbreak of hostilities in Viet Nam, the French government has been overthrown over a dozen times; French commanders-in-chief have been replaced five or six times; French troops have been worn down; France's finances have dwindled with every passing day. The French people's anti-war movement has spread ever more extensively. Our people have grown ever more united and resolute.

Now the French colonialists have openly admitted that *they are exhausted and cannot prolong the war unless they are helped by the USA.*

While begging for US help, they are afraid lest the Americans oust them from Indochina, as the Japanese did a few years ago.

Ever since the war started, the *Americans have done their best to help the French.* But at present they go one step further by *directly interfering in Viet Nam.*

So, apart from our principal enemy, the French colonialists, we have now *another foe, the American interventionists.*

As far as we are concerned, the war of resistance waged these last few years *has won Viet Nam the greatest success in her history :* the two largest countries in the world, the Soviet Union and People's China, and the new

democracies, have recognized the Democratic Republic
of Viet Nam as an equal member in the great family of
democratic countries of the world. This means that we
have definitely joined the democratic camp and the eight
hundred million people fighting against imperialism.

Surely these political successes will pave the way for
future military victories.

*
* *

The USSR and the new democratic countries are
growing ever more powerful.

China has defeated the US interventionists and the
reactionary Kuomintang clique, and is embarking on the
path of new democracy.

The Korean people have risen against the US interventionists and all their satellites. They make up a huge
allied force supporting our Resistance for national salvation and especially our struggle against the US interventionists.

The US reactionaries have failed in face of the unity
in struggle of the Chinese people. They will fail in face
of the unity in struggle of the peoples of Viet Nam, Korea
and the world.

Facts over the past years have demonstrated that *our
long war of resistance will certainly end in victory.*

This is beyond all question.

But *victory and long Resistance must go hand in hand :*

"He who wishes to gather fine fruit should plant good
trees" ; this saying expresses eternal truth.

Therefore, our urgent tasks are :

— to strengthen our *unity* even further ;

— to *unite all our people in a patriotic emulation movement for general mobilization* in order promptly to switch over to the general counter-offensive ; first and foremost to encourage the supply of manpower and food ;

— to urge the National Defence Army, regional forces, militia and guerilla units to emulate one another in *wiping out enemy forces and performing brilliant exploits ;*

— to urge the workers and peasants to *vie with one another in production ;*

— to urge the youth to *rival one another in all fields :* enlistment in the army, production, transport, study, etc ;

— to encourage all administrative and mass organization cadres to put into practice the motto : *industry, thrift integrity, uprightness ;*

— to urge our compatriots living in enemy-controlled areas to get ready to fight the enemy and support our troops.

*
* *

Dear fellow-countrymen !

Dear soldiers !

The *August Revolution* brought us unity and independence. At that time, apart from our spirit of solidarity, we possessed only small forces ; but we carried the day.

Now we are waging a long war of resistance to defend our unity and independence ; we have powerful forces and enjoy favourable national and international conditions : we are bound to win.

However, we must be aware of the following :

— The enemy will grow even more reckless and ferocious, they will probably extend their attacks even more before being wiped out.

— We shall meet with even greater difficulties and hardships before winning final victory.

Therefore we must be vigilant and resolute ; we shall neither be discouraged by temporary setbacks, nor grow arrogant when winning big victories; neither shall we grow complacent and underestimate the enemy.

Thanks to the oneness of mind of our government and people, of our soldiers and civilians, to the unity and dauntlessness of our entire people, to the support of the peoples of democratic countries and of justice-loving personalities in the world,

Our long war of resistance will certainly end in victory !

National reunification and independence will certainly be achieved !

POLITICAL REPORT AT THE SECOND NATIONAL CONGRESS OF THE VIET NAM WORKERS' PARTY

(February 1951)

I. THE INTERNATIONAL SITUATION IN THE PAST FIFTY YEARS

The year 1951 marks the closing of the first half and the opening of the second half of the Twentieth Century. We are at a moment of great importance in the history of mankind.

Quicker and more important changes have occurred in the past fifty years than in many previous centuries added together.

The cinema, radio, television and atomic energy have been invented or discovered in the course of these fifty years. Mankind has thus made a big stride in harnessing the forces of nature. In this same period, capitalism has passed from free competition to monopoly, to imperialism.

In these fifty years, the imperialists have unleashed two *world wars*, the most terrible wars in history. As a result of these wars, the Russian, German, Italian and Japanese imperialists have been annihilated ; the British and French imperialists have gone downhill, while the US capitalists have become the leading imperialists, the leading reactionaries.

Most important of all was the triumph of *the Russian October Revolution*. The Soviet Union, a socialist country, was established, covering one-sixth of the area of the globe. Nearly half of the human race has taken the path of *new democracy*. The oppressed peoples have risen up one after another against imperialism, for independence and freedom. The Chinese Revolution was successful. The workers' movement in the imperialist countries has grown ever stronger.

In the same period, in Viet Nam, *our Party* was born, twenty-one years ago. Our country regained her *independence* six years ago. Our *protracted war of resistance* has proceeded vigorously and is now in its fifth year.

In a word. many events of great importance have occurred in the first half of the Twentieth Century, but we can predict that thanks to the efforts of the revolutionaries, even greater and more glorious changes will take place in its second half.

II. THE BIRTH OF OUR PARTY

After World War One (1914-1918), to make up for their heavy losses the French colonialists invested more capital in our country in order to intensify their exploitation of our wealth and manpower. On the other hand, the triumph of the Russian Revolution and the revolutionary effervescence in China were exerting deep and extensive influence. As a result, *the Vietnamese working class* matured, grew politically conscious, began to struggle, and needed a vanguard, a general staff, to lead it.

On January 6, 1930 * *our Party came into being.*

After the success of the Russian October Revolution, the *Communist International* was set up under Lenin's leadership. Since then, the international proletariat and

* The Third National Congress of the Viet Nam Workers' Party passed a resolution correcting the date of the founding of the Indochinese Communist Party and fixing it as February 3, 1930.

the world revolution have become one great family, and our Party is one of its youngest members.

Due to the French colonialists' policy of savage persecution, our Party was born in very difficult circumstances. However, immediately after its founding our Party led a fierce struggle against the French colonialists, which climaxed in the days of the Nghe An Soviets.

This was the first time our people held local power and began to put democratic policies into effect, though only over a small area.

The Nghe An Soviets failed, but they had a great influence. Their heroic spirit was kept alive in the hearts of the masses and paved the way for subsequent victories. From 1931 to 1945, always under the leadership of our Party, the revolutionary movement in Viet Nam had ups and downs, rising, then ebbing, then rising again. These fifteen years can be divided into three periods:

        1. Period from 1931 to 1935;

        2. Period from 1936 to 1939; and

        3. Period from 1939 to 1945.

III. PERIOD FROM 1931 TO 1935

From 1931 to 1933, the French colonialists pursued a policy of savage terror. Many Party cadres and sympathizers were arrested and killed. Almost all Party and mass organizations were destroyed. As a result, the revolutionary tide temporarily ebbed.

Thanks to the loyalty and devotion of the remaining comrades, the determination of the Central Committee and the assistance of the friendly Parties, from 1933 onwards the revolutionary movement again rose gradually.

At that time, the Party strove, on the one hand, to consolidate its underground organizations and, on the other, to combine underground work with legal activity, propaganda and agitation in the press and in the municipal councils, regional councils, etc.

In 1935, the *Party held its First Congress* in Macao. The Congress assessed the situation in our country and in the world, reviewed the work done and mapped out a programme for the coming period.

But the policies worked out at the Macao Congress were not in keeping with the revolutionary movement in the world and in our country at that time. (They advocated distribution of land to the agricultural workers, and failed to grasp the anti-fascist task and be aware of the danger of fascist war, etc.)

IV. PERIOD FROM 1936 TO 1939

In 1936, at the Party's First National Conference, Comrades Le Hong Phong and Ha Huy Tap rectified these errors and worked out new policies in line with the resolutions of the Seventh Congress of the Communist International (setting up of the Democratic Front; semilegal activity of the Party).

At that time, in France, the Popular Front was in power. Our Party launched a movement for democracy and set up the Indochinese Democratic Front.

The Democratic Front movement was fairly strong and widespread. The people struggled openly. This was a good point. But there were shortcomings: The Party's leadership was not close enough; so in many localities our cadres were affected by narrow-mindedness, legalism, and were intoxicated by partial successes to the extent of neglecting the consolidation of the Party's underground organization. The Party failed to make clear its standpoint on the question of national independence. A number of comrades engaged in unprincipled co-operation with the Trotskyites. When the Popular Front in France collapsed and World War Two broke out, the Democratic Front movement in our country was repressed by the colonialists, and our Party was thrown into confusion for a time.

However, this movement left our Party and the present National Front invaluable experiences. It taught us that whatever conforms to the people's aspirations will receive support from the masses, who will whole-heartedly struggle for it, and as such is a real mass movement. It also taught us to avoid at all costs subjectiveness, narrow-mindedness, etc.

V. PERIOD FROM 1939 TO 1945

The great changes that occurred in this period in our country and in the world were only ten years back. Many of us witnessed them, many still remembered them. I shall recall only some principal ones :

A. **In the world** :

In 1939, *World War Two* broke out.

At first, it was an imperialist war between the German, Italian and Japanese fascist imperialists on one side and the British, French and American imperialists on the other.

In June 1941, the German fascists attacked the Soviet Union, the fortress of the world revolution, which had to fight back and to ally itself with the British and Americans against the fascist camp. Thenceforward, the war became one between the democratic camp and the fascist camp.

Owing to the immense forces of the Red Army and the Soviet people, and to Comrade Stalin's correct strategy, in May 1945, Germany was crushed and in August 1945, Japan surrendered. *The democratic camp had won complete victory.*

In this victory, the *greatest success* in the military field as well as in the political and moral field was that of *the Soviet Union.*

Thanks to the success won by the Soviet Union, the countries of Eastern Europe, which formerly were bases or parts of fascist Germany, have become *new democracies.*

Thanks to the success won by the Soviet Union, semi-colonial countries such as China, and colonial countries such as Korea and Viet Nam have driven out or are driving out the aggressive imperialists to wrest back freedom and independence.

Thanks to the success won by the Soviet Union, national liberation movements in other colonies are rising.

The United States was successful in the financial field. While the other countries were pouring their forces into the war and were devastated by it, the United States made big profits.

After the war, the German, Italian and Japanese fascists were annihilated. The British and French imperialists were going downhill. The Soviet Union very quickly recovered, and developed its work of socialist construction. But treading in the steps of Germany, Italy and Japan, the US has now become the ringleader of the fascist imperialists.

B. **In our country:**

After the outbreak of World War Two, the Party Central Committee met in November 1939, and worked out these policies: to set up *a united front* against the French colonialists and the imperialist war and to prepare for an insurrection; not to put forward the slogan "Confiscate the landlords' land for distribution to the tillers" in order to draw the landlord class into the National Front.

After France's capitulation to fascist Germany, Japan encroached upon French power in Indochina and used the French colonialists as agents for repressing the revolution in our country.

In that period, our people launched three uprisings: in Bac Son, Nam Ky and Do Luong.

In May 1941, the *Party Central Committee* held its *Eighth Plenum*. The main question was to regard the present revolution in Viet Nam as one for national liberation; to set up the League for the Independence of Viet Nam (the Viet Minh) with the following slogan: To unite the entire people, oppose the Japanese and the French and wrest back independence; to postpone the agrarian revolution.

The name *Viet Nam Doc Lap Dong Minh* (League for the Independence of Viet Nam) had a very clear and practical meaning, and corresponded to the aspirations of the entire people. Besides, it set forth a simple, practical and comprehensive programme in ten points, as expounded in a propaganda ditty:

The programme comprises ten points:

All in the interests of the country and the people.

These ten points include points common to the whole nation and others dealing with the struggle for the interests of the workers, peasants and various strata of the population.

As a result, the Viet Minh was warmly welcomed by the people, and thanks to the efforts made by the cadres to keep in close touch with the people, it developed very rapidly and vigorously. Hence the Party also expanded. The Party also helped progressive intellectuals to found the Viet Nam Democratic Party in order to attract young intellectuals and civil servants and to accelerate the disintegration of the pro-Japanese Dai Viet.

In the world, the Soviet Union and the Allies scored repeated victories. In our country, the Japanese and the French were in conflict. Under the Party's leadership, the Viet Minh had grown fairly strong. In that context, the Standing Bureau of the Central Committee held an *enlarged session* in March 1945. The main resolution was to *push forward the anti-Japanese movement and to prepare for the general insurrection*. By that time, power had already fallen from the hands of the French colonialists into those of the Japanese fascists.

In May 1945, Germany capitulated. In August, Japan surrendered. The Soviet Union and the Allies had won complete victory.

Early in August, the Party held its *Second National Conference* at Tan Trao to decide on a plan of action and on participation in the *National People's Congress* convened by the Viet Minh, to be held at Tan Trao in the same month.

The National People's Congress approved the plan set forth by the Viet Minh and the order for general insurrection, and elected the Central National Liberation Committee which was to become the Provisional Government of our country.

Because the Party's policy was correct and was carried out in a timely and flexible way, the August General Insurrection was crowned with success.

VI. FROM THE AUGUST REVOLUTION UP TO NOW

The triumph of the August Revolution was due to the clear-sighted and resolute leadership of our Party and the unity and fervour of the entire people, both inside and outside the Viet Minh.

Comrades,

Not only our own toiling classes and people but also the toiling classes and oppressed peoples of other countries can be proud of this fact : for the first time in the revolutionary history of colonial and semi-colonial peoples, *a party barely fifteen years old has led the revolution to success and seized power throughout the country.*

For our part, we must bear in mind that our success was due to the great victory of the Soviet Red Army over the Japanese fascists, to the friendly assistance of international solidarity, to the close unity of our entire people and to the heroic sacrifices of our revolutionary predecessors.

Our comrades, like Tran Phu, Ngo Gia Tu, Le Hong Phong, Nguyen Thi Minh Khai, Ha Huy Tap, Nguyen Van Cu, Hoang Van Thu and thousands of others, placed the interests of the Party, the revolution, the class and the nation above and before everything else. They had deep confidence in the immense forces and glorious future of the class and the nation. They willingly sacrificed everything, even their lives for the sake of the Party, the class and the nation. They watered with their blood the tree of Revolution which has now bloomed and borne fruit.

In order to become truly deserving revolutionaries, all of us must follow these examples of heroism, of utter devotion to the public interest and complete selflessness.

The August Revolution overthrew the centuries-old monarchy, broke the chains of the nearly one hundred years of colonial rule, gave back power to the people and built the basis for an independent, free and happy Democratic Republic of Viet Nam.

This is an extremely great change in the history of our country.

The triumph of the August Revolution has made us a member of the great democratic family in the world.

The August Revolution has exerted a direct and very great influence on two friendly nations : Cambodia and

Laos. After the success of the August Revolution, the
Cambodian and Lao peoples also rose up against the
imperialists and claimed independence.

On September 2, 1945, *the Government of the Democratic Republic of Viet Nam* declared to the world the
independence of Viet Nam and put into effect democratic
freedoms in the country. One fact should be stressed
here : At the time of the setting up of the Provisional
Government some comrades, members of the Central
Committee elected by the National People's Congress,
should have taken part in the Government ; yet, of their
own accord they withdrew in favour of patriotic personalities who were not members of the Viet Minh. This
is a selfless, magnanimous gesture by men who do not
care for position, who put the interests of the nation, of
the national union above individual interests. This is a
gesture worthy of praise and respect, one that should
serve us as an example.

VII. THE DIFFICULTIES ENCOUNTERED
BY THE PARTY AND THE GOVERNMENT

As soon as the people's power came into existence it
met with great difficulties.

Due to the policy of ruthless exploitation by the
Japanese and the French, within only half a year (end
of 1944 and beginning of 1945) more than two million
people in the North had died of starvation.

Hardly a month after our declaration of independence
British troops entered the South. Under the pretence of
disarming the Japanese army, they acted as an expeditionary corps helping the French colonialists in their
attempts to re-occupy our country.

Chinese Kuomintang troops entered the North, allegedly
also to disarm the Japanese, but actually in pursuit of
three wicked aims :

— to destroy our Party.
— to smash the Viet Minh,
— to help the Vietnamese reactionaries overthrow the people's power and set up a reactionary government at their beck and call.

In the face of that grave and pressing situation, our Party had to do everything that was necessary in order to keep itself in existence, work and develop, to give more discreet and effective leadership, and to gain time in order gradually to consolidate the forces of the people's power and strengthen the National United Front.

At that time the Party could not hesitate : hesitation would have meant failure. The Party had to take quick decisions and adopt measures — even painful ones — likely to save the situation.

In spite of many great difficulties, the Party and the Government guided our country through dangerous rapids and implemented many points in the programme of the Viet Minh :

— holding general elections to elect the National Assembly and draw up the Constitution ;
— building and consolidating the people's power ;
— annihilating the Vietnamese reactionaries ;
— building and consolidating the people's army and arming the people ;
— promulgating labour legislation ;
— reducing land rent and interest rates ;
— building people's culture ;
— broadening and consolidating the National United Front (setting up of the Lien Viet).

Mention should be made here of the *Preliminary Agreement of March 6, 1946,* and the *Modus Vivendi of September 14, 1946,* because they were regarded by a number

of people as manifestations of a *rightist policy* and caused
some grumbling on their part. But in the opinion of our
comrades and compatriots in the South this policy was
correct. And correct it was, because our Southern comrades and compatriots cleverly availed themselves of
this opportunity to build up and develop their forces.

Lenin said that one should make a compromise even
with bandits if it was advantageous to the revolution.

We needed peace to build our country, and therefore
we forced ourselves to make concessions in order to
maintain peace. Although the French colonialists broke
their word and unleashed war, nearly one year of temporary peace had given us time to build up our basic
forces.

When the French deliberately provoked war and we
could no longer put up with them, the nation-wide war
of resistance broke out.

VIII. THE PROTRACTED WAR OF RESISTANCE

The enemy schemed for a *lightning war*. They wanted
to attack swiftly and win swiftly. For our part, our Party
and Government set forth the motto: *Protracted war of
resistance.* The enemy plotted to sow dissensions among
us, so our watchword was: *Unity of the entire people.*

Thus, right from the start, our strategy prevailed over
the enemy's.

To wage a protracted war of resistance, there must be
an adequate supply of arms and munitions to the army.
of food and clothing to the troops and the people. Our
country is poor and our technical level low. Cities and
towns with some industry are all occupied by the enemy.
We must seek to offset our material deficiencies by the
enthusiasm of our entire people. So the Party and the
Government have promoted *patriotic emulation.* Emulation

covers all fields but it is aimed at three main objectives: to get rid of famine, liquidate illiteracy and annihilate the foreign invaders.

Our workers have emulated one another in manufacturing weapons for our troops, who have trained hard and scored good results. Our recent victories in battle are proof of this. Our people have ardently emulated one another and recorded satisfactory results. Although our country is economically backward, we have been waging the war of resistance for nearly 5 years and can keep fighting without suffering too many privations. This is a fact. The majority of our population have been freed from illiteracy. This is a brilliant achievement admired by the world. I suggest that our Congress send cordial thanks and praise to our troops and fellow-countrymen.

However, concerning the work of organization and supervision and the exchange and summing up of experiences we are still weak. These are shortcomings. From now on we should strive to overcome them; then the emulation movement will certainly reap more and better results.

Military activity is the keystone in the war of resistance.

When the war of resistance began *our army* was still in its infancy. Though full of heroism, it lacked weapons, experience, officers, everything.

The enemy army was well-known in the world. It had land, naval, and air forces. Moreover it was supported by the British and American imperialists, especially the latter.

The discrepancy between our forces and the enemy's was so great that at the time some people likened our war of resistance to a fight between "a grasshopper and an elephant".

And such a fight it would be if things were looked at with a narrow mind, solely from the angle of material strength and in their present state. Indeed against the enemy's airplanes and artillery we had only bamboo sticks. But our Party is a Marxist-Leninist one. We look not only at the present but also to the future and have firm confidence in the spirit and strength of the masses, of the nation. Therefore we resolutely told those wavering and pessimistic people:

Yes, it's now grasshopper versus elephant,
But tomorrow the elephant will collapse.

Facts have shown that the colonialist "elephant" is getting out of breath while our army has grown up into a powerful tiger.

Although at the beginning, the enemy was so strong and we still so weak, we none the less fought with the greatest energy, scored many successes, and kept firm confidence in our final victory. This is because our cause is just, our troops courageous, our people united and undaunted, and because we are supported by the French people and the world democratic camp. This is also because our strategy is correct.

Our Party and Government have estimated that our war of resistance includes three stages:

— *In the first stage,* which went from September 23, 1945, to the end of the Viet Bac campaign in autumn-winter 1947, our efforts were aimed at preserving and increasing our main forces.

— *In the second stage,* from the end of the Viet Bac campaign in 1947 up to now, we have actively contended with the enemy and prepared for the general counter-offensive.

— *The third stage* is to be that of the general counter-offensive.

On this last point, because they did not grasp the policy of the Party and the Government, a number of comrades got wrong ideas. Some thought that the slogan of "preparation for general counter-offensive" was premature. Others wanted to know the day and hour of the general counter-offensive. Still others believed that the general counter-offensive would certainly be launched in 1950, etc.

These wrong conceptions were harmful to our work. We must first of all keep in mind that *the war of resistance will be long and hard, but will certainly end in victory.*

The war of resistance must be a protracted one because our population and territory are small and our country poor. Long and all-round preparations have to be made by our entire people. We must always bear in mind that in relation to us the French invaders are quite strong, and, in addition, they are assisted by the British and Americans.

They are like a "tangerine with a thick rind" and so we must have time to "sharpen our finger-nails" in order to peel it.

We must also understand that each stage is linked up with others: it succeeds the one that precedes it and produces seeds for the one that follows.

Many changes occur in the course of the passage from one stage to another. Each stage also contains changes of its own.

It is possible to determine major stages on the basis of the general situation but it is not possible to separate one stage completely from the other, like slicing a cake. The length of each stage depends on the situation at home and in the world, and on the changes in the enemy's forces and in ours.

We must understand that protracted resistance is closely connected with preparations for a general counter-offensive. As the war of resistance is a long one, long preparations are also needed for a general counter-offensive. Whether the general counter-offensive will come early or late depends on changes in the enemy's forces and in ours, and also on changes in the international situation.

In all circumstances, the more careful and complete the preparations, the more steadily and favourably the general counter-offensive will proceed.

The slogan *"To prepare for a vigorous switch to the general counter-offensive"* was set forth early in 1950.

Did we make preparations during that year?

Yes, we did. The Government issued the general mobilization order and launched the movement for patriotic emulation. As is well-known, our troops and our people have made active preparations and have obtained good results.

Did we make the move in 1950?

Yes, we did and are still doing it. The great diplomatic successes scored early in 1950 and the great military victories won towards the end of that year were proof of this.

Have we launched the general counter-offensive?

We have been preparing to switch over vigorously to the general counter-offensive, but have not yet actually launched it. We must fully grasp the meaning of the words, "To prepare for a vigorous switch to..."

Once *the preparations are fully completed* we will launch the general counter-offensive. The more complete, the more fully complete, the preparations, the sooner the general counter-offensive will come and the more favourable the conditions for its success.

We should avoid precipitation, rashness and impatience. The troops, the people, the cadres, everybody and every branch must *strive to make fully complete preparations*. When our preparations are completed we will launch the general counter-offensive and then it will certainly be successful.

IX. CORRECTION OF SHORTCOMINGS AND MISTAKES

Our Party has recorded many achievements but has also committed *not a few mistakes*. We must sincerely engage in self-criticism in order to correct them. Efforts must be made to correct our mistakes so as to progress.

Before speaking of our shortcomings we must recognize that our Party has cadres — especially those in the zones still temporarily under enemy control — who are very heroic and devoted, who, in spite of all hardships and dangers, always keep close to the people, stick to their work without fear or complaint, and are ready to sacrifice even their lives.

They are model fighters of the nation, meritorious sons and daughters of the Party.

It can be said that since the founding of the Party, *its policies on the whole have been correct*. If they were not, how could we have recorded such tremendous achievements ? But we have also shown major shortcomings and weaknesses :

Doctrinal studies are still inadequate, many Party cadres and members are not yet mature ideologically and their theoretical level is still low. As a result, in the carrying out of the policies of the Party and the Government there have occurred erroneous tendencies, either "leftist", or rightist (as in problems relating to land, the Front, the national minorities, religion, the administration, etc.)

Our organizational work is also still weak, and often cannot ensure correct implementation of the policies of the Party and the Government.

Therefore, *to study our doctrine, sharpen our ideology, raise our theoretical level and perfect our organization* are urgent tasks for the Party.

Besides, in leading organs at all levels there still exist fairly prevalent and grave mistakes in the style of work, measures adopted and manner of guiding. These are *subjectiveness, bureaucracy, commandism, narrow-mindedness* and *arrogance.*

Subjectiveness manifests itself in the belief that the long-term war of resistance can turn out to be a short-term war.

Bureaucracy is evidenced by red tape, divorce from the masses and by failure to conduct investigations and surveys, to engage in control and supervision, and learn from the experiences of the masses.

Commandism reveals itself in reliance on administrative compulsion to get things done, and failure to conduct propaganda and explanatory work to make the people work on their own.

Narrow-mindedness is apparent in judging non-Party people with undue severity, or slighting them and refusing to discuss with them or ask for their opinion.

As for *arrogance,* it is revealed in the following :

— To boast of one's past achievements, extol oneself and consider oneself the "saviour" of the people and the "meritorious servant" of the Party. To ask for position and honour. Unable to fulfil major tasks, one is unwilling to accept minor ones. Arrogance is very harmful to solidarity both within and without the Party.

— To rely on one's position as Party member to make light of discipline and hierarchy in mass organizations or government organs.

The comrades affected by this disease do not understand that each Party member must be a model of discipline, not only Party discipline but also that of mass organizations and organs of revolutionary power.

The Central Committee is partly responsible for that disease and others which affect Party members, because it has not paid adequate attention to *control work*. Ideological training has not been given to all, nor in sufficient amount. Inner Party democracy has not been broadly practised. Criticism and self-criticism have not yet become a regular habit.

However, these defects are being corrected to a certain extent. The recent critical reviews and the movement for criticism and self-criticism have yielded good results in spite of a few deviations.

Stalin said that a revolutionary party needs criticism and self-criticism just as a human being needs air. He also said that close control can help avoid many grave mistakes.

From now on the Party must try to dispense doctrinal education in order to raise the political standards of its members. *A collective style of work* must be promoted. *Relations between the Party and the masses* must be strengthened. *Observance of discipline, respect of principles and Party spirit* must be heightened in every Party member. The Party must widen the movement for criticism and self-criticism within the Party, the State organs, the mass organizations, in the press and among the people. Criticism and self-criticism must be conducted regularly, in a practical and democratic way, from top to bottom and from the bottom upwards. Lastly there must be close control by the Party.

By so doing, we shall commit fewer errors and make quicker progress.

X. NEW SITUATION AND NEW TASKS

A. New situation :

As is well-known the world is at present divided into two distinct camps :

— The *democratic camp* headed by the Soviet Union, and comprising the socialist countries and the new democracies in Europe and in Asia. It also embraces the oppressed nations which are struggling against aggressive imperialism and the democratic organizations and personalities in the capitalist countries.

The democratic camp is a powerful camp which is growing in strength. The following few points are sufficient evidence of this :

Let us look at a map of the world : From Eastern Europe to Eastern Asia the USSR and the new democracies form an immense bloc of 800 million people. In this bloc the nations are united, pursue the same goal and are not divided by any antagonisms. It is the symbol of progress and of the bright future of mankind. It is an extremely powerful force.

At the Second Congress of the Peace Front held in the Polish capital in November 1950, the representatives of 500 million peace fighters in 81 countries pledged their determination to safeguard world peace and to oppose imperialist wars. This is the *United Front* of the peaceful and democratic world. This is a very powerful force whose strength is growing with every passing day.

— The *anti-democratic camp* is headed by the US. Immediately after the end of World War Two, the US became the ringleader of world imperialism and reaction. Britain and France are its right- and left-hand men and the reactionary governments in the East and the West its henchmen. The handlbars of world realthism

Aspiring to world hegemony, the US holds out dollars in one hand to entice people and brandishes the atomic bomb in the other to menace the world. The Truman Doctrine[17], Marshall Plan[18], NATO Pact, and Programme[19] for Southeast Asia are all US manoeuvres aimed at preparing for a third world war.

But the US ambitions have run into a tremendous obstacle: the immense force of the Soviet Union, the movement for democracy and peace, and the movement for national liberation seething all over the world.

At present, the US policy is as follows:

— In Asia, to assist the reactionaries such as Chiang Kai-shek, Syngman Rhee, Bao Dai, etc.; to help the British imperialists repress the resistance forces in Malaya and the French colonialists crush the Resistance in Viet Nam, while the US itself is waging an aggressive war against Korea and is occupying Taiwan in an attempt to undermine the Chinese revolution. ＼ filthy culture

— In Europe the US has, through the Marshall Plan and NATO, seized control over the Western countries in the military, political and economic fields, and at the same time has been striving to arm them and compel them to supply cannon-fodder, as in the plan for setting up 70 divisions in Western Europe under an American commander-in-chief.

However, the US camp has a great many weaknesses:

Besides the strength of the democratic camp, the US camp faces another threat: economic crisis.

There are many contradictions in the US camp. For example: The US wants Western Germany to set up an army of ten divisions but this has been opposed by the French people. Britain covertly opposes the US because the two are contending for oil in the Near-East and for influence in the Far-East.

The people, especially the toiling sections in countries "aided" by the US, hate it for encroaching upon their economic interests and the independence of their countries.

The US is too greedy. It schemes to set up bases all over the world. It helps every reactionary group and every reactionary government. Its front extends beyond measure, consequently its forces are spread thin. Clear proof of this is supplied in Korea, where the United States together with 40 of its vassals are suffering defeats at the hands of the country they have invaded. The US helped the reactionary clique in China, the Kuomintang headed by Chiang Kai-shek, but Chiang was defeated. The US helps the French colonialists in Viet Nam, yet the Vietnamese Resistance is winning.

In short, we can foretell that the reactionary imperialist camp will certainly be defeated and the camp of peace and democracy will certainly be victorious.

Viet Nam is a part of the world democratic camp. It is at present a bastion against imperialism, against the anti-democratic camp headed by the US.

Since the beginning of our war of resistance, Britain and the US have helped the French colonialists. And since 1950, the US has openly intervened in our country.

At the end of 1950, Britain and France prepared to set up a "united" front to join forces against the resistance in Malaya and in Viet Nam.

Thus, the international situation is closely related to our country. Every success of the democratic camp is also ours, and every success won by us is also one for the democratic camp. Therefore, at present our main slogan is: *"To crush the French colonialists and defeat the US interventionists in order to regain unity and complete independence and safeguard world peace."*

B. New tasks :

The comrades of the Central Committee will report on such important questions as the Party's political pro-gramme and constitution, the military question, the administration, the National United Front, the economy, etc. This report will only emphasize some main tasks among our new ones :

1. To bring the war of resistance to complete victory.

2. To organize the Viet Nam Workers' Party.

1. Efforts must be made to develop the strength of the troops and the people in order to win success after success and advance towards the general counter-offensive.

This task aims at these main points :

— *In the building and development of the army*, all-out efforts must be made towards the organization and con-solidation of *political and military* work among our troops. Their political consciousness, tactics and techniques, and *self-imposed discipline* must be heightened. Our army must become a genuine *people's* army.

Simultaneously, the *militia and guerilla units* must be developed and consolidated in organization, training, leadership and combat strength. They must make up a vast and solid steel net spread all over the country so that wherever the enemy goes he will get enmeshed.

— *To enhance patriotism* — Our people are inspired by ardent patriotism. This is an invaluable tradition of ours. At all times, whenever the Fatherland is invaded, this patriotism forms an immensely powerful wave sweeping away all dangers and difficulties and drowning all traitors and aggressors.

Many great wars of resistance in our history are proofs of our people's patriotism. We can be proud of the glorious pages of history written by our people in the days of the Trung Sisters, Lady Trieu, Tran Hung Dao,

Le Loi, Quang Trung. etc. We must engrave in our minds the achievements of our national heroes because they are the symbols of a heroic nation.

Our fellow-countrymen today are worthy of their forefathers. White-haired folk, children, people residing abroad, people living in the areas still under enemy control, in the plains, in the highlands — all are imbued with ardent love for the country and hatred for the aggressor. Fighters at the front go hungry for days on end in order to remain in contact with the enemy and annihilate him. Government employees in the rear go hungry for the sake of the troops. Women urge their husbands to enlist in the army while they themselves help to transport supplies. Combatants' mothers take care of the troops as they would their own children. Workers and peasants of both sexes emulate one another to increase production, shrinking from no hardships in order to contribute their part to the Resistance. Landowners offer their lands to the Government. These lofty gestures are all different; yet they are similar for they stem from the same ardent patriotism. Patriotism is like valuable objects. Sometimes these are exhibited in a glass or a crystal vase and are thus clearly visible. But at other times they may be discreetly hidden in a trunk or a suitcase. Our duty is to bring all these hidden valuables into full view. That is, every effort must be made in explanation, propaganda, organization and leadership so that the patriotism of all may find expression in work benefiting the country and the Resistance.

Genuine patriotism is altogether different from the chauvinism of the reactionary imperialists. It is part and parcel of internationalism. It was thanks to their patriotism that the army and the people of the Soviet Union crushed the German and Japanese fascists and safeguarded their socialist Fatherland, thereby helping the working class and the oppressed peoples of the world. It was thanks to their patriotism that the Chinese Liberation Army and the Chinese people destroyed the traitorous Chiang Kai-shek clique and drove out the American imperialists. It is thanks to their patriotism that the Korean troops and people, together with the Chinese Volunteers, are routing the American imperialists and their henchmen. It is also thanks to their patriotism that our troops and people have for long years endured untold sufferings and hardships, determined to smash the colonialist aggressors and the Vietnamese traitors, and to build an independent, re-unified, democratic, free, and prosperous Viet Nam, a new democratic Viet Nam.

— *To step up patriotic emulation.* First, let the troops emulate one another to exterminate the enemy and score feats of arms ; second, let the people emulate one another *to increase production.* We must devote ourselves heart and soul to these two tasks.

. — In the great work of carrying on the war of resistance and engaging in national construction, *the Lien Viet-Viet Minh* Front, the trade-unions, the peasants' associations and other mass organizations exert great influence. We must help them develop, strengthen and work vigorously.

— *Concerning the land policy,* in the free zones, we must strictly implement the reduction of land rent and interest rates, confiscate lands belonging to the French and the Vietnamese traitors and temporarily distribute them to the poor peasants and the families of armymen, with a view to improving the livelihood of the peasants, heightening their spirit, and fostering their forces for the Resistance.

— *Concerning the economy and finance*, we must safeguard and develop our economic bases and fight the enemy in the economic field. There must be an equitable and rational tax system. A balance must be achieved in receipts and expenditures in order to ensure supplies for the army and the people.

— *Cultural work* must be speeded up to form the new man and train new cadres for the Resistance and for national construction. All vestiges of colonialism and the enslaving influence of imperialist culture must be systematically rooted out. Simultaneously, we must develop the fine traditions of our national culture and assimilate the new in world progressive culture in order to build a Vietnamese culture with a national, scientific and popular character.

Following our victories, the *areas still under temporary enemy control* will be liberated one after another. Therefore, preparations must be made to consolidate the newly-liberated areas in all respects.

— The life and property of *foreign residents* who abide by the Vietnamese law will be protected. *Chinese residents* should be encouraged to take part in the Resistance. If they volunteer to do so they will enjoy every right and fulfil every duty of a Vietnamese citizen.

We are waging our war of resistance, the brotherly Cambodian and Lao nations are also waging theirs. The French colonialists and the American interventionists are the common enemy of our three nations. Consequently, we must strive to help our Cambodian and Lao brothers and their wars of resistance, and proceed to set up a Viet Nam-Cambodian-Lao Front.

— Our successes in the Resistance are partly due to the sympathy of the *friendly countries* and of the people of the world. Therefore, we must strengthen the friendship between our country and the friendly countries, and that between our people and the people of the other countries in the world.

2. To carry these points into effect, we must have a legal party organized in a way consistent with the situation in the world and at home in order to lead our people's struggle to victory. This party is named the *Viet Nam Workers' Party.*

As regards its *composition,* the Viet Nam Workers' Party will admit the most enthusiastic and most enlightened workers, peasants, and intellectuals.

As regards its *doctrine,* it adheres to Marxism-Leninism.

As regards its *organization,* it adopts the system of democratic centralism.

. As regards *discipline,* it has an iron discipline which is at the same time a self-imposed one.

As regards its law of *development,* it makes use of criticism and self-criticism to educate its members and the masses.

As regards its *immediate goal,* the Viet Nam Workers' Party unites and leads the entire people to wage the war of resistance, take it to complete victory and win back national unity and complete independence; it leads the entire people to realize new democracy and create conditions for the advance to socialism.

The Viet Nam Workers' Party must be a great party — powerful, firm, pure and thoroughly revolutionary.

The Viet Nam Workers' Party must be the clear-sighted, determined, and loyal leader of the working class and toiling people, of the Vietnamese people, whose aim is to unite and lead the people in the resistance until complete victory, and to realize new democracy.

In the present stage, the interests of the working class and toiling people and those of the nation are at one. It is precisely because it is the party of the working class and toiling people that the Viet Nam Workers' Party must be the Party of the Vietnamese people.

The first task, the most urgent task of our Party today, is to *lead the war of resistance to victory*. The other tasks must be subordinated to it.

Our task is immense, our future glorious. But we shall have to experience many more difficulties. The war has its difficulties; victory has its own For example:

— Ideologically, our cadres, Party members and people are not yet mature enough to cope with all developments at home and abroad.

— The American imperialists may give the French aggressors even greater assistance, causing the latter to act even more rashly.

— We are facing more and more work, but we have not enough cadres and those we have lack ability and experience.

— We must solve economic and financial problems in the most rational way, one that is the most beneficial to the people, etc.

We do not fear difficulties. But we must foresee them, clearly realize them, and be prepared to overcome them.

With the solidarity and unity of mind, the determination and dauntless spirit of our Party, Government and entire people, we will certainly surmount all difficulties and gain complete victory.

The October Revolution triumphed. The building of socialism in the Soviet Union has been successful. The Chinese Revolution was victorious. These great successes have opened the way to success for the revolution in our country and many other countries in the world.

We have a great, powerful Party. Its greatness and strength is due to Marxism-Leninism, to the constant efforts of all our Party members, and to the love, confidence and support of our entire army and people.

That is why I am convinced that we will fulfil our heavy but glorious tasks, which are

— To build the Viet Nam Workers' Party into a most powerful one ;

— To bring the Resistance to complete victory ;

— To build a new democratic Viet Nam ; and

— To contribute to the defence of democracy in the world and a lasting peace.

AT THE CONGRESS FOR THE
UNIFICATION OF VIET MINH AND LIEN VIET
(March 3, 1951)

Venerables, delegates, and friends,

I am very glad to have the honour of winding up the opening ceremony of this National Congress for the Unification of Viet Minh and Lien Viet.

First of all, on behalf of the Presidium, I send my greetings to our fighters and to the cadres of Viet Minh and Lien Viet and express my sympathy to our compatriots living in the zones still under temporary enemy occupation and to those residing abroad. *(Applause.)*

Today, happiness is shared by our entire people, by this entire Congress, but my own joy is at the same time easy to understand and hard to describe.

It is the joy felt by a man who has struggled with you for many years to build up the entire people's unity and today sees the forest of unity bloom and bear fruit. Its roots have penetrated deep into the masses. It will "know eternal spring and never grow old". *(Laughter.)*

What makes me even happier is that not only the entire people of Viet Nam are united, but the entire people of the two brotherly nations, Cambodia and Laos, have also achieved broad unity. *(Long applause.)* The good news of this unity has been personally brought to us by the Cambodian and Lao delegates.

Thus the Vietnamese people have achieved broad union ; so have the Cambodian people and so have the Lao people. We shall surely arrive at a broad Vietnamese-Cambodian-Lao union. *(Long applause.)*

Because our three fraternal nations are of one heart and one mind we will overcome all difficulties and hardships, smash the French colonialist aggressors, the American interventionists and any other invaders. *(Applause.)*

At this Congress, you will thoroughly discuss and reach clear-sighted decisions on the programme and constitution of the National United Front. I will only stress a few points to help the Congress in its debate.

1. The Front must advance ever further on the road of democracy.

2. The Front should not have too many irons in the fire at once and must concentrate on a cardinal task. This cardinal task is patriotic emulation.

3. The parties, organizations and personalities within the Front must closely unite, cordially help one another, sincerely learn from one another's merits and criticize one another's shortcomings in order to progress together.

This Congress is composed of representatives of all strata, religious beliefs, nationalities, old and young people, men and women, and is like a great united family. After the Congress, this unity and cordiality will no doubt develop and consolidate itself among the entire people. This great unity will develop to include the people of the friendly countries, of France and peace- and democracy-loving people throughout the world.

This prodigious force will help us not only bring the resistance to victory and successfully carry out national construction but also make our contribution to the defence of world peace and democracy.

Venerables, delegates, friends,

Early last year, we won a great political victory: the recognition of our Government by the Soviet Union, China and the people's democracies, which led to our great victory along the border and in the Midlands.

Early this year, we won another great political victory, the founding of the Viet Nam Workers' Party and the Viet Minh-Lien Viet unification: this will surely lead to even greater military victories.

Long live the unity of the entire people!

Long live the Lien Viet Front!

Long live the Vietnamese-Cambodian-Lao great unity!

The resistance will certainly be victorious!

The camp of peace and democracy will certainly be victorious!

TO THE ARTISTS ON THE OCCASION OF THE 1951 PAINTING EXHIBITION
(December 10, 1951)

Dear friends,

Being informed of the holding of your exhibition, I regret that owing to pressure of work, I cannot visit it. I send you my cordial greetings and take this opportunity to express some of my views on art for you to think over

Literature and art are also a fighting front. You are *fighters* on this front.

Like other fighters, you combatants on the artistic front have definite responsibilities: to serve the Resistance, the Fatherland and the people, first and foremost the workers, peasants and soldiers.

To fulfil your tasks, you must have a *firm political stand* and a *sound ideology;* in short you must place the interests of the Resistance, the Fatherland and the people above all.

With regard to your *creative work,* you must understand, get in close touch with and go deeply into the people's life. Only by so doing will you be able to depict the heroism and determination of our soldiers and people and to contribute to the development and heightening of these qualities. Our Resistance has made great progress; our soldiers and people have made vigorous and continuous strides forward; so must you, artists, by means of criticism and self-criticism.

Some of you may think : President Ho is trying to link art to politics.

That is right. Culture and art, like all other activities, cannot stand aloof from economics and politics, but must be included in them.

Our people's future is most glorious, and the future of our art is very bright. I wish you good health, progress and success in your work.

Cordial greetings. We shall win.

TO PRACTISE THRIFT AND OPPOSE EMBEZZLEMENT, WASTE, AND BUREAUCRACY

(1952)

Comrades,

The working programme of our Goverment and Party this year is still epitomized in these words : "Protracted war of resistance, self-reliance."

For a correct implementation of this programme, the Government and the Party have stressed the following main points :

To emulate one another in wiping out enemy forces, increasing production and practising thrift, and

— to oppose embezzlement ;

— to oppose waste ;

— to oppose bureaucracy.

Concerning the *movement of emulation to wipe out enemy forces and score feats of arms,* the High Command has worked out a comprehensive plan and sent it down to all Party branches and all members of the National Defence Army, regional forces, militia and guerilla units for them to study, grasp, and implement

With regard to the *emulation movement to increase production,* the Government has drawn up a comprehensive general plan. On the basis of it, the different branches, localities and families will work out their own particular plans which must be realistic and well-coordinated. and strive to fulfil them at all costs.

The comrades in charge will give a clear account of these two matters. Here I will only speak of the *emulation movement to practise thrift and oppose embezzlement, waste and bureaucracy.*

I. THRIFT

First of all, let us ask some questions :
— What is thrift ?
— Why must we practise thrift ?
— What kind of thrift must be practised ?
— Who must practise thrift ?

1. To practise thrift does not mean to be stingy, "to consider a coin as big as a drum", not to do things worth doing, not to spend sums worth spending ; to practise thrift does not mean to impose privations on our armymen, cadres and people. On the contrary, to practise thrift is essentially aimed at helping to increase production, and as a result to raise their living standards. Scientifically speaking, to practise thrift is a positive, not a negative act.

2. Our country was plundered by the French for 30 years and then by the Japanese imperialists, that is why our economy is poor and backward. Now we must have a strong economy to wage the war of resistance and reconstruct the country.

To build our economy we must have funds. To get these, the capitalist countries use three means: to raise loans abroad ; to pillage their colonies ; and to exploit their peasants and workers. We cannot resort to such means. Only by increasing production and practising thrift can we secure more funds for economic construction and development.

3. We must *save time*. For example : by improving organization and raising efficiency, we can finish in one day what used to be done in two.

We must *save labour*. For instance : with better organization and higher efficiency, a job which used to require ten persons can now be done with five.

We must *save money*. For example : by cutting down on manpower, time and raw materials we now spend only 10,000 *dong* on what used to cost 20,000.

In brief, we must streamline organization so that one person can do the work of two, one day is enough to finish the work of two, and one *dong* can be as useful as two.

4. Everybody must *practise thrift*. First of all, in public services, the army, and in enterprises. Some people may ask : How can the army practise thrift since it only concerns itself with fighting the enemy and scoring feats of arms and is not a service of production ?

In the army, such services as the Commissariat, the Ordnance Corps, the Transport Department, etc., must practise thrift. For instance :

Previously, suppose each fighter used 60 cartridges on an average per enemy soldier killed, now he uses only 10 as a result of diligent training and better marksmanship. Thus, he saves 80 per cent on cartridges, and the raw materials and manpower saved can be used to produce other weapons. Previously, the Transport Department had to use 100 trucks to carry cartridges, now it only needs 20, thus saving on vehicles, petrol and lubricants ; and if fewer vehicles are in service, less manpower will be needed to mend the roads, etc.

In the various military campaigns we have captured a lot of booty (ammunition, food, arms). Our armymen take good care of them and use them against the enemy ; in this way they also *increase production*.

Some may ask : Besides growing crops and raising livestock for their own use how can the public services (for example the judicial service) practise thrift ?

Any public service must and can practise thrift. For example, all public services use envelopes; if every envelope is used twice or three times, each year the Government can save tens of tons of paper. If the judicial cadres raise their efficiency, they will help people who have dealings with the judicial service to save time to increase production.

5. *Results from thrift* :

The above-mentioned examples show that *if we know how to save manpower,* resources and time, with what we have now our production as well as our forces in every field can be increased several times.

In the *Soviet Union,* due to thrift, the funds invested in the Five-Year Plan (1946-1950) increased by 26,000 million roubles, that is by one-third.

For example, in 1948. a garment shop in Moscow saved more than 34,000 metres of fabric, enough to make 20,000 more shirts.

Time is saved when efficiency is raised. Formerly it took 20,000 work-hours to make a big airplane, now only 12 700 hours are needed; formerly 8,000 work-hours were necessary to make a big tank, now only 3,700 hours.

In *China,* in 1951, due to increased output and thrift, the people of the North-East produced 14 million more tons of foodstuffs. This year, the workers and the population of this zone have promised Chairman Mao Tse-tung that they would save 22 million tons.

Thanks to thrift the North-West has got an increase of one million tons of foodstuffs, 600,000 metric quintals of cotton, 350,000 head of buffaloes and oxen, etc. ; the other zones have achieved similar results.

Time saving and higher productivity go hand in hand. Previously a weaver had to make more than 5,200 steps in two hours. Now, after the popularization of the *Xich*

Kien Tu method only 2,300 steps are needed. Fatigue is lessened, while output is raised. *Xich Kien Tu*, the author of this method of rationalization, is a girl-weaver of 17.

Thanks to emulation in both production and *thrift*, only five years after World War II the economy of the Soviet Union has made prodigious leaps. While in the capitalist countries, the cost of living is rising, and the people have to suffer ever more privations, in the Soviet Union prices have been cut four times, and the people are getting happier and happier.

The triumph of the Chinese revolution dates back only a few years but thanks to increased production and thrift, the economy has been developed, finances unified, prices stabilized, and the people's living standards improved very rapidly.

We are waging a war of resistance, our conditions are more difficult. But if we are determined to increase production and practise thrift we shall certainly succeed in doing so.

II. TO WIPE OUT EMBEZZLEMENT, WASTE AND BUREAUCRACY

To have a good crop we must weed the field, otherwise the rice will grow badly in spite of careful ploughing and abundant manuring. To be successful in increasing production and practising thrift, we must also weed the field, that is, root out embezzlement, waste and bureaucracy. Otherwise they will harm our work.

A. **What is embezzlement ?**

— *For the cadres, embezzlement means :*

To rob public property, to extort money from the people, to pick and steal from Army funds, to falsify expenditure reports. To abuse public property and Government funds, and divert them to the benefit of one's locality or one's unit is also embezzlement.

— *On the side of the people, embezzlement means :*

To rob the people's property; to make collective fraudulent reports.

B. **What is waste ?**

Waste takes on many forms :

Waste of labour : Because of lack of the sense of responsibility or bad organization, a large number of people are assigned to a job which can be done by a few.

This shortcoming exists in the army, public services and enterprises. For example : Owing to defective organization there is much waste in the use of civilian manpower in the repair of roads and bridges, and in serving military campaigns.

Waste of time : Several days are spent for a job which can be done in one day or even half a day. For instance : Meetings may last three or five days instead of only one, because the cadre in charge has not prepared the programme carefully and because those who attend the meeting have not reflected upon the matter to be debated.

Waste of public property : It assumes many forms, of which here are but a few examples:

— Waste of materials by public services.

— Bad use of machines and raw materials in enterprises.

— The Transport Department does not take good enough care of its vehicles, and does not save enough on petrol and lubricants.

— Granaries under the Department of Storehouses are not carefully built; the keepers have a poor sense of responsibility, and so the paddy is damp and damaged.

— The State Trading Department is not careful in its arrangements and calculations, thus suffering damage and losses.

— Armymen do not take good care of their weapons, equipment, and the booty captured.

— Money is badly managed by the Bank and does not help increase production.

— Plans worked out by economic organs are not practical and in harmony with the situation, thus causing losses to the revolution.

— People let their lands lie fallow, burn votive offerings to the spirits, pawn their buffaloes and sell their fields for costly weddings and funerals, etc.

Embezzlement is robbery and pillage. Waste is not, but its consequences are none the less ruinous to the people and the Government, sometimes even more ruinous than embezzlement.

Embezzlement and waste stem from bureaucracy, from the fact that leading individuals and organs at all levels fail to get down to brass tacks, to supervise and educate the cadres, and to get in close touch with the masses. They pay undue attention to matter of form and fail to tackle their jobs in detail and in depth. They only like to convene meetings, write instructions and read reports, but *control nothing thoroughly.*

In short, leading individuals and organs affected with bureaucracy have eyes, but do not see clearly, ears, but do not hear distinctly; regulations and discipline are not observed, and as a result, bad elements and irresponsible cadres are given a free rein to indulge in embezzlement and waste.

Thus bureaucracy fosters, tolerates and protects embezzlement and waste. Hence to wipe out embezzlement and waste, one must first and foremost eliminate bureaucracy.

III. EMBEZZLEMENT AND WASTE ARE ENEMIES OF THE PEOPLE

A. Embezzlement, waste and bureaucracy are enemies of the people, the army, and the Government.

They are quite dangerous enemies because they wield no swords and guns, but lie in our own organizations to spoil our work.

Whether they are committed deliberately or not, embezzlement, waste, and bureaucracy are allied with colonialism and feudalism because they hamper our war of resistance and our national reconstruction. They spoil the integrity of our cadres and their determination to overcome difficulties. They undermine our revolutionary virtues: industry, thrift, integrity, and uprightness

To contribute to the success of the war of resistance and of national construction, our fighters have shed their blood, and our compatriots their sweat. But those who commit embezzlement, waste and bureaucracy sap the spirit, waste the strength and squander the wealth of the Government and the people; this is a crime as serious as that committed by traitors and spies.

For these reasons, the struggle against embezzlement, waste, and bureaucracy is as important and urgent as the fight on the front! This is the ideological and political front.

As on other fronts, to succeed on this one, we must have plans, organization, leadership and activists.

B. To oppose embezzlement, waste and bureaucracy are revolutionary acts.

To wage a revolution is to destroy the bad, and build the good. Our revolution aims at destroying the colonial and feudal regime and building a new democracy.

If after the colonialists and feudalists have been annihilated, the evils left by them (embezzlement, waste, bureaucracy) still subsist, our revolutionary work is not yet completed, because these evils still undermine and sabotage the constructive work of the revolution.

There are people who are enthusiastic and faithful in struggle; they fear neither dangers, hardships, nor the enemy, thus they have *served the revolution well;* but as soon as they hold some authority, they grow arrogant and luxurious, indulge in embezzlement, waste, and unconscious bureaucracy, thus *becoming guilty in the eyes of the revolution.* We must save them, help them recover their revolutionary virtues. Others, while pretending to serve the Fatherland and the people, indulge in embezzlement and waste. and harm the Fatherland and the people. We must educate them, and lead them to the revolutionary path.

Embezzlement, waste, and bureaucracy are evils left by the old society. They spring from self-interest and selfishness. They are begotten by the regime of "exploitation of man by man."

We want to build a new society, a free society where all men are equal, a society where industry, thrift, integrity and uprightness prevail, hence we must wipe out all bad habits of the old society.

C. **To oppose embezzlement and waste is democracy.**

Our armymen unstintingly shed their blood and our compatriots their sweat to save the country. Our fighters entrust their lives, our compatriots their labour and wealth to the Government and the Party to wage the war of resistance and reconstruct the country. This is a form of *democratic centralism.*

The Government and the Party give the cadres authority to command the army, and use money and resources in the war of resistance and national reconstruction. The duty of the cadres is to love and take care of every fighter and to value and save every cent, every bowl of rice, every work-hour of their compatriots. Our fighters and compatriots have the right to demand that the cadres fulfil this task, and to *criticize* those who do not.

Democracy means to rely on the masses, correctly to follow the mass line. Hence, to be successful, the movement against embezzlement, waste and bureaucracy must *rely on the masses.*

By the masses we mean all armymen, all workers in the factories, all civil servants in the public services, etc., and the entire people. As in any other work, only by *mobilizing the masses, implementing democracy,* making the masses understand and enthusiastically participate in this movement, can we be certain of success. The greater the participation of the masses, the more complete and rapid the achievements.

The *task of the masses* is to participate enthusiastically in the movement against embezzlement, waste and bureaucracy. The fighters contribute their exploits and the people their wealth to fight the enemy and save the country. Embezzlement, waste and bureaucracy are a kind of "internal enemy". If our fighters and people, while striving to oppose *the enemy from outside,* forget to fight the enemy from inside, they will not have fulfilled their task. Therefore they must zealously participate in this movement.

At all echelons, we must act as one man and join forces in this struggle. Success will help us strengthen our solidarity and raise productivity even further. It will help our cadres remould themselves ideologically, heighten their political consciousness, become imbued with revolutionary virtues, and whole-heartedly serve the army and the people. It will help purify our administration and make it worthy of our fighters' and compatriots' confidence and sacrifices. It will help us fulfil the plan of the Government and the Party for increased production and thrift and complete our preparations for the general counter-offensive.

INSTRUCTIONS GIVEN AT A CONFERENCE ON GUERILLA WARFARE
(July 1952)

I. All of you here have to various degrees made efforts, scored achievements, endured hardships. For this you deserve praise. However you should remember that *these accomplishments belong not to any one individual but to all our army and compatriots*. Without their assistance, your talents would have been of no avail.

II. Since the Hoa Binh Campaign guerilla warfare in the enemy's rear has greatly developed compared with last year; in particular, *our compatriots and cadres are confident that they can by themselves defeat the enemy*. This is a correct assessment and a very good change.

You must know that *our war of resistance is a long and hard, but surely victorious, one*. It is long because it will last till the enemy is defeated, till he "quits". The 80-year-long oppression by the French imperialists is like a chronic disease that cannot be cured in one day or one year. Don't be hasty, don't ask for an immediate victory : this is subjectiveness. A long resistance implies hardships, but will end in victory.

This long and hard war of resistance *calls for self-reliance*. This is especially true when operating in the enemy's rear. The assistance of friendly countries is of course important, but we should not be dependent on it and stay idle. A nation which does not rely on its own strength but merely looks for help from other peoples does not deserve to be independent.

In this long resistance what should the guerillas in the enemy's rear do? What is their task? *Guerilla warfare, too, is protracted warfare. The present task is to foil the enemy's scheme of "feeding war with war, and using Vietnamese to fight Vietnamese".* The enemy, being unable to grab manpower and material resources in the free zones, is trying to do so in the zones in his rear. We must frustrate this scheme. By so doing, we shall effectively contribute to the preparation for a general counter-offensive. The enemy will be gradually weakened and finally defeated.

III. Operating in the enemy's rear, you have shown many good qualities: perseverance, courage and solidarity. I shall not expatiate on your strong points. Let me only stress a few shortcomings that should be redressed:

1. *The cadres of the army, mass organizations, administration, and Party have not studied with sufficient care, in sufficient detail, and in sufficient depth the orders and directives from the Party Central Committee and the Government.* This is a serious shortcoming. The Central Committee and the Government see far and wide. Their directives are the results of careful study of situations and experiences all over the country. The cadres of the army, mass organizations, administration and Party must carefully study these directives so as to apply them to the concrete situation of each locality. Individual regions have only a limited range of vision; they can only see the tree but not the forest, they can grasp only part of the situation, not the whole of it. And so a job deemed a success by a given region may turn out to be a failure when viewed in the general context. This is due to inadequate study of directives from the Government and the Party Central Committee.

2. *The regular, regional and guerilla forces should not content themselves with fighting the enemy.* To fight the enemy is a good thing ; but *to confine oneself to fighting him* without paying due attention to politics, economics, propaganda and education of the people is to know only one aspect of things, for fighting cannot be dissociated from politics and economics. If we only think of fighting without caring for economics, we won't be able to fight when we run short of rice. So, let us fight of course, but fighting alone will not do, other things must also be thought of.

3. Another shortcoming lies in the fact that *the regular, regional and guerilla forces are all eager to fight big battles and win great victories* while failing to conduct a careful study of the situation and a detailed assessment of our own possibilities as well as those of the enemy so as to determine appropriate targets and combat methods. As a result, hitches have developed in practice. Wherever you may be, attack only when you are sure of winning ; do not engage the enemy when you are not, especially when you are surrounded by enemy forces.

4. *Army cadres concern themselves solely with military affairs, Government cadres with administrative jobs, Party cadres with Party business.* They are like men standing on one leg. It is wrong for a cadre to be acquainted only with one field. He will not be truly proficient because army, mass, government and party work forms a whole which would not be strong and complete should one of its components come to miss. Party and government cadres seem to rely entirely on the army for fighting the enemy, unaware that the Party should exercise overall leadership and that, in combat, victory can come only if there is close co-ordination of all elements.

5. As regards Party cadres in particular, partly because of unfavourable conditions but mostly because they do

not grasp the main link, i.e. the basis of the Party organization, the Party bases in the areas still under temporary enemy control are not yet very strong. It should be known that if the Party is strong, everything will get along well.

6. *Security* measures are not yet satisfactorily carried out, state secrets not yet well kept.

7. *Propaganda and agitation work among puppet troops* has recorded some achievements but has not yielded steady results. Good work is done in places where the cadres show resourcefulness ; but things slacken wherever they lack initiative. The enemy has rigged up units of village guards and security forces. These brambles should be got rid of. You should exchange experiences and step up this political work among puppet troops.

8. As regards *propaganda in the enemy's rear*, let us remember that before the August Revolution, in spite of the presence of the Japanese, the French and the Vietnamese traitors, we succeeded in carrying out propaganda work among the people. This was due to our resourcefulness ; besides verbal propaganda, we also used press publications. At present, the Central Committee and the Government are trying to send such papers as *Cuu Quoc* (National Salvation) and *Nhan Dan* (the People) into enemy-occupied zones. But this is not enough and we have met with difficulties. In the enemy's rear we must circulate papers printed from lithographic stone or clay which need neither be of large size nor be issued every day ; the main purpose being to popularize the government's line and policies and carry out a *practical propaganda* among the people about our successes as well as the enemy's crimes and failures. There lies the educational work of the Party.

IV. Now about the jobs to be done :

1. First of all, there must be close internal unity, i.e.
our army, people, government and party must be closely
united. For whatever we do, there should be careful
study and discussion, unity of thought and action, mutual
help and sincere criticism and self-criticism with a view
to common progress.

2. The orders and directives from the Central Committee and the Government must be carefully studied,
correctly applied and thoroughly carried out.

3. What matters the most is that our armed forces, be
they regulars, regionals or guerillas, must hold fast to
the people ; divorce from the latter will surely lead to
defeat. To cling to the people means to win their hearts,
gain their confidence and affection. This will allow us
to overcome any difficulty and achieve sure success. To
this end, we must protect, assist and educate the people.
Educating the people does not mean to thrust books into
their hands and compel them to learn ; if we act in this
way, we shall go counter to their interests and those of
the revolution. This is bureaucratic commandism. We
must persuade the people so that they will do things of
their own accord ; coercion would only produce temporary results but no lasting effects.

4. Regular forces operating in the enemy's rear must
assist regional and guerilla forces in organization and
training ; they should assist them, not do things in their
place. Furthermore they must help the people ; some
units have managed to do so, but others have not. As
goes a saying of ours : "One should curl up when inside
a sphere and stretch out when inside a tube." When
fighting in an enemy-occupied area, we must use guerilla tactics, not fight regular warfare as in the free

zones. We must absolutely not go in for large-scale battles and big victories, unless we are 100 per cent certain of success.

5. The aim of guerilla warfare is not to wage large-scale battles and win big victories, but to nibble at the enemy, harass him in such a way that he can neither eat nor sleep in peace, to give him no respite, to wear him out physically and mentally, and finally to annihilate him. Wherever he goes, he should be attacked by our guerillas, stumble on land mines or be greeted by sniper fire. Here is what French soldiers say in their letters: "In Viet Nam, death is lying in wait for us in every cave, every bush, every pond..."

If you manage to redress your shortcomings and do as I said, you will surely gain successes. However, you should bear in mind that so long as a single enemy soldier remains on our land, our victory is not yet complete. The failures of the enemy forces, in spite of their better equipment and greater experience, have been due to their subjectivity. So, if you guard against subjectivity and are careful not to underrate the enemy, you will win.

Back in your home localities, you must urge people to emulate one another in all fields: to fight the enemy and accomplish deeds, to organize propaganda and agitation work among the enemy troops and their puppets, to increase production and practise thrift. A saying goes: "Adequate food, strong army." We shall not have enough food for our war of resistance if we do not boost production and practise economy. Can you promise to do as I told you? (All said yes in a loud voice.) You have made a pledge you must fulfil it at all costs.

Another point: you must report our troops' and our compatriots' accomplishments to the Central Committee and the Government for commendation and reward which is also a means of education and exhortation. Those commended will be encouraged while the others will actively emulate them. So far, the local authorities have sent but very few reports ; from now on, you must make up for it.

Lastly, I ask you to transmit my best wishes and those of the Central Committee and the Government to our compatriots, our cadres and fighters, particularly to our elderly guerillas, women guerillas and children of the resistance. The Central Committee, the Government and I myself are glad and confident that our army and compatriots in the enemy's rear will correctly implement the line and policies of the resistance so as to achieve quick victory.

REPLIES TO A SWEDISH CORRESPONDENT

(November 1953)

QUESTION : *The debate in the French National Assembly has shown that a great number of French politicians are for a peaceful settlement of the conflict in Viet Nam through direct negotiations with the Vietnamese Government. This desire is spreading among the French people. Is it welcomed by yourself and your Government ?*

ANSWER : The war in Viet Nam was launched by the French Government. The Vietnamese people were obliged to take up arms and have heroically struggled for nearly eight years now against the aggressors, to safeguard their independence and their right to live in freedom and peace. If the French colonialists continue their aggressive war, the Vietnamese people are determined to carry on their patriotic resistance until final victory. However, if the French Government have drawn a lesson from the war they have been waging these last few years and want to negotiate an armistice in Viet Nam and solve the Viet Nam problem by peaceful means, the people and Government of the Democratic Republic of Viet Nam are ready to meet this desire.

QUESTION : *Will a ceasefire or an armistice be possible ?*

ANSWER : An armistice can take place in Viet Nam, provided that the French Government ends its war of aggression in Viet Nam. The basis for such an armistice is that the French Government should show sincere respect for the genuine independence of Viet Nam.

QUESTION : *Would you agree to mediation by a neutral country for a meeting between you and representatives of the High Command of the other side ? May Sweden offer such a mediation ?*

ANSWER : If some neutral countries try to help bring a speedy end to the hostilities in Viet Nam by means of negotiations, such an effort will be welcomed. However, the negotiation for an armistice essentially concerns the Government of the Democratic Republic of Viet Nam and the French Government.

QUESTION : *In your opinion, is there any other way to end the hostilities ?*

ANSWER : The war in Viet Nam has brought havoc to the Vietnamese people and at the same time has caused much suffering to the French people. That is why the French people have been struggling for an end to this war.

I have constantly shown my sympathy and esteem for the French people and the French peace fighters. At present not only is the independence of Viet Nam seriously encroached upon but the independence of France itself is also gravely threatened. On the one hand, the US imperialists are pressing the French colonialists to continue and expand the aggressive war in Viet Nam, hoping thus to weaken France more and more and eventually replacing it in Indochina; on the other, they oblige France to ratify the European defence treaty, which means the revival of German militarism.

Therefore, the struggle of the French people for independence, democracy and peace and for an end to the war in Viet Nam, constitutes one of the important factors of a peaceful settlement of the Viet Nam question.

REPORT TO THE THIRD SESSION OF THE FIRST NATIONAL ASSEMBLY

(December 1st, 1953)

Deputies to the National Assembly,

On behalf of the Government I am happy to welcome you to this special session of the National Assembly.

I send my cordial greetings to the deputies who cannot attend it on account of their resistance work.

On behalf of the Government, I pay respectful homage to those members of the National Assembly who have heroically laid down their lives for the Resistance, for the Fatherland.

On behalf of the Government, I also welcome the delegates of the Front coming to greet the National Assembly.

Deputies,

For the last eight years, our entire people have been carrying out the greatest task of all : the resistance.

From now on, we have another central task : land reform.

We must push forward the war of resistance to ensure success for land reform.

We must strive to implement land reform in order to secure complete victory for the war of resistance.

At this special session, the National Assembly will hear a report on the resistance during the last few years, discuss the land reform policy and approve the land reform law.

Our country is a part of the world. The situation in our country has an effect on the world and the situation in the world also exerts an influence on our country. For this reason, before reporting on the resistance and the land reform policy, I shall report briefly on the situation in the world and in our country.

THE WORLD SITUATION

We can say right away that our camp is growing stronger with every passing day while the enemy camp is becoming weaker and weaker.

The *Soviet Union,* the bulwark of peace and democracy in the world, is vigorously advancing from socialism to communism. Mankind's dream of happiness for so many centuries is being gradually realized on one-sixth of the globe.

To safeguard world peace, the Soviet Union also possesses A bombs and H bombs, but it has time and again proposed the banning of these weapons.

With the wholehearted assistance of the Soviet Union, the *East-European people's democracies* are devoting all their effort to building socialism.

China has gained great successes in the fight against the US imperialists to help Korea, and has repeatedly recorded great achievements in the first year of the Five-Year Plan and in all construction work.

The great electoral successes of the Italian Communist Party and the French Communist Party, the mammoth strikes (August and September 1953) in these two countries, the struggle waged by the toiling class in various countries, and the national-liberation movement in Malaya, the Philippines, North Africa, Central Africa Guiana, etc., have proved that the struggle waged by the people throughout the world is developing.

The Conference for Peace in Asia and the Pacific (held in October 1952) and the World Conference for the Defence of Peace (held in November 1952) have shown the tremendous strength of the world camp of peace and democracy.

During the recent period, the greatest success gained by the world camp of peace and democracy was the cessation of hostilities in Korea. In their most heroic struggle, the Korean army and people, hand in hand with the Chinese volunteers, have annihilated more than one million soldiers of the USA and its camp. For their part, the forces of democracy and peace in the world are extremely powerful. Like a pair of pincers, these two forces have forced the USA and its camp to accept an armistice in Korea.

Last October, the Third World Congress of Trade Unions, on behalf of more than 88 million workers in 79 countries, took the resolution that the 19th of December this year will be "the Day of Solidarity with the Heroic Vietnamese People and of Struggle for the Cessation of the Aggressive War in Viet Nam". This is an expression of warm internationalism, of positive class feelings; it inspires our people with more enthusiasm to carry on the war of resistance, and more confidence in final victory.

That is a summary of the situation in our camp.

What about the imperialist camp headed by the USA ? *The USA and sixteen countries of its camp* (including Great Britain and France) have suffered an ignominious defeat in Korea. Ever since the late 19th century, the USA has repeatedly relied on war to enrich itself and become a chieftain. This is the first time (but it will not be the last) it has suffered a great failure, losing not only men (more than 390,500 American soldiers dead and wounded), and money (more than 20,000 million

dollars), but also its face before the other countries
The position of the USA in the United Nations is growing
weaker, its camp is becoming more and more divided and
its economy is plunged into an ever more acute crisis.

The capitalist countries dependent on the USA, such
as Great Britain and France, are facing ever greater
economic and political difficulties due to their arms race
policy, the people's movement at home and the movement
of national liberation in their colonies.

The present US scheme is to kindle war in the hope
of gaining world hegemony.

In Asia it sabotages the convening of the political
conference, seeking to rekindle war in Korea; rearms
Japan; prevents China from joining the United Nations;
and interferes more actively in the war in Viet Nam,
Cambodia and Laos.

In Europe, it frustrates the unification of Germany,
and rearms West Germany with a view to turning it into
the mainstay of the "European Army".

*
*   *

Our camp is becoming ever stronger and more united
in the front of democracy and peace headed by the
Soviet Union.

Our present *main goal* is to relax international tension;
we advocate that all international disputes be solved by
means of negotiations.

The present task of the world's people is to consolidate
their achievements, maintain vigilance and guard against
US schemes, and strongly push forward the world peace
movement.

The world situation is favourable to us. We support
the world peace movement. But we must not harbour

the illusion that peace can be realized easily. It can be gained only through hard struggle. As the French colonialists and American interventionists are persisting in their aggressive war in our country, we must overcome all difficulties, rely essentially on our own forces and strongly push forward the war of resistance until complete victory is won.

THE DOMESTIC SITUATION

A. **On the enemy's side :**

In the military field: The enemy has suffered great losses (about 320,000 men by November 1953). There is growing shortage of European and African manpower. On the main battlefields, the enemy's passive posture has worsened. Recently, he has tried to launch a few thrusts into the free area in the Third Interzone and into some coastal localities in the Fourth Interzone, but he is basically passive.

However, at present the enemy still has strong forces. We must not underestimate him.

Political situation. Contradictions are becoming ever more acute between the Americans and the French, between the French and the puppets, and between the pro-French puppets and the pro-American puppets.

In the areas still temporarily occupied by the enemy, his policies of deception and exploitation are resolutely opposed by our people.

In France, the anti-war movement is spreading.

Economy and finance. The enemy has incurred ever greater expenditures (from 1946 up to now, he has spent more than 3,000 billion francs).

But he can still get rubber and coal, export a certain quantity of rice, collect taxes and plunder the people's property in areas still under his temporary control. In addition he is given "assistance" by the Americans.

On the other hand, he is doing his utmost to destroy our production and communications in the free areas, guerilla bases and guerilla zones.

In the cultural and social fields. In the areas still under his temporary occupation, the enemy strives to disseminate a depraved culture and hooliganism in order to poison our people, especially our youth. He seeks to use religions to divide our people.

His main scheme is to *"use Vietnamese to fight Vietnamese and feed war with war."*

*

* *

What is the enemy doing at present and what are his intentions ?

The Americans are interfering more and more in the war in Viet Nam, Cambodia and Laos, and giving the French and the puppets ever more money and weapons. They buy over the Vietnamese, Cambodian and Lao puppets and speed up the organization of puppet armed forces. They force the French to make concessions to the puppets, that is, to them. They have a plan to replace the French step by step, but continue to use the latter as stooges for the implementation of their war policy.

Apart from their economic exploitation and plundering, the French and American imperialists practise such deceitful policies in the political field as :

— Declaring sham "independence" and "democracy", holding fraudulent elections.

— Pretending to carry out "land reform" to deceive the peasants in areas still under their temporary occupation.

— Setting up "yellow" trade-unions to mislead the workers.

— Advancing a peace fable to hide the truth from the French people and the world, and to deceive our people.

Meanwhile, General Navarre feverishly mustered his mobile forces to attack us, disturb our rear areas, expand commando activities and intensify intelligence activities.

In short, the French and the Americans are striving to implement their scheme, which is to extend the war by "using Vietnamese to fight Vietnamese and feeding war with war".

We must not be subjective and underestimate the enemy. We must always be vigilant and ready to frustrate his schemes. But we can say that his activities betray weakness, not strength. He is afraid of our policy of protracted resistance. He is afraid of the world peace movement.

In order to foil the enemy's schemes, we must push ahead with our war of resistance. To this end, we must carry out land reform.

B. **On our side.**

In the military field. From the autumn-winter of 1950 up to now, we have gained great victories in seven military campaigns and held the initiative on the main fronts. We have liberated the greater part of the vast Northwest area. The guerilla movement has developed strongly everywhere.

The ideological remoulding and technical training drives in the army have brought good results. Our army has grown up rapidly in both number and quality.

Many regular, regional and guerilla units have recorded heroic and glorious military feats.

Political situation. The ideological remoulding courses for cadres within and without the Party have had good results (nearly 15 800 cadres from central to village levels have attended these courses).

The Lien Viet (National United Front) has been consolidated and enlarged.

The alliance between Viet Nam, Cambodia and Laos has grown closer.

The diplomatic activities of our Government and people have expanded and have won the sympathy and support of the people of the world, especially the people of the friendly countries and of France.

Economy and finance. Our people have overcome many difficulties, emulated one another in production, and contributed greatly in manpower and wealth to the war of resistance. Our finances have gradually stabilized. We have established commercial relations with China, which is very advantageous to our people.

In the cultural and social fields. An ever greater number of toiling people are now engaged in study. The number of general education schools and that of students have increased many times. The training of specialists has been gradually reorganized and expanded.

On the whole, the position of the enemy is weakening with every passing day while ours is growing ever stronger.

The above is a summary of the major achievements of our people, Government and Party, but our work has also shown shortcomings: in the previous stage of our land policy we were too much concerned about achieving unity with the landlords for the sake of the Resistance and did not attach due importance to the peasant question and the agrarian question.

Recently, our Government and Party have corrected this shortcoming, and much progress has been made. But in some localities the policy of the Central Committee has not been strictly implemented. A number of cadres think and act contrary to the policy of the Government and Party; they lack the sense of organization and discipline. Other cadres attach importance only to fighting feudalism and neglect the struggle against imperialism.

We must set right these shortcomings and prevent both "leftist" and rightist deviations.

LAND REFORM

Concerning this problem, I only wish to stress the following points:

The significance of land reform:

Our revolution is a people's democratic national revolution against aggressive imperialism and its prop, feudalism.

Our slogan during the war of resistance is "All for the front, all for victory!" The more the war of resistance develops, the more manpower and wealth it requires. Our peasants have contributed the greatest part of this manpower and wealth to the resistance. We must liberate them from the feudal yoke and foster their strength in order fully to mobilize this huge force for the resistance and win victory.

The key to victory for the resistance lies in consolidating and enlarging the National United Front, consolidating the worker-peasant alliance and the people's power, strengthening and developing the Army, consolidating the Party and strengthening its leadership in all respects. Only by mobilizing the masses for land reform can we carry out these tasks in favourable conditions.

The enemy actively seeks to use Vietnamese to fight Vietnamese and to feed war with war. They are doing their utmost to deceive, divide and exploit our people. Land reform will exert an influence on our peasant compatriots in the enemy's rear areas and will encourage them to struggle even more vigorously against him in order to liberate themselves, and to give even more enthusiastic support to the democratic Government of the Resistance ; at the same time it will have an impact on the puppet armed forces and cause their disintegration because the absolute majority of the puppet soldiers are peasants in enemy-occupied areas.

The overwhelming majority of our people are peasants.

Over these last years, it is thanks to their forces that the war of resistance has been going on successfully. It is also thanks to the peasant forces that it will gain complete victory and our country will be successfully rebuilt.

Our peasants account for almost 90 per cent of the population but they own only 30 per cent of the arable land ; they have to work hard all the year round and suffer poverty all their lives.

The feudal landlord class accounts for less than 5 per cent of the population but they and the colonialists occupy about 70 per cent of the arable land and live in clover. This situation is most unjust. Because of it our country has been invaded and our people are backward and poor. During the years of resistance, the Government has decreed the reduction of land rent, the refunding of excess land rent and the temporary distribution of land belonging to the French and the Vietnamese traitors and that of communal land to the peasants in the free areas. But the key problem remains unsolved : the peasant masses have no land or lack land. This affects the forces of the resistance and the production work of the peasants.

Only by carrying out land reform, giving land to the tillers, liberating the productive forces in the countryside from the yoke of the feudal landlord class can we do away with poverty and backwardness and strongly mobilize the huge forces of the peasants in order to develop production and push the war of resistance forward to complete victory.

The goal set for land reform is to wipe out the feudal system of land ownership, distribute land to the tillers, liberate the productive forces in the countryside, develop production and push forward the war of resistance.

The general line and policy is to rely entirely on the landless and poor peasants, closely unite with the middle peasants, enter into alliance with the rich peasants, wipe out feudal exploitation step by step and with discrimination, develop production, and push forward the war of resistance.

To meet the requirements of the resistance and the National United Front, which consist in satisfying the land demands of the peasants while consolidating and developing the National United Front in the interests of the resistance and production, in the course of land reform we must apply different kinds of treatment to the landlords according to their individual political attitudes. This means that depending on individual cases we shall order confiscation or requisition with or without compensation, but not wholesale confiscation or whole-sale requisition without compensation.

The *guiding principle for land reform* is boldly to mobilize the peasants, rely on the masses, correctly follow the mass line, organize, educate and lead the peasants to struggle according to plan, step by step, with good discipline and under close leadership.

The dispersion of land by landlords after the promul-gation of the land rent reduction decree (July 14, 1949) is illegal (except for particular cases mentioned in the circular issued by the Prime Minister's Office on June 1, 1953).

The land confiscated or requisitioned with or without compensation is to be definitively allotted to the peasants who have no or not enough land. These peasants will have the right of ownership over the land thus distributed.

The *guiding principle for land distribution* is to take the village as unit, to allot land in priority to those who have been tilling it, to take into consideration the area, quality and location of the land, so as to give a fair share to everyone; especial consideration must be given to the peasants who have previously tilled the land to be distributed. As for the diehard elements bent on sabotaging land reform, the traitors, reactionaries, and local despots, those among them who are sentenced to 5 years' imprisonment and more will not receive any land.

*

* *

The mass mobilization launched this year gives experience in preparation for the land reform drive to be carried out next year. From this experience we have drawn a number of lessons. In general, in those localities where the Party and Government policies have been firmly grasped and the mass line correctly followed (in spite of mistakes and deviations by some cadres in some places), satisfactory results have been recorded.

But failures have happened wherever the movement has been launched hurriedly by hot-headed local cadres before the decision had been taken by the central authorities.

Land reform is a policy to be applied throughout the country, but it must be carried out step by step, in accordance with local conditions.

After the land reform law has been approved by the National Assembly, the Government will, next year, fix the dates and the places in the free zone for land reform to be carried out.

The Government will later on take decisions concerning the regions inhabited by national minorities, the Fifth Interzone, Nam Bo, and the guerilla bases. In guerilla and enemy-occupied areas, land reform will be carried out after their liberation.

In those localities where mass mobilization has not yet been launched for radical land rent reduction, the latter must be completed before land reform is undertaken. This is in order to organize the peasants, raise their political consciousness, build up their political supremacy in the villages and at the same time to train cadres, adjust organization and prepare the political conditions for land reform.

No locality is allowed to start mass mobilization for land reform without authorization by the Government.

Land reform is a peasant revolution, a class struggle in the countryside; it is a large-scale, hard and complex struggle which requires careful preparations, clearly mapped-out plans, close leadership, judicious choice of places, strict time-table and correct implementation. These are conditions for success.

The experience gained in other countries shows that a successful land reform will help overcome many difficulties and solve many problems.

In the *military field*, our peasant compatriots will join the resistance even more enthusiastically, hence it will be easier to build up the army and recruit voluntary civilian manpower. Our soldiers, with their minds at peace about their families, will fight even more resolutely.

In the *political field*, political and economic power in the countryside will be in the hands of the peasants, the people's democratic dictatorship will be truly carried into effect, the worker-peasant alliance will be consolidated, the National United Front will include more than 90 per cent of the people in the countryside and will become prodigiously great and strong.

In the *economic field*, liberated from feudal landlordism, the peasants will enthusiastically carry out production and practise thrift, their purchasing power will increase, industry and commerce will develop and the national economy as a whole will expand.

Thanks to the development of production, the livelihood of the peasants, workers, soldiers and cadres will be improved more rapidly.

In *the cultural and social field,* the large majority of the people, now having enough food and clothing, will study even harder, in accordance with the saying: "One must have enough to eat before one could practise the good doctrine." Good customs and habits will develop. The experience drawn from localities where mass mobilization has been launched shows that our compatriots are very fond of study and that there are good opportunities for the intellectuals to serve the people.

As said above, land reform is an immense, complex and hard class struggle. It is all the more complex and all the harder because we are conducting a war of resistance. But it is precisely because we want to push the resistance forward to victory that we must be determined to make land reform a success.

Because it is a complex and hard struggle, a number of cadres, whether they are Party members or not, might commit mistakes and deviations in their thoughts and deeds while implementing it. To prevent and set right these shortcomings and mistakes, we must firmly grasp the policies of the Party and the Government, completely rely on the masses and correctly follow the mass line.

The Government and the Party call on all cadres and Party members to abide by the policies of the Government and the Party, keep discipline, side entirely with the peasants, lead them in struggle. Whenever their own private interests or those of their families run counter to the interests of the resistance and those of the peasant masses, they must sacrifice the former to the latter.

We must mobilize the entire Party, the entire Army and the entire people to ensure the implementation of land reform, to fulfil this great task.

For the Party members and the cadres, for the democratic parties and the patriotic personalities, this is a tremendous trial. All of us must win this trial, just as we are winning this other immense trial: the war of resistance against aggressive imperialism.

So our two central tasks in the next year will be: to fight the enemy and to carry out land reform.

We must fight the enemy on all fronts, annihilate as much of his force as possible, and smash his new military schemes.

We must mobilize the masses to carry out land reform in the regions fixed by the Government.

To carry out land reform is aimed at securing victory for the war of resistance.

To fight the enemy and to annihilate his forces is aimed at securing success for land reform.

All other undertakings must be focused on those two central tasks and serve them. In 1954, we must pay particular attention to three great tasks, combining them with land reform:

To strengthen the armed forces (the regular army, the regional forces, the militia and guerilla units) in all respects: organization, training, raising of their political consciousness, technical level and combat strength.

To train cadres and raise their ideological level, promote them to appropriate posts, reorganize the Party bases in the countryside.

To develop agricultural production; to meet the requirements of the resistance and supply food to the people; to push forward the national economy.

The full implementation of these two central undertakings and three great tasks will create more favourable conditions for the carrying out of other duties : firmly to maintain and develop the struggle in the enemy's rear areas, to consolidate the people's democratic power in the villages, to reorganize the security service, to develop and consolidate the National United Front, to collect agricultural taxes, to develop our economy and finances, to intensify propaganda and education and to promote work in the cultural and social fields.

*

* *

Our strength lies in the tens of millions of our peasant compatriots who are ready to organize themselves under the leadership of the Government and the Party and to rise up and smash the feudal and colonial yoke. With skilful organization and leadership, these forces will shake heaven and earth and sweep away all colonialists and feudalists. We can conclude that under the firm and correct leadership of the Government and the Party and with the whole-hearted assistance of the National Assembly and the Front, the successful completion of land reform will take us a long way towards victory for the resistance and success for national construction.

LETTER OF COMMENDATION TO THE ARMY, CIVILIAN WORKERS, YOUNG VOLUNTEERS AND PEOPLE IN THE NORTHWEST ON THE OCCASION OF THE GLORIOUS VICTORY OF DIEN BIEN PHU

(May 8, 1954)

Our army has liberated Dien Bien Phu. The Government and I convey our cordial greetings to you, cadres, fighters, civilian workers, young volunteers and local people, who have brilliantly fulfilled your tasks.

This victory is a resounding one, but it is only the beginning. We must not grow vainglorious and subjective and underestimate the enemy. We are waging a resolute war of resistance to gain independence, national unity, democracy and peace. Whether our struggle is on the military or diplomatic plane, we shall have to fight long and hard before complete victory is achieved.

The Government and I will reward those cadres, soldiers, civilian workers, young volunteers and local people who have performed especially brilliant deeds.

Cordial greetings. We shall win!

REPORT TO THE 6TH PLENUM OF THE VIET NAM WORKERS' PARTY CENTRAL COMMITTEE

(July 15, 1954)

The 6th Plenum of the Central Committee has been enlarged to include a number of high-ranking cadres and is to discuss the new situation and the new tasks.

On behalf of the Central Committee, I express my cordial regards to our fighters and cadres on all fronts, my encouragement to our compatriots in the free and the newly-liberated zones, and my sympathy to those living in areas still under enemy control.

On behalf of the Central Committee I thank the fraternal Parties and the peoples of the friendly countries for having assisted us in our war of resistance and struggle for peace, and peace-loving people all over the world for their support to our cause.

Now I shall report on the new situation and the new tasks.

I. THE NEW SITUATION

1. *World situation*

Owing to the all-sided development, consolidation and advance of the Soviet Union, China and the People's Democracies, the world movement for peace and democracy is growing ever stronger. Thanks to the skilful and wise diplomacy of the Soviet Union, the imperialists, and above all the American imperialists, have been compelled to attend the Berlin and the Geneva Conferences. The holding of these two conferences alone is in itself a victory for our side and a defeat for the imperialists.

The inner contradictions of the US-headed imperialist camp have steadily deepened and widened. For instance :

Contradictions between Britain and the United States : conflict of interests in the Mediterranean and in the Middle East and Near East. The United States has pulled Pakistan, New Zealand and Australia away from the British and to its own side. In the Far East, British policy towards China and Japan runs counter to that of the United States, etc.

Contradictions between the United States and France : outwardly, the United States is helping France, but this is done with the intention of putting pressure on it. It has done its utmost to force France into signing the Franco-German treaty and that on the organization of a European army. But it would be suicidal for France to do so. In Indochina, these two countries seem united in coping with our resistance, but in fact the United States wants to have the puppets well in hand in order to oust the French, and has already put Ngo Dinh Diem — its zealous valet — at the head of a puppet government.

The American policy of a treaty on a "European Army" has sown discord among and within the Western European countries. The people of these countries oppose their pro-American governments, and contradictions crop up between the pro-American capitalists and the others. In Asia, the United States wants to set up S.E.A.T.O. with a view to using Asians to fight Asians. However, this extremely reactionary policy has met with repeated failures. The Americans practise a "policy of force" and brandish their A and H bombs to threaten the other

countries. But the world peace movement opposing their
policy of violence and their A and H bombs becomes
stronger day by day. Even the Pope has been forced to
oppose the use of such weapons. Thus the peace movement has drawn support from the vast majority of the
people in the world, from many members of the bourgeoisie in various countries, and from the Pope himself.

Faced with the Geneva Conference and our victory at
D:en Bien Phu, the United States plotted to issue a "joint
declaration" with France, Britain and a number of other
countries to intimidate China, charging it with intervention in the Indochina war. But due to opposition from
Britain and reluctance from the other countries, the move
failed. Then the Americans proposed "joint action" to
save France at Dien Bien Phu but Britain and the other
countries again disagreed, and this scheme also failed.
The Americans have used every means to sabotage the
Geneva Conference. The US Secretary of State attended
the Conference for only a few days then left, but the
Conference has continued none the less and has led to some
results.

For all their setbacks, the Americans are still obdurate
and are speeding up the formation of S.E.A.T.O. Their
failure means success for our camp. *US imperialism is
the main enemy of world peace,* consequently we must
concentrate our forces against it.

2. *Home situation*

The Vietnamese, Cambodian and Lao peoples are
united and their resistance grows ever more vigorous.
Our guerilla forces in South, Central and North Viet
Nam, not only have stood firm but have grown ever
stronger. From the Border Campaign to the Hoa Binh,
Tay Bac and other campaigns, our regular forces have
recorded repeated successes. These victories plus the
major one at Dien Bien Phu have brought about an im-

portant change in the situation. The fiasco of the Navarre plan has led to the collapse of the Laniel-Bidault cabinet and the shrinking of French-occupied zones.

We owe our successes to the correct policy of our Party and Government, the heroism of our armed forces and people, and the support of the fraternal countries and the world's people. Our successes also belong to the world movement for peace and democracy.

Besides military successes, initial ones have also been scored on the anti-feudal front. The former have had a good effect on the mobilization of the masses to implement our land policy and the latter, on our struggle against imperialism. Our successes inspirit our people and the peoples of the world and reinforce our diplomatic position at Geneva ; they have compelled our enemy to enter into talks with us. Compared with what Bollaert put forward in 1947, France's attitude at present has noticeably changed. Thus, since the start of the resistance, our posture has grown stronger and the enemy's weaker. But we should bear in mind that this should be understood in a relative, not absolute, sense. We must guard against subjectiveness and not underrate our enemy. Our successes have awakened the American imperialists. After the Dien Bien Phu campaign, the latter's intentions and plan for intervention have also undergone changes aimed at protracting and internationalizing the Indochina war, sabotaging the Geneva Conference, and ousting the French by every means, in order to occupy Viet Nam, Cambodia and Laos, enslave the peoples of these countries and create further tension in the world.

Therefore, *the US imperialists* not only are the enemy of the world's people but are becoming the *main and direct enemy of the Vietnamese, Cambodian and Lao peoples.*

These changes in the world and domestic situation have led to the Geneva Conference. This Conference has further exacerbated the contradictions between the imperialist countries, with France willing to negotiate. Britain wavering, and the United States bent on sabotaging the talks. The Americans have grown ever more isolated.

Viet Nam, China and the Soviet Union are closely united. Owing to contradictions among the imperialists, to our own efforts and to those of our camp, we have managed to secure a few fairly important agreements. The French Government being now in the hands of those who stand for peace, there are better chances for an end to the Indochina war.

During the recess of the Geneva Conference, the chief delegates have returned home, leaving things in the hands of their deputies. Availing himself of this occasion, Comrade Chou En-lai, Prime Minister of the People's Republic of China, has visited India and Burma. Comrade Chou and the prime ministers of India and Burma have issued a joint peace declaration. Though briefly worded, the five principles stated in the declaration are very clearly set forth and most judicious, and are warmly approved of by the peoples of the world and particularly of Asia ; at the same time they frustrate the US imperialists' scheme of sabotaging solidarity among the Asian nations.

These five principles are :

1. Mutual respect of sovereignty and territorial integrity.
2. Non-aggression.
3. Non-interference in each other's internal affairs.
4. Equality and friendship in mutual relations.
5. Peaceful coexistence.

My meeting with Comrade Chou has also been fruitful. The friendly meetings between Comrade Chou En-lai and the representatives of India, Burma and Viet Nam have tightened solidarity among the Asian nations. This is a success for our camp.

The present situation in the world, in Asia and at home holds out prospects of peace for our country. However, the US imperialists are bent on sabotage; in France there remain bellicose groups; the pro-American puppets also strive to wreck the peace; and so the war may still go on.

That is the characteristic feature of the new situation in our country.

II. NEW TASKS

The new situation has set new tasks, new guidelines and new tactics. Over nearly nine years of resistance, under the leadership of our Party and Government, our people and army have overcome difficulties, fought heroically, and won glorious victories. Our forces have made headway in all respects. Thanks to the correct policy of our Party and Government, we have recorded good achievements.

At present the situation has changed; so have our tasks and consequently so should our policy and slogans. Up to now we have concentrated our efforts on wiping out the forces of the French imperialist aggressors. But now the French are having talks with us while the American imperialists are becoming our main and direct enemy; so our spearhead must be directed at the latter. Until peace is restored, we shall keep fighting the French; but the brunt of our attack and that of the world's peoples should be focused on the United States. US policy is to expand and internationalize the Indochina war. Ours is to struggle for peace and oppose the US war policy. For some nine years now, our Party has made clear its programme: Complete independence for

12 SW.

Viet Nam, Cambodia and Laos, which must be freed from the French yoke; to refuse to recognize the French Union, drive out all French troops from Indochina, destroy the puppet administration and armed forces, confiscate all properties of the imperialists and the traitors, launch a drive for the reduction of land rents and interest rates as a step towards agrarian reform, bring democracy to the whole nation, and carry our war of resistance through to final victory. This programme has won many successes. It is a correct one.

However, in the new situation we cannot maintain the old programme. Our previous motto was "Resistance to the end". At present, we must put forward a new one: "Peace, Unity, Independence, Democracy". We must take firm hold of the banner of peace to oppose the US imperialists' policy of direct interference in, and prolongation and expansion of, the war in Indochina. Our policy must change in consequence: formerly we confiscated the French imperialists' properties; now, as negotiations are going on, we may, in accordance with the principle of equality and mutual benefit, allow French economic and cultural interests to be preserved in Indochina. Negotiations entail reasonable mutual concessions. Formerly we said we would drive out and wipe out all French aggressive forces; now, in the talks held, we have demanded and the French have accepted, that a date be set for the withdrawal of their troops. In the past, our aim was to wipe out the puppet administration and army with a view to national reunification; now we practise a policy of leniency and seek reunification of the country through nation-wide elections.

Peace calls for an end to the war; and to end the war one must agree on a cease-fire. A cease-fire requires regrouping zones, that is, enemy troops should be regrouped in a zone with a view to their gradual withdrawal, and ours in another. We must secure a vast area where we would have ample means for building, consolidating and developing our forces so as to exert influence over other regions and thereby advance towards reunification. The setting up of regrouping zones does not mean partition of the country; it is a temporary measure leading to reunification. Owing to the delimitation and exchange of zones, some previously free areas will be temporarily occupied by the enemy; their inhabitants will be dissatisfied; some people might fall prey to discouragement and to enemy deception. We should make it clear to our compatriots that the trials they are going to endure for the sake of the interests of the whole country, for the sake of our long-range interests, will be a cause for glory and will earn them the gratitude of the whole nation. We should keep everyone free from pessimism and negativism and urge all to continue a vigorous struggle for the complete withdrawal of French forces and for independence.

To set up regrouping zones as a step towards peace, to hold nationwide elections to achieve national reunification, such is our policy. The aims of our war of resistance are independence, unity, democracy and peace. The very restoration of peace is aimed at serving the cause of reunification, independence and democracy. The new situation requires a new policy for securing new successes.

At any juncture, peace or war, we must firmly hold the initiative, show foresight and be in full readiness.

To secure peace is not an easy task; it is a long, hard and complex struggle; with advantageous conditions but also with difficulties. The advantageous conditions: the friendly countries support us, so do the world's people; our people are full of spirit and confidence in our Party and Government, under whose wise leadership they will certainly unite and struggle in peace as in war. The difficulties: the United States is trying its hardest to sabotage the restoration of peace in Indochina, the partisans of peace in France have not completely freed themselves from American influence.

The new situation is not only a difficult but also a complex one. Here are some instances : we should apply different policies to the old free areas and the newly-liberated areas ; to our own free zone and to the zone temporarily reserved for regrouped enemy troops ; in the past we only worked in the countryside, at present we must have a policy for cities. The present policy with regard to France should be different from the past. Policies are not the same with respect to the pro-American traitors and the pro-French traitors. In the past we only had to care about home affairs and relations with friendly countries ; now we have extended our foreign relations to other countries.

We should make a distinction between immediate and future interests, between local interests and over-all interests.

The situation is undergoing great changes ; furthermore difficulties and complications have cropped up ; as a result, changes are also happening in the minds of the people and cadres. Failing good preparations and timely leadership, confusion might be thrown into thought and action.

The following ideological errors may be committed : *Leftist deviation*. Some people, intoxicated with our repeated victories, want to fight on at all costs, to a finish ; they see only the trees, not the whole forest ; with their attention focused on the withdrawal of the French they fail to detect their schemes ; they see the French but not the Americans ; they are partial to military action and make light of diplomacy. They are

unaware that we are struggling in international conferences as well as on the battlefields in order to attain
our goal. They will oppose the new slogans, which they
deem to be rightist manifestations and to imply too
many concessions. They set forth excessive conditions
unacceptable to the enemy. They want quick results,
unaware that the struggle for peace is a hard and
complex one. Leftist deviation will cause one to be
isolated, alienated from one's own people and those of the
world, and suffer setbacks. *Rightist deviation* will lead
to pessimism, inaction and unprincipled concessions. It
causes one to lack confidence in the people's strength
and to blunt their combative spirit; to lose the power
to endure hardships and to aspire only to a quiet and
easy life.

Leftist and rightist tendencies are both wrong. They
will be exploited by the enemy; they will benefit them
and harm us.

TASKS AND WORK

The new situation has set us three new responsibilities :

1. To secure and consolidate peace; to achieve unity,
independence, and democracy for the whole country.

2. To strengthen the people's armed forces and build
up a mighty people's army capable of meeting the
requirements of the new situation.

3. To keep implementing the slogan : land to the tiller.
To strive to restore production and to prepare for national
reconstruction.

These three responsibilities entail ten tasks :

1. To create unity of mind in the whole Party and
among the entire people as regards the new situation and
the new tasks.

2. To strengthen leadership in diplomatic struggle.

3. To strengthen the people's army.

4. To take over the newly-liberated zones; especial attention to be paid to the taking over and management of the cities.

5. To give a new orientation to work in the zone temporarily reserved for regrouped enemy forces.

6. To keep consolidating the former free zones.

7. To mobilize the masses vigorously for land reform.

8. To improve economic and financial work and prepare conditions for the reconstruction of the country.

9. To assist the Pathet Lao and Khmer forces.

10. To continue the work of reorganization and ideological rectification of the Party in the newly-liberated areas.

These 10 tasks are under the leadership of the Central Committee. Each locality and each branch will not necessarily have to carry out all ten but each will be assigned a certain number of tasks.

Of the above ten tasks, ideological leadership is the most important. For both members and non-members of the Party, only a clear grasp of the new situation and the new tasks can bring about unity of mind, which will lead to unity of action. If all of us, both inside and outside the Party and at all levels, are at one in thought and action, we will successfully carry out our tasks, however difficult and complex.

At present, the US imperialists are the main enemy of the world's people and the main and direct enemy of the Indochinese people and so all our actions must be directed against them. Any person or country that is not pro-American can (even temporarily) join us in a united front. Our unalterable goal is peace, independence, unity and democracy. We must unswervingly stick to principles but show flexibility in tactics. All our activities should be inter-related and well co-ordinated, each par't being integrated into the whole. Each task should be done in accordance with the concrete situation in each locality at a given moment.

Thanks to the correct leadership of our Party and Government, the unity and efforts of all our cadres and people, the sympathy and support of the people of the friendly countries and peace-loving people all over the world we will surely fulfil the above three responsibilities and ten tasks.

PART THREE

(1954 — 1969)

APPEAL ON THE OCCASION OF THE
8th ANNIVERSARY OF THE OUTBREAK
OF THE NATION-WIDE RESISTANCE

(December 19, 1954)

Fellow-countrymen, soldiers and cadres at home and Vietnamese residents abroad,

After nearly nine years of a most arduous and valiant resistance, we have won a brilliant victory: the war has ended and peace has been restored, making it possible for us to rebuild our country.

Today, for the first time we celebrate Resistance Day in peace. But we must realize that, like the armed struggle waged during the resistance, the political struggle to be conducted in peacetime will be long and hard, and even more arduous and complex.

Therefore, our people, soldiers and cadres must not be subjective and complacent, but must keep up their combativeness and heroism.

Thanks to our solidarity, struggle, vigilance and faith, we were victorious in our resistance. Now, we must bring about a broad national union and closely unite with the people of the friendly countries and peace-loving people throughout the world. We must further enhance our fighting spirit, heighten our vigilance and have even firmer confidence in the powerful strength and glorious future of our people. We shall in this way successfully carry out our task of consolidating peace, achieving national reunification and bringing independence and democracy to all our country.

CLOSING ADDRESS AT THE CONGRESS OF THE NATIONAL UNITED FRONT[20]

(September 10, 1955)

Dear members of the Presidium,
Dear delegates,
After days of hard work and an'mated discussion, the Congress has unanimously adopted the new Programme of the Front. This is a success.

We can say that this is a Programme of *broad union,* the aim of which is to struggle for peace, reunification, independence and democracy for the whole country.

Everybody must recognize that the Programme of the Front is very firm, broad and practical.

It is *practical* because it is in perfect agreement with the deep aspirations of our countrymen from North to South. Apart from a handful of individuals who have sold their conscience to the U.S. imperialists, all Vietnamese want their country to be reunified, and reunified through peaceful means. Therefore, if all members of the Front endeavour through propaganda and explanation to make the people understand the significance of the Programme, the great majority of them will certainly welcome and support it.

The Programme is a *broad* one because the Front is ready to welcome into its ranks all those who are sincerely opposed to the US-Diem scheme of dividing the country, and sincerely stand for national reunification.

The Front is ready to unite with all patriots whatever their political tendencies, religions, etc. Thus it will include all persons who now sincerely want to serve the Fatherland, whatever parties or groups they may have belonged to in the past.

It is a *firm* one because the Front is based on the workers and the peasants, who make up the overwhelming majority of our people, and at the same time pays attention to all strata of our society, without exception.

At home, the Front is supported by the great majority of our people. In the world, it will be supported by all peace-loving people.

The Front's practical, broad and firm **Programme** will ensure for it a glorious future.

I avail myself of this occasion to express a few ideas:

— The Front has produced a correct Programme. This is very good for the coming struggle. But this is only the first step on the road leading to complete victory. From now on, we must struggle hard to carry the Programme into effect. This struggle is fraught with difficulties and hardships. We must show tenacity and determination. The first and urgent thing we have to do is to give everyone a good grasp of the Programme, to conduct a vast campaign of in-depth and wide-ranging propaganda and explanation from North to South, so that everyone will fully understand its spirit and content and wholeheartedly support it.

— The North is the foundation, the root of our people's struggling forces. Only when the foundation is solid does the house stand firm. Only when the root is strong will the tree grow well. To carry the Front's Programme into effect we must endeavour to consolidate the North in *every way,* strengthen it and make it progress; we should certainly not lay lesser emphasis on the consolidation of the North.

To strengthen the North and make it progress is to serve the interests of the South effectively.

— Some people say: "The Front has produced a good Programme. But if the U.S.-Diem clique refuse to budge, what shall we do?"

Here is the answer: By its very nature, a stone will not budge of itself. But when many people join hands, a stone, however big and heavy, can be moved aside.

We are united and resolved to consolidate the North, to carry into effect the Front's Programme; we make up an immensely powerful thrusting force. And the U.S. Diem clique, although they refuse to budge, will be moved aside.

That is why we should not ask: "What if the US-Diem clique refuse to budge?" Instead, each of us should ask himself: "What efforts have I made? To what extent have I done my duty?" If all of us endeavour to consolidate the North and to put into practice the Front's Programme, we will, with the support of peace-loving people in the world, force the US-Diem clique to move aside.

Dear delegates,

History has shown in the last few years that the force of our people's unity is invincible, and that the National United Front has won many victories.

The Viet Minh brought about the triumph of the August Revolution.

The Viet Minh-Lien Viet United Front helped to bring the war of resistance to victory.

We may be sure that with the efforts of all of us, with the support of the entire people, the Fatherland

Front will fulfil its glorious task of contributing to the building of a peaceful, re-unified, independent, democratic, and prosperous Viet Nam.

Please convey the Government's and my own greetings to all our fellow-countrymen and in particular, to our compatriots in the South who are now engaged in heroic struggle.

TO THE NATION

(July 6, 1956)

Dear fellow-countrymen,

For nearly a century, our people heroically struggled against the colonialists. The result was the triumph of the August Revolution and the founding of the Democratic Republic of Viet Nam.

But the perfidious colonialists provoked war in an attempt to reconquer our country. After nearly nine years of extremely heroic and hard struggle by our entire people, the resistance was victorious. The Geneva Agreements restored peace, recognized Viet Nam's independence, sovereignty, unity and territorial integrity and stipulated that free general elections be held throughout the country in July 1956 to reunify the country.

Strictly implementing the Geneva Agreements, the Government of the Democratic Republic of Viet Nam has repeatedly proposed to the South Viet Nam authorities the holding of a consultative conference with a view to organizing free general elections to reunify the country.

But the U.S. imperialists and the pro-American authorities in South Viet Nam, scheming to divide our country permanently, have prevented the holding of free general elections at the time prescribed by the Geneva Agreements. They are acting against the interests of our Fatherland and our people's wishes.

Faced with this situation, our sacred *duty* is to continue to struggle with determination for the implementation of the Geneva Agreements, the reunification of our country by peaceful means on the basis of independence and democracy, and for the completion of the glorious task of national liberation.

Our present line is closely and broadly to unite the entire people from North to South within the Viet Nam Fatherland Front, endeavour to consolidate the North and make it a strong base for the struggle for national reunification.

All honest Vietnamese can only approve of and support this noble aim. That is why we advocate a broad union of all Vietnamese at home and abroad who love their Fatherland and stand for peace and unity. On the strength of this unity, we will make continuous efforts to bring the North and the South ever closer to each other, and will struggle with determination to consolidate peace, achieve reunification, and bring independence and democracy to the whole country.

Our present political struggle is a long, hard and complex one, but it will certainly be victorious. Victory is certain because our cause is just, our people are closely united and of one mind, our fellow-countrymen in both South and North are struggling with heroism, the peoples of the world are supporting us and the world peace movement is growing stronger every day, while the imperialists' warlike schemes have suffered ever more serious failures.

To meet our people's ardent wishes, which are to consolidate peace and achieve national reunification on the basis of the Geneva Agreements, the Government of the Democratic Republic of Viet Nam proposes these practical measures:

1. *To restore normal relations* and free movement between the two zones; to create the required conditions for contacts between political, economic, cultural and social organizations of the North and of the South.

2. *To hold a consultative conference* between representatives of the two zones in order to discuss the question of free general elections to reunify the country on the basis of the Geneva Agreements.

Dear fellow-countrymen at home and abroad,

Viet Nam will certainly be reunified. Our people of South and North will certainly be reunited. Let all unite closely and broadly on the basis of the Programme of the Viet Nam Fatherland Front, participate whole-heartedly in the patriotic emulation movement, endeavour to consolidate the North and struggle with determination and perseverance for a peaceful, reunified, independent, democratic and prosperous Viet Nam.

Reunification is our people's road to salvation. Broad unity is an invincible force. Thanks to broad unity, our revolution has triumphed, our resistance has been victorious. With broad unity, our political struggle will certainly win, our country will certainly be reunified.

ON REVOLUTIONARY MORALITY
(1958)

Ever since the beginning of its existence mankind has had to *struggle* against nature — wild beasts, the weather, etc. — in order to survive. To succeed in this struggle each individual must rely on the force of large numbers of people, on the collective, on *society*. Alone, he cannot get the better of nature and subsist.

In order to survive, man must also *produce* to get food and clothing. Production, too, must rely on the collective, on society. Alone, the individual cannot produce.

Our era being a civilized, revolutionary era, one must rely all the more on the force of the collective, of society, in all undertakings. More than ever the individual cannot stand apart but must join the collective, join society.

Therefore, *individualism* goes counter to *collectivism* ; collectivism and socialism will certainly prevail while individualism will surely disappear.

The mode and forces of production ceaselessly develop and change ; so do, therefore, man's thinking, social systems, etc. All of us know that from the past to the present, the mode of production has evolved from the use of tree branches and stone axes to that of machines, electricity and nuclear energy. Social systems have also developed from primitive communism through slave-ownership and feudalism to capitalism, and today nearly half of mankind is progressing to socialism and communism.

No one can stop this development and progress.

With the coming into being of private ownership, society has been divided into *classes* — exploiting classes and exploited ones —, hence the emergence of social *contradictions* and class *struggle*. Any person necessarily belongs to one class or another and no one can stand outside the classes. At the same time, each individual represents the *ideology* of his own class.

In the old society, the feudal landlords, capitalists and imperialists mercilessly oppressed and exploited the other social strata, especially the workers and peasants. They plundered the common property produced by society, turned it into their own private property and lived in clover. But they kept ranting about "virtue", "freedom", "democracy"...

Refusing to endure this oppression and exploitation for ever, the workers, peasants and other toiling people have risen up and made the *revolution* in order to liberate themselves and transform the wicked old society into a fine new one, in which all labouring people would live happily, and from which the exploitation of man by man would be banned.

To succeed, the revolution must be *led by the working class* — the most advanced, conscious, resolute, disciplined and best organized class — with the proletarian party as its staff. This has been incontestably borne out by the revolution in the Soviet Union and in the other socialist countries.

To make the revolution, to transform the old society into a new one is a very glorious, but also an extremely heavy task, a complex protracted and hard struggle. Only a strong man can travel a long distance with a heavy load on his back. A revolutionary must have a solid foundation of *revolutionary morality* in order to fulfil his glorious revolutionary task.

Born and brought up in the old society, we all carry within ourselves, to varying extent, traces of that society in our thinking and habits. The worst and most dangerous vestige of the old society is *individualism*. Individualism runs counter to revolutionary morality. The least remaining trace of it will develop at the first opportunity, smother revolutionary virtues and prevent us from wholeheartedly struggling for the revolutionary cause.

Individualism is something very deceitful and perfidious; it skilfully induces one to backslide. And everybody knows that it is easier to backslide than to progress. That is why it is very dangerous.

To shake off the bad vestiges of the old society and to cultivate revolutionary virtues, we must study hard, and educate and reform ourselves in order to progress continuously. Otherwise we shall retrogress and lag behind, and shall eventually be rejected by the forward-moving society.

It is not only by going to school or attending training courses that we can study and educate and reform ourselves. In every revolutionary activity, we can and must do it. Underground revolutionary activities, the general insurrection, the war of resistance, the present building of socialism in the North and the struggle for national reunification are very good schools where we can acquire revolutionary virtues.

People with revolutionary virtues fear neither difficulties, hardships nor failures; they neither waver nor step back. For the sake of the interests of the Party, the revolution, the class, the nation and mankind, they never hesitate to sacrifice their own interests, and if need be, even their own lives. This is a very clear and lofty expression of revolutionary morality.

In our Party, Comrades Tran Phu, Ngo Gia Tu, Le Hong Phong, Nguyen Van Cu, Hoang Van Thu, Nguyen Thi Minh Khai and many others have laid down their lives for the sake of the people and the Party, thus setting brilliant examples of total dedication to the public interest and complete selflessness.

People with revolutionary virtues remain simple, modest, and ready to face more hardships, even when meeting with favourable conditions and winning successes. "Worry about work before the others, think of enjoyment after them". We must think of how best to fulfil our task, not of how to get the greatest reward. We must avoid boasting about past achievements and claiming special prerogatives, or indulging in bureaucratism, conceit and depravation. This also is an expression of revolutionary morality.

*

* *

In brief, revolutionary morality consists of the following:

To devote one's life to struggling for the Party and the revolution. This is the most essential point.

To work hard for the Party, observe Party discipline, and implement Party lines and policies.

To put the interests of the Party and the labouring people before and above one's own interests. To serve the people wholeheartedly. To struggle selflessly for the Party and the people and to be exemplary in every respect.

To endeavour to study Marxism-Leninism and constantly use self-criticism and criticism to heighten one's ideological standard, improve one's work and progress together with one's comrades.

Each revolutionary must deeply realize that our Party is the most advanced and close-knit organization of the working class, the leader of the latter and the labouring people at large. At present, our working class, though still not very numerous, is developing with every passing day. In future, agricultural co-operatives will be organized everywhere, machines will be widely used in the countryside, and peasants will become workers. The intellectuals will become well acquainted with manual labour and the difference between brain and manual workers will be gradually wiped out. Our country's industry will develop day by day. Hence, the workers will be ever more numerous, their strength will grow, and the future of the working class is great and glorious. It will reform the world and itself as well.

The revolutionary must clearly realize this and firmly stick to the *stand* of the working class so as to struggle whole-heartedly for socialism and communism, for the working class and all the labouring people. *Revolutionary morality consists in absolute loyalty to the Party and the people.*

Our Party pursues no other interests than those of the working class and the toiling people. Therefore, its immediate objective is to struggle for the gradual building of socialism in the North and the reunification of the country.

Under the Party's leadership our people have fought heroically, overthrown the colonial and feudal domination, and completely liberated the North of our country. This was a great success. But the revolution is not yet totally victorious, and the present aim of the Party is to struggle for national reunification in order to build a peaceful, reunified, independent, democratic and prosperous Viet Nam, to eliminate exploitation of man by man all over the country and build a new society with happiness and abundance for all.

However, our industry is still backward. Thanks to the devoted help of the fraternal countries, first of all the Soviet Union and China, it is developing. For our effort to succeed, our workers must emulate one another and strive to produce ever more, faster, better and more economically, observe labour discipline and actively participate in the management of their enterprises: we must oppose waste and embezzlement, and our cadres must be truly industrious, thrifty, honest and upright, and join the workers in labour.

Land has been allotted to our peasants, whose life has been partially improved. But the mode of production is still scattered and backward; hence the yields have not yet increased much and living conditions have improved but slightly. The movement for setting up work-exchange teams and co-operatives in our countryside must be extensively and firmly pushed forward in order to bring about a firm increase in production; only then can our peasants escape poverty and see their condition improved.

Therefore, *revolutionary morality consists in striving to achieve the Party's objective,* faithfully serving the working class and the toiling people, and never wavering.

Most members of the Party and the Working Youth Union and most cadres have done so, but some have not. They wrongly think that now that the colonialists and feudalists have been got rid of in the North, the revolution has been successfully completed. That is why they let individualism develop within themselves, demand enjoyment and rest, and want to pick their own work instead of fulfilling the tasks entrusted to them by their organization. They want high positions but shirk responsibilities. Their combativeness and energy gradually weaken, and so do their revolutionary courage and noble virtues. They forget that the prime criterion of a revolutionary *is his resolve to struggle all his life for the Party and the revolution.*

We must realize that the successes recorded by us so far are only the first steps on a thousand-league road. We must advance further, the revolution must make further progress. Otherwise, we shall regress, and the successes we have gained cannot be consolidated and developed.

To advance to socialism, we must wage a long and hard struggle. We must have revolutionaries for there still exist *enemies*, who oppose the revolution.

There are three kinds of enemies:

Capitalism and imperialism are very dangerous ones.

Backward habits and traditions are also big enemies: they insidiously hinder the progress of the revolution. However, we cannot repress them, but must seek to correct them with caution, perseverance and over a long period of time.

The third enemy is *individualism*, the petty-bourgeois mentality which still lurks in each of us. It is waiting for an opportunity — either failure or success — to rear its head. It is the ally of the two above-mentioned categories.

Therefore *revolutionary morality* consists, in whatever circumstances, in resolutely struggling against all enemies, maintaining one's vigilance, standing ready to fight, and refusing to submit, to bow one's head. Only by so doing can we defeat the enemy, and fulfil our revolutionary tasks.

It is due to its correct policy and unified leadership that our Party can lead the working class and the entire people to socialism. This unified leadership springs from the unity of thought and action of all its members.

Without this unity we would be like "an orchestra in which the drums play one way and the horns another." It would not be possible for us to lead the masses and make revolution.

The Party members' words and deeds have a great bearing on the revolution for they exert great influence on the masses. For instance: the present policy of our Party and Government is broadly and closely to organize *work-exchange teams and co-operatives*, to carry out agricultural co-operation. But a number of Party and Working Youth Union members do not join them, or, having joined them, do not actively contribute to their building and consolidation. It is *individualism* which has led those comrades to do as they please and to go counter to the Party's organization and discipline. Wittingly or unwittingly, their actions impair the prestige of the Party, hinder its work and impede the advance of the revolution.

All the Party's policies and resolutions aim at serving the people's interests. Therefore, for a Party member revolutionary morality consists in *resolutely implementing them,* whatever the difficulties, and setting an example for the masses. Each Party member must heighten his sense of responsibility to the people and the Party. He must guard against and resolutely oppose individualism.

Our Party represents the *common interests* of the working class and the entire labouring people, not the private interests of any group or individual. This everyone knows.

The working class struggle not only to free themselves, but also to liberate mankind from oppression and exploitation. Therefore, their interests and those of the people are at one.

The Party member, in the name of the Party, represents the interests of the working class and the labouring people. That is why his own interests lie within, not without, those of the Party and the class. Success and victory for the Party and the class means success and victory for the militant. Separated from the Party and the class, no individual, however talented, can achieve anything.

Revolutionary morality, for a Party member, consists in *putting the Party's interests above everything else,* in all circumstances. If the Party's interests are in contradiction with those of the individual, the latter must absolutely give way to the former.

For having not cleansed themselves of individualism some Party members still boast of "their services to the Party," for which they claim the Party's "gratitude". They want to enjoy favour, honour, rank and privilege. If their desires are not satisfied they bear resentment against the Party, complaining that they have "no future" and are "sacrificed". They gradually drift away from the Party; worse still, they sabotage its policies and discipline.

Many cadres and fighters in the period of underground struggle and the war of resistance heroically laid down their lives; many labour heroes and elite workers have done their utmost to increase production. Those comrades have never asked for rank and honour, never demanded thanks from the Party.

Our Party has a mass character, and hundreds of thousands of members. Owing to the situation in our country the bulk of Party members spring from the petty bourgeoisie. There is nothing surprising in it. In the beginning, under the influence of bourgeois ideology the stand of some Party members may lack firmness, their outlook may be confused and their thinking not quite correct, but owing to the fact that they have been tempered in the revolution and the war of resistance, our Party members are by and large good militants, faithful to the Party and the revolution.

Those comrades know that those Party members who commit errors will lead the masses into error; therefore, they stand ready to correct any mistake they may make, and this in a timely way, and do not allow small errors to accumulate into big ones. They sincerely practise criticism and self-criticism, which makes it possible for them to progress together.

This conforms to revolutionary morality. During its many years of underground activity, our Party, although harshly repressed by the colonialists and meeting with numerous difficulties and dangers, developed and grew stronger with every passing day, and then led the revolution and the war of resistance to victory. This is due to its effective use of this sharp weapon: *criticism and self-criticism.*

However, there still remain some Party members who, unable to shake off individualism, become arrogant and conceited and keep flaunting their merits. While criticizing others, they do not like being criticized; they avoid self-criticism or practise it without sincerity and seriousness. They are afraid they might lose face and prestige. They pay no attention to the opinion of the masses, and make light of non-Party cadres. They do not realize that it is difficult not to commit any errors in one's work. We are not afraid of possible mistakes, but of failure to correct them resolutely. To redress them, we must listen to criticism by the masses and practise sincere self-criticism. Otherwise we shall lag behind and regress, which will lead to our being cast aside by the masses. This is the inevitable consequence of individualism.

The forces of the work'ng class and the labouring people are immense, boundless. But they must be led by the Party if they are to win. At the same time the Party must stay close to the masses, and sk lfully organize and lead them, if the revolution is to triumph.

*

* *

Revolutionary morality consists in uniting with the masses in one bcdy, trusting them and paying attention to their opinion. By their words and deeds, Party and Working Youth members and cadres win the people's confidence, respect and love, closely unite them around the Party organize, educate and mcb lize them so that they will enthusiastically implement the Party's policies and resolut'ons.

That is what we have done during the revolut'on and the war of resistance.

But at present, individualism is haunting a number of our comrades. Claiming to be clever in everything they stray from the masses, refuse to learn from them and want only to be their teachers. They are reluctant to engage in organization, propaganda, and education work among the masses. They become infected with bureaucratism and commandism. As a result, the masses neither trust nor respect them, much less love them. Eventually, they can do nothing good.

*

* *

The North of our country is advancing to socialism. This is the urgent aspiration of millions of labouring people. This is the collective undertaking of the toiling masses under our Party's leadership. Individualism is a big obstacle to the building of socialism. Therefore, *the success of socialism cannot be separated from that of the struggle for the elimination of individualism.*

To struggle against individualism is not "to trample on individual interests". Each person has his own character, his fortes, his private life and that of his family. There is no harm when the interests of the individual do not go counter to those of the collective. But one must realize that only under the socialist regime can each person improve his private life and develop his personality and his strong points.

No system equals socialism and communism in showing respect for man, paying due attention to his legitimate individual interests and ensuring that they be satisfied. In a society ruled by the exploiting class only the individual interests of a few people belonging to this class are met, whereas those of the toiling masses are trampled underfoot. But in the socialist and communist systems, of which the labouring people are the masters, each man is a part of the collective, plays a definite role in it and contributes his part to society. That is why the interests of the individual lies within those of the collective and are part of them. Only when the latter are secured can the former be satisfied.

The interests of the individual are closely tied to those of the collective. If there is any contradiction between them, revolutionary morality demands that the former yield to the latter.

The revolution unceasingly progresses. So does the Party. And so must the revolutionary.

The revolutionary movement involves hundreds of millions of people. Revolutionary work involves thousands of extremely complex and difficult tasks. In order to be able to assess all complex situations, clearly see the contradictions, and correctly solve the various problems, we must *strive to study Marxism-Leninism.*

Only by so doing can we consolidate our revolutionary morality, firmly maintain our stand, raise our theoretical and political level, and fulfil the tasks entrusted to us by the Party.

To study Marxism-Leninism is to learn the spirit in which one should deal with things, with other people and with oneself. It means to study the universal Marxist-Leninist truths in order to apply them creatively to the practical conditions of our country. We must study with a view to action. Theory must go hand in hand with practice.

But some comrades only learn by heart a few books on Marxism-Leninism. They think they understand Marxism-Leninism better than anyone else. Yet, when faced with practical problems, they either act in a mechanical way or are thrown into confusion. Their deeds do not match their words. They study books on Marxism-Leninism but do not seek to acquire the Marxist-Leninist spirit. They only want to show off their knowledge, not to apply it to revolutionary action. This is also *individualism.*

Individualism spawns hundreds of dangerous diseases: bureaucratism, commandism, sectarianism, subjectiveness corruption, waste... It ties up and blindfolds its victims whose every action is guided by their desire for honour and position, not by concern for the interests of the class and the people.

Individualism is a cruel enemy of socialism. The revolutionary must do away with it.

At present, the task of our Party and people is to endeavour to increase production and practise thrift in order to build up the North, gradually take it to socialism, and turn it into a strong base for the reunification of the country. This is an extremely glorious task. Let all members of the Party and the Working Youth Union, let all cadres within and without the Party be resolved to devote all their lives to serving the Party and the people. This is the noble virtue of the revolutionary, this is revolutionary morality, the Party and class spirit, which ensures victory for the Party, the class and the people.

Revolutionary morality does not fall from the sky. It is developed and consolidated through persevering daily struggle and effort. Like jade, the more it is polished the more it shines. Like gold, it grows ever purer as it goes into the melting pot.

What can be a greater source of happiness and glory than to cultivate one's revolutionary morality so as to bring a worthy contribution to the building of socialism and the liberation of mankind!

I earnestly hope that all members of the Party and the Working Youth Union and all cadres within and without the Party will strive hard and progress.

REPORT ON THE
DRAFT AMENDED* CONSTITUTION

Members of the Presidium,
Deputies,

At its 6th session, the National Assembly decided to amend the 1946 Constitution and to set up a Committee entrusted with preparing a draft amended Constitution and submitting that draft to its approval.

The drafting of the amended Constitution has been a long process of careful preparation and study. Following completion of the first draft in July 1958, we submitted it to discussion by high and middle-ranking cadres in the army, mass organizations, administrative departments and Party offices. The draft was then improved and on April 1st, 1959, was made public for the entire people to discuss it and contribute constructive suggestions. These discussions lasted four consecutive months. Everywhere, in government offices, factories, schools and other people's organizations, in both town and countryside, the study and discussion of the draft Constitution proceeded in an enthusiastic atmosphere and became a broad mass movement with the participation of all sections of the people. In the press, the discussions were also lively and fruitful. The Committee for the Amendment of the Constitution received many letters carrying the views of individual people and

---

* Presented to the First National Assembly, 11th session, (December 18, 1959).

groups, including letters from our dear compatriots in the South and Vietnamese nationals residing abroad.

The views contributed by the people have been carefully studied and debated by the Committee for the Amendment of the Constitution and, on that basis, we have again improved the draft.

On behalf of the Committee for the Amendment of the Constitution, I am presenting to the National Assembly this report on the draft Constitution.

I

IMPORTANT SIGNIFICANCE OF THE AMENDED CONSTITUTION

Viet Nam, our Fatherland, has been built in the course of thousands of years of industrious labour and heroic struggle of our people.

In the middle of the 19th century, the French imperialists began to invade our country. The feudal kings and mandarins surrendered to the aggressors and sold out our country to the French imperialists. For nearly a century the latter colluded with the local feudal class to rule over our country in an extremely cruel manner. Right in the beginning, our people had risen up to fight the French imperialists in order to win back national independence. Thanks to their spirit of selfless struggle, the movement for national liberation developed unceasingly. However, after nearly half a century of struggle, the imperialist and feudal domination was not yet overthrown and our country was not yet independent.

It was then that the Russian October Revolution broke out and won glorious victory. The Union of Soviet Socialist Republics was founded. The colonial system of imperialism began to collapse. The Soviet Union brought to the oppressed peoples a model of equal relationships between the nations.

The oppressed peoples of the world saw that only by relying on socialist revolution and following the line of the working class was it possible to overthrow the imperialists, win back complete national independence and realize genuine equality among the nations. The Russian October Revolution welded the socialist revolutionary movement and the revolutionary movement for national liberation into an anti-imperialist front.

In Viet Nam, following World War I, the national bourgeoisie and the petty bourgeoisie were unable to lead the movement for national liberation to success. The Vietnamese working class, in the light of the October Revolution, charted the course of the Vietnamese revolution. In 1930, the Indochinese Communist Party, the political party of the working class, was founded and showed that the Vietnamese revolution should go through two stages: the national democratic revolution and the socialist revolution. For the first time, the Vietnamese revolution was provided with a comprehensive political program worked out by the Party of the working class. And ever since then, under the unified leadership of the working class and its political party, it has developed rapidly and steadily.

The 1930 Nghe Tinh Soviets and the 1936-1939 democratic action movement gave a strong impetus to the Vietnamese revolution and strengthened even more the ties between the working class and its party on the one hand and the peasants and other sections of the people on the other.

In 1939, World War II broke out. The French imperialists and Japanese militarists worked hand in glove to rule over our country. Under the leadership of the

Party, our people rose up to fight the aggressive imperialists in a most heroic manner. The Bac Son and Nam
Ky* uprisings were the harbingers of a widespread
revolutionary movement. In 1941, the Party established
the Viet Minh with the task of "driving out the
Japanese and the French in order to make the country
fully independent and build the Democratic Republic of
Viet Nam".

In 1945, the Soviet Union and the democratic forces
of the world defeated the fascists and the Second World
War came to an end. Seizing this opportunity, the Party
led the August Revolution to victory. The imperialist
and feudal yoke was thrown off. The people's power
was established throughout the country. On September 2,
1945, the Democratic Republic of Viet Nam was founded.
The independence of our country was solemnly proclaimed before the peoples of the world. After nearly a
century of slavery, our Fatherland was liberated and
our people emancipated. An extremely glorious chapter
began in the history of our nation.

*
* *

After the victorious August Revolution, our people
began building the nation in order to consolidate and
develop the fruits of the revolution. On January 6, 1946,
in free nation-wide general elections, our people elected
our first-ever National Assembly. On November 9,
1946, the National Assembly adopted the first Constitution of our country.

The preamble to the 1946 Constitution pointed out:

The task of our people in this stage is to preserve
territorial integrity, win complete independence and

* Cochinchina in French times (Ed.).

build the country on a democratic basis. The Vietnamese Constitution must record the glorious achievements of the Revolution and must be built on the principle of unity of the entire people ; it must guarantee democratic freedoms and set up a strong people's power.

The regime instituted by the 1946 Constitution guaranteed national independence and broad democracy for the people. Right after its establishment under the leadership of the Party, the people's power promulgated labour legislation, reduced land rent, confiscated land belonging to the French colonialists and the Vietnamese traitors and distributed it to the peasants. The right of the people to vote and stand for elections and to participate in the affairs of the State was guaranteed, and democratic freedoms carried into effect. This was the regime of new democracy.

However, the French imperialists provoked war in an attempt to reconquer our country. Our people, closely united around the Party and the Government, waged a long and hard war of resistance, and resolutely smashed the enslaving schemes of the imperialists and the traitors, their henchmen. In 1953, while our people were waging the war of resistance, the National Assembly adopted the law on land reform in pursuance of the principle : "Land to the tillers."

The Dien Bien Phu victory and the success of the Geneva Conference brought the extremely heroic resistance of our people to a glorious end; North Viet Nam was completely liberated.

For the first time in history, an oppressed nation defeated the aggression of a mighty imperialist power, won back national independence, brought land to the tillers and genuine democratic rights to the people. This victory was due to the ardent patriotism and valiant struggle of our army and people, the close unity of our entire people with'n the National United Front, the reliance of our people's power on the worker-peasant alliance led by the working class and the Party, and the support of the fraternal countries in the socialist camp and the forces of peace and democracy throughout the world.

The victory of the August Revolution and the great war of resistance proves that even a small and weak nation can most certainly defeat the imperialist aggressors, if it is closely united ·under the leadership of the working class and its Party and correctly follows the Marxist-Leninist line.

*

* *

Following the victory of the war of resistance and the restoration of peace, the Vietnamese revolution moved on to a new stage. Under the people's democratic regime, North Viet Nam, completely liberated, entered a period of transition to socialism. But South Viet Nam is still under the imperialist and feudal yoke and our people must carry on the national democratic revolution in the new conditions of our country.

In North Viet Nam, following its complete liberation, rapid progress has been achieved in all fields.

In the three years from 1955 to 1957, we healed the wounds of war and rehabilitated our economy.

In 1958, we began a three-year economic plan aimed at developing and transforming the national economy along the socialist line.

The 14th plenum of the Central Committee of the Viet Nam Workers' Party pointed out that "the socialist forces in North Viet Nam have now become definitely stronger than the capitalist forces."

In the economic and cultural fields, we have achieved great progress. For instance :

From 1955 to 1959, in agriculture, paddy output increased from 3.6 million tons to 5.2 million tons. In industry, starting with only 17 factories in 1955, we have 107 State factories in 1959.

Agricultural co-operatives of the lower level now embrace 43.9 per cent of peasant households and most of the rest have joined work-exchange teams.

53 per cent of craftsmen have joined co-operative organizations.

In culture, we have basically eliminated illiteracy. Compared with 1955, the number of students has increased twofold in general-education schools, sixfold in secondary vocational schools, and sevenfold in colleges and universities. The number of medical doctors has increased by 80 per cent, etc.

We are advancing to a socialist economy. Along with these successes, class relations in North Viet Nam have changed. The feudal landlord class has been overthrown. The working class is growing day by day and is strengthening its leadership over the State. The peasantry has taken the co-operative path. The worker-peasant alliance has been further strengthened. The revolutionary intellectuals are contributing an active part to national construction. The national bourgeoisie, generally speaking, accept socialist transformation. The various sections of our people are united ever more closely within the National United Front. Compared with 1946, when the first Constitution of our country was adopted, the situation in present-day North Viet Nam has undergone very important and favourable changes.

While the North has been advancing to socialism, in the South the US imperialists and their henchmen have undermined the Geneva Agreements and refused to hold the consultative conference on general elections to reunify the country. They are enforcing an extremely cruel and autocratic policy, robbing the people of their property, and repressing and persecuting them in the most barbarous manner. They seek to perpetuate the division of our country and turn the South into a colony and a military base of the US imperialists, with a view to a new war in Indochina.

But our compatriots in the South have shown great heroism and the struggle there has been carried on and expanded. They demand improved living conditions, the development of the national economy, democratic freedoms, peace and national reunification ; they oppose oppression, exploitation and American "aid", terror and massacre, military build-up and war preparations.

North Viet Nam's advance to socialism powerfully stimulates the patriotic movement in South Viet Nam. The thoughts of our southern compatriots are constantly turned to the North and to our government, and their confidence in national reunification is all the more strengthened.

In short, the Vietnamese revolution has moved on to a new stage. We have new tasks to perform. Conditions both at home and in the world are favourable.

The 1946 Constitution — the first democratic Constitution of our country — conformed to the situation and the revolutionary tasks of that period. It has completed its mission. It is no·longer compatible with the new situation and the new revolutionary tasks. That is why we must amend it.

The draft amended Constitution clearly records the great successes of our poeple in the past years and clearly outlines the new revolutionary tasks in the new historical period.

II

THE MAIN POINTS IN THE DRAFT AMENDED CONSTITUTION

I present below a summary of the main points in the draft amended Constitution :

1. Character of the Democratic Republic of Viet Nam.
The character of the State is the fundamental question in the Constitution. This is the question of the class content of State power. In whose hands is power and whose rights and interests does it serve ? This question determines the whole content of the Constitution.

The Vietnamese State established after the August Revolution was already a people's democratic State, led by the working class. The Preamble of the draft amended Constitution points out :

"Our State is a people's democratic State based on the worker-peasant alliance and led by the working class."

In order to build socialism and struggle for the country's reunification, we must unceasingly strengthen the leadership of the working class over the people's democratic State.

The worker-peasant alliance is the foundation of the Democratic Republic of Viet Nam. The peasantry constitutes a very big productive force and at the same time a very great revolutionary force. In the people's democratic national revolution, the peasants have energetically followed the Party and have risen up side by side with the working class to overthrow imperialism and feudalism. At present they are enthusiastically joining the agricultural co-operation movement. This is due to their own active revolutionary spirit and the patient and ceaseless education by the Party and the working class. Therefore, in building socialism, our State strives to help the peasantry and consolidate the worker-peasant alliance.

The working class unites with craftsmen and small traders because they are working people ; they willingly take the path of co-operation, approve of and support the socialist revolution.

The socialist revolution is intimately linked with the scientific and technical development and the cultural development of the people. Our intellectuals contributed a valuable part to the resistance. They have been constantly assisted by the Party, which has allowed them to progress. That is why they are for socialism. The working class closely unites with the intelligentsia to help them serve the revolution and socialism.

Under the leadership of the working class, the Vietnamese national bourgeoisie have supported the people's democratic national revolution. Since the restoration of peace they have contributed their part to economic rehabilitation. At present we have the conditions to transform them along socialist lines. In the northern part of our country, the socialist economic forces have grown definitely superior to the capitalist economic forces. We have the people's power. The revolutionary struggle of the working masses is becoming ever more powerful. The national bourgeoisie are ready to accept transformation to contribute to national construction and the building of socialism.

Our country is a united multi-national country. All nationalities living on Vietnamese territory are equal in rights and duties.

All the nationalities in our country are fraternally bound together ; they share a common territory and in the course of our long history have worked and fought side by side in order to build our beautiful Fatherland.

Imperialism and feudalism deliberately sought to undermine the solidarity and equality between the nationalities and to sow discord among them and carried out a "divide-

and-rule" policy. Our Party and Government have constantly called on the nationalities to forget all enmities caused by imperialism and feudalism and to unite closely on the basis of equality in rights and duties. The minority nationalities have, side by side with their brothers of the majority nationality, fought against their common enemies, and brought the August Revolution and the war of resistance to success. Since the restoration of peace, our State has helped the brotherly nationalities to achieve further progress in the economic, cultural and social fields. The Viet Bac and the Thai Meo Autonomous Regions have been established. Closely united under the leadership of the Party and the State, the nationalities are enthusiastically taking part in the emulation movement for national construction.

Our nationalities policy is aimed at achieving equality and mutual assistance between the nationalities so as to allow them to advance together to socialism. Autonomous regions may be established in areas where minority nationalities live in dense communities.

2. General line of advance to socialism

For nearly a century, Viet Nam was a colonial and semi-feudal country. The economy was very backward and heterogeneous ; production was little developed and the people's material and cultural living standards were low. To get out of this situation of poverty, North Viet Nam must advance to socialism.

Article 9 of the draft amended Constitution points out the line of advance to socialism : "The Democratic Republic of Viet Nam will advance step by step from people's democracy to socialism by developing and transforming the national economy along socialist lines, transforming its backward economy into a socialist economy with modern industry and agriculture and advanced science and technology. The economic policy of the Democratic Republic of Viet Nam is continuously to develop production with the aim of constantly raising the material and cultural standards of the people."

At present in our country these are the main forms of ownership of the means of production :

— Ownership by the State, that is, ownership by the entire people ;

— Ownership by the co-operatives, that is, collective ownership by the working people ;

— Ownership by individual working people ; and

— Ownership of a few means of production by the capitalists.

The aim of our regime is to eliminate the forms of non-socialist ownership, to turn the present heterogeneous economy into a homogeneous one based on the system of ownership by the entire people and collective ownership.

Under article 12 of the draft amended Constitution, the State economic sector is owned by the whole people ; it leads the national economy, and the State must give priority to its development.

Under article 13, the sector of co-operative economy is collectively owned by the working people ; the State is to provide encouragement, guidance and assistance for its development.

We must develop the State economic sector to create the material foundation for socialism and stimulate socialist transformation.

— Agricultural co-operation is the prime mover of socialist transformation in the North. Past experiences have shown that agricultural co-operation in our country must pass through the forms of work-exchange teams and agricultural producers' co-operatives. This is very necessary

If we steadily develop step by step the work-exchange teams and the co-operatives, agricultural co-operation will certainly be successful.

— As regards craftsmen and other individual workers the State protects their right to ownership of their means of production, actively guides and helps them to improve their trades and encourage them to organize producers' co-operatives in accordance with the principle of voluntariness.

— As regards bourgeois traders and industrialists, the State does not cancel their right to ownership of their means of production and other property but actively guides their activities to keep them in line with the interests of the State and the people's welfare and the State economic plan. At the same time the State encourages and helps them to transform themselves along socialist lines through joint State-private ownership and other forms of transformation.

Under article 10 of the draft amended Constitution, the State leads the economic activities according to a unified plan. It uses State organs and relies on trade-unions, co-operatives and other organizations of the working people to map out and execute its economic plan.

Following the restoration of peace and the start of economic restoration, we gradually took the economy in the North along the path of planned development. We had a three-year programme for economic rehabilitation (1955-1957). At present we are carrying out a three-year plan for initial economic and cultural development and paving the way for our first five-year plan. The three-year plan aims particularly at promoting the socialist transformation of the individual economy of the peasants, craftsmen and other individual working people and the private capitalist sector ; at the same time it enlarges and reinforces the State economic sector and stimulates economic development along socialist lines.

3. Organization of the State in the Democratic Republic of Viet Nam

In order to fulfil its revolutionary tasks, our State must develop the democratic rights and political activities of the entire people so as to promote their ardour and creativeness and cause all citizens of Viet Nam to take effective part in managing State affairs, endeavour to build socialism and struggle for national reunification.

Our revolutionary regime has been established for near-ly fifteen years. The 1946 Constitution set up the People's Parliament and People's Councils at various levels. The National Assembly is the People's Council of the entire country. There are People's Councils at the local level. The National Assembly and the People's Councils are composed of representatives elected by the people through universal suffrage. The National Assembly decides the most important affairs of the State. The People's Councils decide the most important affairs of the localities.

During the resistance, the National Assembly and the Government united and guided our people, and brought the patriotic and anti-imperialist war to glorious victory. The National Assembly adopted the law on land reform aimed at completing the anti-feudalist revolution. In the localities the People's Councils contributed to the mobilization of the people in the anti-imperialist and anti-feudalist revolution.

Since the restoration of peace, the National Assembly has adopted the three-year programme for economic rehabilitation, the three-year plan for initial economic and cultural development, the policies on economic development and transformation along the socialist lines, the laws on democratic freedoms, etc. These are most important problems relating to the national interest and the people's welfare.

Under article 4 of the draft amended Constitution, all powers in the Democratic Republic of Viet Nam belong to the people. The people exercise their authority through the National Assembly and the People's Councils at various levels, which are elected by the people and responsible to the people.

Our electoral system is democratic and at the same time realizes unity among the entire people. All citizens from the age of 18 upward have the right to vote, and from the age of 21 upward have the right to stand for election. Elections will be held on the principle of universal, equal, direct and secret suffrage.

The people have the right to dismiss deputies to the National Assembly and to the People's Councils, should the latter show themselves unworthy of their trust. This principle guarantees the people's right of control over their representatives.

Article 6 of the draft amended Constitution stipulates that it is the duty of all organs of the State to rely upon the people, keep close contact with them, carefully listen to their opinions and submit to their supervision.

The National Assembly is the supreme organ of State power. The People's Councils are organs of State power in the localities.

The National Assembly elects the President of the country, the Standing Committee of the National Assembly and the Government Council. The Government Council is the organ entrusted with enforcing the laws and decisions of the National Assembly and the highest administrative organ of the State. It is responsible to the National Assembly and reports to it on its work. In the period between two sessions of the National Assembly the Gov-

ernment Council is responsible and reports to the National
Assembly Standing Committee.

The National Assembly is the only organ having legis-
lative power. The most important affairs of the State on
a national scale are decided by the National Assembly.

The People's Councils elect the administrative committees at various levels. These are executive organs of the
People's Councils. They are responsible to the People's
Councils and report to them on their work. At the same
time they are placed under the direct leadership of the
administrative committees of higher levels and the unified
leadership of the Government Council.

The most important local affairs are decided by the
People's Councils.

Our economic and social system aims at fully realizing
the democratic rights of the people on the basis of the increasing development of the socialist economy, the gradual
elimination of capitalist exploitation, and the improvement
of the material and cultural standards of the people. Thus
all conditions are gathered for our people to take effective
part in the management of the State.

*

*   *

Article 4 of the draft amended Constitution clearly stipulates that the principle governing the organization of
our State is democratic centralism. The National Assembly, the People's Councils, the Central Government and
other State organs all follow the principle of democratic
centralism.

Our State ensures the fullest development of democracy,
because it is a people's State. Only through the fullest
development of democracy can all forces of the people be
mobilized to take the revolution forward. At the same time
the highest centralism must be ensured to lead the people
in building socialism.

4. Basic rights and duties of the citizen

The draft amended Constitution clearly stipulates the basic rights and duties of the citizens of our country. These stipulations demonstrate the genuinely democratic character of our regime.

The capitalists often boast that their Constitutions guarantee the rights of the individual, democratic liberties and the interests of all citizens. But in reality, only the bourgeoisie enjoy the rights recorded in these Constitutions. The working people do not really enjoy democratic freedoms; they are exploited all their life and have to bear heavy burdens in the service of the exploiting class.

The capitalists often circulate the slander that our socialist regime does not respect the personal interests of the citizen. But in reality, only our regime really serves the interests of the people, first and foremost the working people, safeguards all interests of the people and develops democracy to enable the people to take effective part in the management of the State. That is why our people devote all their energies to their duties as the masters of the country, in order to build socialism and make our country strong and our people prosperous.

The draft amended Constitution clearly points out that the citizens of the Democratic Republic of Viet Nam have:
— the right to work ;
— the right to rest ;
— the right to study ;
— the right to personal liberty ;
— freedoms of opinion, of the press, of assembly, of association ; the right to hold demonstrations ;
— freedom of religious belief, to adhere or not to adhere to any religion ;
— the right to elect and stand for election, etc.

All citizens are equal before the law. Women enjoy equal rights with men in every respect : political, econom-

ic, cultural, social and familial. The State pays particular attention to the moral, intellectual and physical
education of the youth.

By virtue of the character of our State and our economic and social system, the State not only recognizes the
interests of the citizens but also guarantees the necessary
material conditions for them to enjoy these interests
effectively.

The State guarantees democratic freedoms to the citizens but strictly prohibits any misuse of these freedoms
to infringe the interests of the State and the people, as
clearly stipulated in article 38 of the draft amended
Constitution.

In our regime the interests of the State, the collective
and the individual, are basically at one. Therefore, while
enjoying rights brought to them by the State and the
collective all citizens must consciously fulfil their duties
to the State and the collective.

The citizens have the duty to respect the Constitution,
the law, labour discipline, public order and the rules of
social life. The citizens have the duty to respect public
property, pay taxes according to the law, do military service, and defend the Fatherland.

Only in a socialist system are the interests of the individual, the State and the collective at one. That is why
only a socialist Constitution can encourage the citizens to
fulfil enthusiastically their duties to the society and the
Fatherland.

III

OPINIONS CONTRIBUTED TO THE DRAFT AMENDED
CONSTITUTION

The two campaigns of debate on the draft amended
Constitution among the people have been very stirring
periods of political activity. Our people have enthusiastic-

ally exercised their democratic rights to participate in the elaboration of the Constitution. People in various localities, government offices, mass organizations, army units, the People's Councils in the provinces, many compatriots in the South and abroad and the press have contributed abundant suggestions. All these suggestions have been carefully studied by the Committee for the Amendment of the Constitution. On this occasion, the Committee expresses its appreciation to our compatriots for their contributions to the draft amended Constitution.

Here is a summary of the main views contributed by our compatriots:

1. Concerning the Preamble of the Constitution, acting upon the people's suggestions, the Committee for the Amendment of the Constitution has made additions to bring out more fully the achievements recorded, the present situation and tasks of the revolution and the heroic struggle of our compatriots in the South, and to point out that the socialist revolution in the North will certainly succeed and our country will certainly be reunified.

2. Article 1 of the draft amended Constitution has been unanimously approved because it stresses, right at the beginning, the unity of our country. At present our country is still temporarily divided, but all our people, both in the North and in the South, are unshakably confident that it will be reunified. Thus, to affirm the unity of our country in the very first article of the draft amended Constitution is fully correct.

3. Many people hold the view that it must be clearly specified that our State is based on the worker-peasant alliance under the leadership of the working class, because this is a great historical reality which has brought our people tremendous revolutionary victories and guarantees the fulfilment of their revolutionary duties in the new

stage. However, as this character has been clearly record-ed in the Preamble it is only necessary to stipulate in article 2 that the Democratic Republic of Viet Nam is a people's democratic State. This is clear enough.

4. Article 3 clearly stipulates that Viet Nam is a unified multi-national State and the task of our State is to pre-serve and develop the solidarity between the nationalities.

5. Democratic centralism is the fundamental organiza-tional principle of State organs under our regime. This is shown in the organization of our State. That is why many people have proposed that this be clearly recorded in our Constitution. We have added this to article 4.

6. There have been suggestions to the effect that the path of advance of our country and its prospects of eco-nomic development should be clearly stated. The Com-mittee for the Amendment of the Constitution has complet-ed article 9 and clearly stipulated that our country will become one possessed of a socialist economy with a mod-ern industry and agriculture and advanced science and technology.

7. There have been many suggestions to the effect that a higher minimum age be required to stand for election than to vote. We have amended article 23 and fixed the minimum age for electors at 18 and that of candidates to elections at 21.

8. We have accepted the suggestion on establishing a National Defence-Council and recorded this in the draft: the President of the Democratic Republic of Viet Nam is President of the National Defence Council. The Vice-President and other members of the Council are appoint-ed by the National Assembly on the proposal of the Pre-sident of the Republic.

9. It has been proposed that the various Commissions to be set up by the National Assembly be recorded in the

Constitution. We have mentioned in the Constitution the Commision for the Scrutiny of the Deputies' Mandate, the Law-Drafting Committee, and the Planning and Budget Committee, and at the same time have stipulated that the National Assembly may set up other commissions whenever necessary to assist it and its Standing Committee.

10. In the opinion of many, it should be stipulated that the President of the country has the right to attend and preside over meetings of the Government Council, whenever he deems it necessary. The Committee for the Amendment of the Constitution has recorded this point in article 66.

Apart from the suggestions which the Committee for the Amendment of the Constitution has approved and has taken as a basis to improve the draft Constitution, there have been others on questions of detail concerning legislation or the activities of State organs. We will transmit them to the responsible organs for study.

Deputies,

Fourteen years ago our people joyfully welcomed the first Constitution of our country. Today our people have again enthusiastically discussed the draft amended Constitution.

In the process of these discussions, they have clearly assessed the difficulties overcome, and have found great inspiration in the successes achieved : the North of our country has been completely liberated, our people hold effective power, the socialist economy is developing at a rapid rate. Our people's material and cultural standards have been improved. Revolutionary morality among our people has been gradually elevated ; solidarity among them has been strengthened day by day. The practice of democracy has been developed to a high degree ; the people are really the masters of the country.

People of all walks of life in the North and in the South alike warmly welcome the draft amended Constitution. Our entire people are firmly convinced that the North and the South will be united in the great family of the reunified Vietnamese Fatherland.

The Constitution will fill our Southern brothers with enthusiasm; they will keep their minds turned towards the National Assembly and the Government and will struggle even more vigorously for the reunification of the Fatherland.

All our people are aware that the present draft amended Constitution is due to the Party — the organizer and leader of the past glorious victories and the guarantor for future great achievements — and to the unity of our entire people and the valiant struggle waged by them for national construction along the Party line.

Since the day our Committee was entrusted by the National Assembly with the task of drafting the amended Constitution, we have worked uninterruptedly and held 27 meetings. The draft has been completed; today our Committee presents it to the National Assembly. We have worked to the best of our ability but cannot claim perfection. We hope that you will debate it and contribute further improvements and that it will be adopted by the National Assembly.

After adoption by the National Assembly, this draft Constitution will become the new Constitution of our country.

This Constitution will further stimulate our people's patriotism and their love of socialism; it will encourage them to unite even more closely and emulate one another even more enthusiastically to build a peaceful, reunified, independent, democratic, and prosperous Viet Nam.

THIRTY YEARS OF ACTIVITY
OF THE PARTY *
(1960)

Our Party is celebrating its thirtieth anniversary. For thirty years, it has waged heroic struggles and reaped glorious successes. On the occasion of this anniversary, we would like to look back at the road travelled and to draw precious lessons in order correctly to determine the revolutionary tasks of the present stage and of the immediate future, and to win still greater, more resounding victories.

Just as the changes that have taken place in our country are inseparable from international developments, so the maturation of our Party is inseparable from the growth of the fraternal Parties.

The triumph of the Russian October Revolution, which destroyed part of the forces of capitalism, opened to the proletariat and the oppressed peoples all over the world the way to liberation. In 1919, under Lenin's leadership, genuine revolutionaries of all countries founded the Third International. Since then Communist Parties have been formed in France, China and many other countries. At the beginning, it was due to the direct help of the Communist Parties of China and France that Marxism-Leninism and the influence of the October Revolution penetrated the iron curtain of French colonialism and reached Viet Nam.

* Article written for the review *Problems of Peace and Socialism* (N° 2 — 1960) on the occasion of the 30th founding anniversary of our Party.

From 1924 on, the revolutionary movement in our country surged up ; our workers waged repeated struggles, advancing from economic actions to political ones.

The union of Marxist-Leninist theory with the workers' movement and the patriotic movement led to the formation, early in 1930, of the *Indochinese Communist Party.**

This event, which marked an extremely important turning point in the history of the Vietnamese Revolution, showed that our working class had matured and was capable of leading the revolutionary struggle.

Broadly speaking, our Party has passed through the following stages:

— Underground activity ;

— Leading the August Revolution to victory;

— Leading the war of resistance to victory; and

— The present stage of leading the socialist revolution in the North, and the struggle for reunifying the country and completing the national democratic revolution throughout the land.

*

* *

At the beginning, for almost fifteen years our Party had to work underground. It faced ceaseless and savage persecution by the French colonialists. The jails of Poulo-Condor, Lao Bao and Son La were filled with Communists. Many Party cadres and members died the death of the brave in the struggle. But we firmly believed in the ultimate victory of the Party and the revolution, and our ranks continued to grow and gain in strength.

Right at its inception the Party held aloft the banner of the national democratic revolution and led the national liberation movement. At that time the feudal class had

* Since March 1951, the Viet Nam Workers' Party *(Tr.)*

capitulated to the imperialists, while the weak bourgeoisie sought to come to terms with imperialism in order to survive. Despite their fervour the petty bourgeois strata were in an ideological impasse. Alone, the *working class*, the most courageous and revolutionary class, kept up the struggle against the colonialist imperialists. Equipped with advanced revolutionary theory and the experience of the international proletarian movement, it proved to be the most able and trustworthy leader of the Vietnamese people.

*

*   *

Imbued with the spirit of Marxism-Leninism, the Party set forth a correct revolutionary line. As early as 1930, in its programme on the bourgeois democratic revolution, it enunciated the task of *struggling against the imperialists and feudalists* for national independence and the realization of the watchword: "Land to the tillers". This programme fully answered the aspirations of the peasants, who made up the majority of our people. In this way our Party succeeded in uniting large revolutionary forces around the working class, while the parties of the other classes either met with failure or found themselves isolated. The leading role of our Party, the Party of the working class, was thus ceaselessly consolidated and strengthened.

Shortly after its formation the Party organized and led a mass movement of unprecedented magnitude in our country: that for the setting up of *Soviets in Nghe An and Ha Tinh provinces*. The workers and peasants in these provinces rose up and threw off the imperialist and feudal yoke, established worker-peasant-soldier rule, and proclaimed democratic liberties for the working people.

Although the movement was drowned by the imperialists in a sea of blood, it testified to the heroism and revolutionary power of the Vietnamese working masses. In spite of its failure, it forged the forces which were to ensure the triumph of the August Revolution.

*

*   *

When, in 1936, the menace of fascism and the threat of a world war became obvious, our Party allied itself with the world anti-fascist democratic front and the Popular Front in France, and initiated a broad mass movement for the formation of a *Democratic Front against fascism and colonial reaction in Indochina*. It led mass actions claiming democratic liberties and better living conditions. This movement embraced millions of people and awakened their political consciousness. The prestige of the Party mounted and struck deep roots among the working people.

Shortly after the outbreak of the Second World War, Viet Nam was occupied by the Japanese aggressors, who sought to dominate the country in collusion with the French colonialists. The Party changed its tactics in time. The *Viet Minh* (League for the Independence of Viet Nam) *and mass organizations for national salvation* were established in 1941 with a view to rallying all patriotic forces in a single anti-fascist and anti-colonial front. The Party temporarily withdrew its slogan for agrarian revolution, and confined itself to advocating lower rents and lower interest rates, the confiscation of land belonging to the imperialists and traitors and its transfer to the peasants. In this way it sought to unite all forces in the struggle against the imperialists and their stooges, win over patriotic elements among the land-owning class and extend the National Front for the Salvation of the Country.

The Party's correct policy furthered the growth of the revolutionary movement. Resistance bases were set up, and the first units of the Vietnamese Army of Liberation formed. The Party started *guerilla warfare against the Japanese invaders,* in co-ordination with the international anti-fascist struggle.

This made it possible in the autumn of 1945, immediately after the Soviet Red Army had smashed fascism, to launch *a national uprising for the conquest of power.* The August Revolution of 1945 triumphed. The Democratic Republic of Viet Nam was born.

In 1945 our Party, which had been formed from a few groups of militants and tempered in hard struggles, had only about 5,000 members, a number of whom were in prison. But it was able to unite the people and lead their uprising to victory. This was a great victory for the Vietnamese people and also the first victory won by Marxism-Leninism in a colony.

*
* *

Soon after the August Revolution the French Government violated the agreements it had signed with us and unleashed an aggressive war.

At that time the country was in dire straits. We had not yet recovered from the terrible famine caused by French imperialism and Japanese fascism. The enemy had considerable land, sea and air forces equipped with modern weapons. We had only small, newly-formed infantry forces, poorly-equipped and with little combat experience. But the Party resolutely decided to organize the resistance, simultaneously leading the patriotic struggle and fostering the people's strength. At the beginning, it carried on the policy of reducing land rents and interest rates. When the resistance became widespread, and the need was felt to increase further the forces of the people, mainly the peasantry, we resolutely mobilized the people *for land reform and the full implementation of the slogan: "Land to the tillers."* Thanks to this correct policy, the resistance forces grew rapidly and won repeated victories.

Our people had been cruelly exploited and oppressed by the French colonialists for nearly eighty years. In the beginning of the patriotic war some units of our army were only armed with bamboo sticks. But we were tempered by nine years of resistance. Our people united into an iron-like bloc. Our regular units, regional detachments and people's militia expanded into an army of heroes, determined to fight and win.

The close unity and heroic sacrifices of our army and people led to the historic victory of Dien Bien Phu in the summer of 1954. The French colonialist troops were shattered, and had to agree to a cease-fire. The agreements signed in Geneva restored peace on the basis of the recognition of the independence, sovereignty and territorial integrity of the peoples of Indochina.

For the first time in history a small colony had defeated a big colonial power. This was a victory not only of our people but also of the world forces of peace, democracy and socialism.

Once again Marxism-Leninism lit the path for the Vietnamese working class and people, and led them to triumph in their struggle to save their country and safeguard their revolutionary gains.

Since the restoration of peace Viet Nam faces a new situation: the country is temporarily divided into two parts. Socialism is being built in the North, now completely liberated, while the imperialists and their underlings now are ruling over the South and trying to turn it into an American colony and military base with the object of rekindling the war. They are savagely repressing patriots in the South, brazenly violating the Geneva Agreements, and stubbornly preventing the convening of a consultative conference to arrange for free elections and the peaceful reunification of the country. They are the most ferocious enemies of our people.

In view of this situation, *two tasks* confront the Vietnamese revolution at present: first, the construction of socialism in the North, and second, the completion of the national democratic revolution in the South. These tasks have a common aim: to strengthen peace and pave the way to reunification on the basis of independence. and democracy.

This is how the Fifteenth Session of the Central Committee of the Viet Nam Workers' Party defined the tasks facing our entire people: "Consolidating national unity, vigorously struggling for the reunification of the country on the basis of independence and democracy, completing the national democratic revolution in the whole country; strengthening the North and leading it to socialism; building a peaceful, reunified, independent, democratic and prosperous state; actively contributing to the defence of peace in Indochina, in Southeast Asia and throughout the world."

*

* *

North Viet Nam is bound to advance to socialism. *The outstanding feature of the transitional period in Viet Nam* is for our economically backward agrarian country to advance *direct* to socialism, bypassing the stage of capitalist development.

The French imperialists left us an economy in a bad state. Small peasant farming with very backward techniques prevailed in the countryside. There were only tiny and scattered industrial undertakings. Fifteen years of war further ruined the economy. The situation was worsened by the economic sabotage carried out by the colonialists before they withdrew from North Viet Nam.

In these conditions our cardinal task is to build the *material and technical basis of socialism,* gradually to take the North to socialism, and to provide it with modern industry and agriculture and advanced culture and science. In this process of socialist revolution we must transform the old economy and create a new one, and constructive labour is the essential task over a long period.

The period between 1955 and 1957 was one of economic rehabilitation. The main task was to restore agriculture and industry in order to heal the wounds of war, stabilize the economy and take the initial steps in improving the people's living standards.

Thanks to the efforts of our entire Party and people and the warm-hearted aid accorded us by the brotherly countries, this task was completed in the main by the end of 1957. The level of industrial and agricultural output was approximately that of 1939. Impressive results were achieved in raising food crops : North Viet Nam, which in 1939 produced less than 2,500,000 tons of paddy, harvested over 4,000,000 tons in 1956.

This period also witnessed radical changes in the *relations of production.* New relations of production gradually replaced the old ones. The agrarian reform abolished the system of feudal land-ownership and released the productive forces in the countryside. The cherished dream of ten-odd million peasants came true: land was distributed to them. The economic monopoly of the imperialists was liquidated. Our State took control of the economic levers, built a State-run economy of a socialist character, and gave leadership to the whole national economy. Thanks to generous and disinterested aid from the socialist states, primarily the Soviet Union and China, twenty-nine old industrial enterprises were rehabilitated and fifty-five new ones built.

In many regions the peasants set up work-exchange teams, an embryonic form of socialism. A number of experimental agricultural co-operatives were formed, and about 10.7% of the craftsmen joined production groups.

Private capitalist industry and trade began to switch over to State capitalism in low or medium forms: working on government orders, using raw materials provided by the State, retailing goods from State-owned wholesale trading organizations, etc.

After the completion of rehabilitation work, the Party led the people for the fulfilment of the three-year plan (1958-1960). This plan aims at the socialist transformation of agriculture, handicrafts, and private capitalist industry and trade, the main link being the transformation and development of agriculture, which will create conditions for the industrialization of the country. Industry and foreign trade can expand only on the basis of a prospering socialist agriculture. In the three-year plan, socialist transformation is the key problem. When completed as a result of our concentrated efforts, it will create favourable conditions for the rapid building of socialism. The Party's policy for the socialist transformation of agriculture is gradually to take the individual peasants from the work-exchange teams (an embryonic form of· socialism) to agricultural co-operatives of the lower (semi-socialist) type and, eventually to co-operatives of the higher (socialist) type.

Densely populated, the North Vietnamese countryside is small in area; farming implements are antiquated, and labour productivity is low. Simply by re-organizing, and improving technique and management, we can already get a higher productivity than the individual farmers. Our peasants are aware of this. They have, besides, revolutionary traditions and great confidence in the Party, and are ready to respond to its calls. That is why they are enthusiastically joining the work-exchange teams and the agricultural co-operatives and taking the socialist path. The co-operatives now account for more than 40 per cent of the peasant households.

The consolidation of socialist relations of production will undoubtedly ensure the advance of agriculture and this, in turn, will further industrial development without which the countryside cannot get the means it needs for water conservation, fertilizers, improved farming implements, agricultural machinery and electric power.

Another task of paramount importance is the *peaceful socialist transformation of the national bourgeoisie.* In the economic field, our policy is to *redeem*, not to confiscate its means of production. In the political sphere the national bourgeoisie is accorded reasonable rights and a place in the Fatherland Front.

In the past, due to the colonial status of our country, our already small and weak national bourgeoisie was bullied by the imperialists and the feudalists and could not develop. For this reason a considerable number of its members joined the working people's anti-imperialist and anti-feudal struggle and took part in the patriotic war. This is its positive side. However, due to its class nature the national bourgeoisie is reluctant to give up exploitation and still nurtures hopes of development along capitalist lines. But our advance to socialism rules out this possibility. The national bourgeoisie realizes that it can retain its place in the great national family only by agreeing to socialist transformation. Most of its members are aware that sincere acceptance of this transformation will allow them to participate in national reconstruction and socialist building by the side of the working people. This is the only honourable path for them.

Our achievements in the sphere of education are appreciable. Whereas over 95 per cent of our population was illiterate under French rule, illiteracy has now in the main been wiped out in North Viet Nam.

Below are a few figures on school enrolment:

	1939 Whole of Indochina	1959-1960 North Viet Nam alone
Universities	582	8,518
Technical schools	438	18,100
General-education schools	540,000	1,522,200

The following data relate to health work:

	1939 North and Central Viet Nam	1959 North Viet Nam alone
Hospitals	54	138
Village health centres	138	1,500
Doctors	86	292
Nurses	968	6,020
Public health personnel in the countryside		169,000

In simple terms, the aim of socialism is to free the working people from poverty, provide them with employment, make them happy and prosperous. It is the duty of the

16 SW.

Party and the people to increase production and practise thrift, to exert every effort to produce more, faster, better and more economically. Then State plans will surely be fulfilled and the people's life will certainly be ceaselessly improved.

On the basis of the progress made, we must get ready for future long-term plans.

*

* *

The above successes are due to the following factors:

1. *Our Party, which has always taken a firm proletarian class stand and shown absolute loyalty to the interests of the class and the people,* has correctly applied Marxist-Leninist theory to Vietnamese conditions and worked out correct lines and policies. It has ceaselessly combated the reformist tendencies of the bourgeoisie and the political adventurism of the petty bourgeois elements in the national movement, the "left" phraseology of the Trotskyites in the workers' movement, and the right and "left" deviations in the Party, in both the elaboration and execution of various revolutionary strategies and tactics at each stage. Marxism-Leninism has helped us to face those trials successfully. This has enabled our Party not only to win leadership of the revolution in the whole country, but also to maintain this leadership in all fields and to frustrate all attempts by the bourgeoisie to contend with us for the leading role.

2. Guided by Marxist-Leninist theory, we have realized that in a backward agrarian country such as Viet Nam the national question is at bottom the peasant question, that the national revolution is, basically, a peasant revolution carried out under the leadership of the working class, and that people's power is essentially worker-peasant power. At each stage, our Party has firmly grasped

and *correctly solved the peasant question and strengthened the worker-peasant alliance*. It has combated the right and "left" deviations which under-estimate the role of the peasants in the revolution, unaware that they are the main force of the revolution, the chief and most trustworthy ally of the proletariat, and the fundamental force which, together with the proletariat, will build socialism. The Party's revolutionary experience shows that in every case when its cadres took correct decisions which satisfied the deep aspirations of the peasants and conformed to the principle of alliance between the working class and the peasantry, the revolution made vigorous progress.

3. The Party has succeeded in assembling all patriotic and progressive forces in the *National United Front* and realizing national unity with a view to the anti-imperialist and anti-feudal struggle. The workers and peasants being the main force in the national union, their alliance forms the basis of the National United Front. In the formation, consolidation and development of the National United Front, the Party has always combated both sectarianism and isolationism on the one hand and unprincipled compromise on the other. Thirty years of experience in uniting the national forces show that only by waging this twofold struggle against these tendencies can we ensure the Party's leading role in the National United Front, reinforce its worker-peasant base, and broaden its ranks.

4. Our Party has matured and developed in the favourable international conditions created by the victory of the Russian Socialist October Revolution. All achievements of our Party and people are inseparable from the fraternal support of the Soviet Union, People's China and the other socialist countries, the international Communist and workers' movement and the national-liberation movement and the peace movement in the world. If we have been

able to surmount all difficulties and lead our working class and people to the present glorious victories this is because the *Party has coordinated the revolutionary movement in our country with the revolutionary movement of the world working class and the oppressed peoples.*

We are sincerely grateful to the Communist Parties of the Soviet Union and China, which have helped us to mould ourselves into a new-type party of the working class. We shall always remember the generous support given to our Party and people in their revolutionary struggle by the Communist Parties of the Soviet Union, China and France.

From now on, while advancing towards new successes in building socialism in North Viet Nam and fighting for the reunification of the country, our Party will continue its efforts to strengthen the international solidarity of the working class, increase the might of the socialist camp headed by the Soviet Union, educate our people in the spirit of socialist internationalism, which is inseparable from genuine patriotism, and extend the contacts between the revolutionary movement in our country and the struggles waged by the working masses and the oppressed peoples of the world for peace, democracy, national independence and socialism.

In the past thirty years, tremendous changes have happened in the world. Great changes have also happened concerning our Party and our people.

Thirty years ago, our people were crushed under the colonial yoke. Our Party was just born, a heroic party but still young and weak. The Soviet Union, the only existing socialist country, was surrounded by imperialism on all sides.

The Chinese Communist Party and Red Army were subjected to fierce attacks by the reactionary Kuomintang. The other fraternal parties were only in their beginnings. Imperialism was ruling the roost over five-sixths of the world and was taking the road to fascism.

In short, most of mankind was then smothered in capitalist oppression.

But now the situation has changed and the world is facing much brighter perspectives.

The Soviet Union, one of the greatest powers on earth, is building communism; it is also the most solid bastion of world peace.

Socialism has become a powerful world system extending from Europe to Asia and comprising more than a billion people. There exist at present 85 Communist and workers' parties with 35 million members resolutely struggling for peace, socialism and communism.

Many former colonial countries have become independent States. The national-liberation movement is surging up everywhere, in Asia, Africa and Latin America. Imperialism is sinking ever more deeply in a quagmire.

The North of our country has been entirely liberated and the Democratic Republic of Viet Nam is proud to be a member of the great socialist family headed by the Soviet Union. Our Party, now comprising hundreds of thousands of members, is organizing and mobilizing our people in building socialism in the North and struggling for the reunification of the country. It is in the van of the revolutionary struggle of our entire people. Raising high the standard of patriotism and socialism, it resolutely leads our people in the struggle to build a peaceful, reunified, independent, democratic and prosperous Viet Nam, thus contributing to the defence of peace in Southeast Asia and the world.

In order to fulfil this difficult but very glorious task, the Party must raise its ideological level and strengthen its organization and *ensure the growth of its ranks* in a cautious, steady and broad fashion among the masses, first and foremost the working class, with the object of strengthening its proletarian core.

All Party members should strive to *study Marxism-Leninism*, strengthen their proletarian class stand, grasp the laws of development of the Vietnamese revolution, *elevate their revolutionary morality, vigorously combat individualism, foster proletarian collectivism*, be industrious and thrifty in the work for national construction, build close contacts with the labouring masses, and struggle whole-heartedly for the interests of the revolution and the Fatherland.

Socialist construction in North Viet Nam demands that our Party have a good grasp of science and technology; therefore Party members should strive *to raise their cultural, scientific and technological level.*

The Party should strengthen its *leadership* in all spheres of activity.

The *Working Youth Union* should be the Party's right hand in organizing and educating the young generation in the spirit of absolute fidelity to the cause of building socialism and communism.

The *Trade-unions* should be a true school of State administration, economic management and cultural guidance for the working class.

The *Women's Union* should be a powerful force helping the Party to mobilize, organize and lead the women in the advance to socialism.

Under the leadership of the Party the *agricultural co-operatives* should become powerful armies grouping more than ten million peasants and fighting to increase production, raise living standards, elevate socialist consciousness and build a prosperous countryside.

It is the duty of our *People's Army* to work assiduously to raise its political and technical level, build itself up into an ever more powerful force and stand ready to defend our country and the peaceful labour of our people.

Under the banner of Marxism-Leninism, let our Party, with the seething spirit of an invincible army, unite even more closely, and lead our working people boldly forward to new victories in the struggle for socialist construction in the North and for the reunification of the country.

Long live the Viet Nam Workers' Party!

Long live peaceful, reunified, independent, democratic and prosperous Viet Nam!

Long live socialism!

Long live world peace!

TALK AT THE
FIRST MEETING OF CULTURAL ACTIVISTS
(February 11, 1960)

To advance to socialism we must develop our economy and culture. Why don't we say : develop our culture and economy ? Because we have a proverb which runs : "One must have enough to eat before one could practise the good doctrine." So economics should come first. But why should our economy and culture be developed ? Because we must raise our people's material and cultural standards. You are active in both production work and cultural activities. That is good. Culture must serve the people in a practical way ; it must contribute to building a pleasant and healthy life for the masses. In consequence, culture must have an educational content. For example, we must educate our people about the new life, about revolutionary virtues. In the "tree-planting" movement at Tet (Lunar New Year — *Tr.*), we must popularize efficient methods of planting and tending trees. In many places, you have composed poems and songs on these matters with an excellent content and good effects. Let me commend you on this. Culture must be closely bound to work and production. Divorced from life and labour it becomes sterile. A cultural cadre must use culture to promote diligence and thrift in building the country, building socialism in the North, and struggling for national reunification. For example, among members of farming co-operatives, cultural work must seek to enhance diligence and thrift in building the co-ops, and attachment to them as to one's home ; it must oppose any tendency towards an individual economy and other backward thoughts harmful to the consolidation and development of the co-operatives. In the enterprises, cultural work must seek to imbue the workers with the sense of being collective masters of their factories, impel the emulation movement to fulfil the State plan, promote diligence and thrift in building the country's industry, oppose embezzlement and waste...

In brief, to serve socialist revolution, culture must be socialist in content and national in form.

Are you resolved to act in this way ?

In the present conditions, we still meet with many difficulties, the cultural level of our cadres and people is still low, which accounts for many limitations in our work and production. Your duty is to make still more efforts so as to raise our people's cultural standards.

THE PATH WHICH LED ME TO LENINISM*
(April 1960)

After World War One, I made my living in Paris, at one time as an employee at a photographer's, at another as painter of "Chinese antiques" (turned out by a French shop). I often distributed leaflets denouncing the crimes committed by the French colonialists in Viet Nam.

At that time, I supported the October Revolution only spontaneously. I did not yet grasp all its historic importance. I loved and respected Lenin because he was a great patriot who had liberated his fellow-countrymen; until then, I had read none of his books.

The reason for my joining the French Socialist Party was because those "ladies and gentlemen" — so I called my comrades in those days — had shown their sympathy with me, with the struggle of the oppressed peoples. But I had no understanding as yet of what a party, a trade-union, socialism and communism, were.

Heated discussions were then taking place in the cells of the Socialist Party, about whether one should remain in the Second International, found a "Second-and-a-half" International or join Lenin's Third International? I attended the meetings regularly, two or three times a week, and attentively listened to the speakers. At first, I did not understand everything. Why should the discussions be so heated? Whether with the Second, Second-and-a-half or

* Article written for the Soviet review *Problems of the East* on the occasion of Lenin's 90th birthday *(Ed.)*

Third International, the revolution could be waged. Why squabble ? And what about the First International ? What had become of it ?

What I wanted most to know — and what was not debated in the meetings — was : which International sided with the peoples of the colonial countries ?

I raised this question — the most important for me — at a meeting. Some comrades answered : it was the Third, not the Second International. One gave me to read Lenin's "Theses on the national and colonial questions" printed in *l'Humanité*.

In those Theses, there were political terms that were difficult to understand. But by reading them again and again finally I was able to grasp the essential part. What emotion, enthusiasm, enlightenment and confidence they communicated to me ! I wept for joy. Sitting by myself in my room, I would shout as if I were addressing large crowds : "Dear martyr compatriots ! This is what we need, this is our path to liberation !"

Since then, I had entire confidence in Lenin, in the Third International.

Formerly, during the cell meetings, I had only listened to the discussions. I had a vague feeling that what each speaker was saying had some logic in it, and I was not able to make out who were right and who were wrong. But from then on, I also plunged into the debates and participated with fervour in the discussions. Though my French was still too weak to express all my thoughts, I hit hard at the allegations attacking Lenin and the Third International. My only argument was : "If you do not condemn colonialism, if you do not side with the colonial peoples, what kind of revolution are you then waging ?"

Not only did I take part in the meetings of my own cell, I also went to other Party cells to defend "my" position. Here I must again say that Comrades Marcel Cachin,

Vaillant-Couturier, Monmousseau and many others helped me to broaden my knowledge. Eventually, at the Tours Congress, I voted with them for our joining the Third International.

At first, it was patriotism, not yet communism which led me to have confidence in Lenin, in the Third International. Step by step, during the course of the struggle, by studying Marxism-Leninism while engaging in practical activities, I gradually understood that only socialism and communism can liberate the oppressed nations and the working people throughout the world from slavery.

There is a legend, in our country as well as in China, about the magic "Brocade Bag". When facing great difficulties, one opens it and finds a way out. For us Vietnamese revolutionaries and people, Leninism is not only a miraculous "Brocade Bag", a compass, but also a radiant sun illuminating our path to final victory, to socialism and communism.

OPENING SPEECH AT THE THIRD NATIONAL CONGRESS OF THE VIET NAM WORKERS' PARTY

(September 5, 1960)

Dear Comrades,

Today, the Third National Congress of our Party opens at a time wheñ our entire people are joyfully celebrating the 15th anniversary of the founding of the Democratic Republic of Viet Nam. It is attended by over 500 delegates representing more than 500,000 Party members throughout the country and personifying the heroic militant tradition of our Party these last thirty years. On behalf of the Central Committee, I extend cordial greetings to you, to all the cherished members of our Party, to the representatives of the Viet Nam Socialist Party, the Viet Nam Democratic Party and the member organizations of the Fatherland Front.

Our Congress is very happy to extend its warm welcome to the comrades delegates of:

The Communist Party of the Soviet Union,
The Communist Party of China,
The Albanian Party of Labour,
The Bulgarian Communist Party,
The Polish United Workers' Party,
The Socialist Unity Party of Germany,
The Hungarian Socialist Workers' Party,
The Mongolian People's Revolutionary Party,
The Rumanian Workers' Party,

The Korean Workers' Party,
The Communist Party of Czechoslovakia,
The French Communist Party,
The Communist Party of India,
The Communist Party of Indonesia,
The Communist Party of Japan,
The Communist Party of Canada,
and other fraternal Communist Parties.

Prompted by lofty internationalist sentiments our comrades have come to take part in our Congress and have brought us the affectionate feelings of the fraternal Parties. So,

Frontiers and mountains stand between us, yet we are
                                        one family.
Proletarians of the whole world are brothers.

On behalf of the Congress, I affectionately commend all the workers, peasants, intellectuals, armymen, cadres, youth and children who have enthusiastically engaged in emulation and have recorded achievements in honour of the Party Congress and the Fifteenth National Day.

Dear Comrades,

Over the past thirty years, large numbers of our comrades and compatriots have heroically made the supreme sacrifice for the cause of the Revolution. During the War of Resistance, how many fighters gave their lives for the Fatherland! Over the last six years, how many brave fighters in the South have laid down their lives for the Nation! Our Party and our people shall forever treasure the memory of their best sons and daughters who have fallen in the fight for the cause of national liberation and the ideal of Communism.

More than nine years have elapsed since our Party's Second National Congress.

Over the past nine years, our Party, implementing the line of the Second Congress, led our people to wage a bitter, difficult and heroic war of resistance. The great and brilliant victory of Dien Bien Phu put an end to the aggressive war unleashed by the French colonialists assisted by the American imperialists. The Geneva Agreements were signed ; peace was restored in Indochina on the basis of international recognition of the sovereignty, independence, unity and territorial integrity of our country. North Viet Nam was completely liberated. Six years have elapsed ; but our country has not yet been reunified as stipulated by the Geneva Agreements. Our Government and people have always correctly implemented the Agreements signed. But the US imperialists and Ngo Dinh Diem have deliberately sought to perpetuate the partition of our country and shamelessly sabotaged the Geneva Agreements, so that the people in the South of our country are still leading a wretched life under their ruthless rule.

That is why our people have never ceased struggling for the peaceful reunification of the country, for the liberation of our compatriots in the South from their atrocious situation. The widespread, deep-going and powerful revolutionary struggle of our compatriots in the South is continuing. The South has proved worthy of its glorious title : "Brass Wall of the Fatherland."

Since the re-establishment of peace, the North, completely liberated, has shifted over to the stage of socialist revolution. This is a change of great significance in the Vietnamese revolution. Under the leadership of the Party, the Land Reform has been victoriously completed ; it has liberated the toiling peasantry and translated the slogan : "Land to the tillers" into reality.

We have successfully rehabilitated our economy and are now victoriously fulfilling the Three-Year Plan for the development of our economy and culture. In the socialist transformation of agriculture, handicrafts and private

capitalist industry and commerce, we have won successes
of a decisive character. We have recorded many achievements on the agricultural and industrial production fronts
and in cultural and educational work, and have brought
about initial improvements in the people's living standards. The North has been more and more consolidated and
has become a firm base for the struggle for national reunification. The big victories won over the past nine years
have testified to our Party's correct line and clearsighted
leadership. They are victories of Marxism in a country
which has suffered imperialist oppression and exploitation. Our Party is worthy of the confidence of our people
from North to South.

Our Party can be proud of being the heir to our people's glorious traditions, and their guide to a bright future.

Dear Comrades,

All those victories are not the work of our Party alone.
They are the common work of our entire people all over
the country. The revolution is the work of the masses, not
of any individual hero. The successes achieved by our
Party are due to the fact that it has organized and developed the boundless revolutionary forces of the people and
led them in battle under the invincible banner of
Marxism-Leninism.

The victories of the Vietnamese revolution are also due
to the wholehearted assistance of the fraternal socialist
coutries, especially the Soviet Union and China. We avail
ourselves of this opportunity to express our warm gratitude to the fraternal socialist countries headed by the
great Soviet Union. We are also sincerely grateful to the
other fraternal Parties, first of all, to the French Communist Party for its active support to our people's just
struggle. We sincerely thank all colonial nations and
peace-loving people throughout the world, who have
always given us their sympathy and support.

The history of the thirty-year-long struggle of our Party has taught us this lesson :

The best guarantee of victory for the revolution lies in a thorough grasp of Marxism-Leninism, absolute loyalty to the interests of the proletariat and the nation, the preservation of solidarity and oneness of mind within the Party, among all Communist Parties and among all countries of the great socialist family.

Our Party has in the past always acted in this way. It will undoubtedly continue to do so in future.

Dear Comrades,

Our Party has won many great victories, but it has not been immune from errors. We have not, however, concealed our mistakes. On the contrary, we have frankly practised self-criticism and actively corrected them. Our successes have not caused us to grow dizzy and self-complacent. Today, armed with our own experiences and those of the fraternal Parties we are resolved to strive for ever greater progress.

The present task of the Vietnamese revolution *is to take the North to socialism and to struggle for national reunification by peaceful means,* to complete the people's national democratic revolution throughout the country.

The decisions of this Congress will guide our whole Party and our entire people in successfully building socialism in the North, endowing the North with modern industry and agriculture· and advanced culture and science, and making our people's life ever more abundant and happy.

The Second Party Congress was the Congress of Resistance. The present Party Congress is the Congress of Socialist Construction in the North and of Struggle for Peaceful National Reunification.

Our people, who showed heroism in the war of resistance, are now showing heroism in their labour for national construction. We will undoubtedly succeed in building glorious socialism in the North.

A prosperous and strong North is a firm base for the struggle for national reunification.

This Congress will shed new light on our people's path of revolutionary struggle leading to peaceful national reunification.

Our nation is one, our country is one. Our people will undoubtedly overcome all difficulties and achieve our aim : "The country reunified, North and South brought together again."

Dear Comrades,

The Vietnamese revolution is a part of the forces of peace, democracy and socialism in the world. The Democratic Republic of Viet Nam is a member of the great socialist family headed by the great Soviet Union.

It is our duty to defend the advanced post of socialism in Southeast Asia and contribute with all our might to strengthening the forces of the socialist camp and safeguarding peace in Southeast Asia and the world.

At present socialism has become a powerful world system, as firm as a brass wall. Our people are immensely encouraged by the momentous achievements of the Soviet Union in the building of communism and the great successes of China and the other fraternal socialist countries in the building of socialism. Our people strongly support the foreign policy of peace of the Soviet Union and the other countries in the socialist camp. Our people also rejoice profoundly at the victories won by the peoples of Asia, Africa and Latin America in their great struggle against the imperialists, especially the American imperialists. It is clear that the forces of peace, democracy, national independence and socialism throughout the world have become definitely stronger than the imperialist camp. The peoples of the world, by uniting closely with one another and struggling actively, will undoubtedly be able to prevent a world war, and establish a lasting peace. The resolute struggle of the oppressed peoples will undoubtedly defeat the imperialists and colonialists. Socialism will ultimately triumph throughout the world.

In this great struggle, the solidarity among the forces of the socialist countries and the unity of mind of the Communist and Workers' Parties of all countries are of the utmost importance. As stressed by the communiqué of the Bucharest Conference, we are confident that "the Communist and Workers' Parties will continue to strengthen the solidarity of the countries of the world socialist system and to preserve it like the apple of their eye in the struggle for peace and the security of all peoples, for the triumph of the great cause of Marxism-Leninism."

In our time, the imperialists can no longer rule the roost in the world as they did before. But so long as imperialism exists there remains the danger of war. The Declaration of the Meeting of Representatives of the Communist and Workers' Parties of the Socialist Countries, held in Moscow in 1957, reminds us that "the Communist Parties regard the struggle for peace as their foremost task... The peoples of all countries must display the utmost vigilance in regard to the war danger created by imperialism". We must also bear in mind that "the broader and stronger the unity of the various patriotic and democratic forces, the firmer the guarantee for victory in the common struggle".

The imperialists have in the past caused our people much suffering ; the Americans and Diem are now seeking to perpetuate the partition of our country, and are trampling on the South. So long as we have not driven the American imperialists out of the South and liberated it from the barbarous US-Diem rule, our people will know no rest. That is why the struggle for the defence of peace and for national reunification cannot be separated from the struggle against American imperialism.

In the common struggle to safeguard peace and national independence in Indochina, the Vietnamese people resolutely support the Lao people's present valiant struggle against American imperialism, a struggle aimed at leading Laos along the road to national concord, independence, unity, peace and neutrality. We sincerely hope that friendly relations between our country and our neighbours, especially Cambodia and Laos, will be established and promoted in a satisfactory manner.

Dear Comrades,

The socialist revolution in the North and the struggle for national reunification, which contribute to the safeguarding of peace in Southeast Asia and the world, set heavy and glorious tasks for our Party. To ensure victory for the revolution, the question of decisive significance is to heighten the fighting capacity of our whole Party and to promote its leading role in all fields.

Our Party has always endeavoured to link Marxism-Leninism closely with the realities of the Vietnamese revolution. In general, our Party cadres and members are of good revolutionary mettle. But we still have many shortcomings, such as : subjectiveness, dogmatism, empiricism, bureaucratic style of work, individualism... These shortcomings are hampering our progress. To overcome them, we must endeavour to study Marxism-Leninism and strengthen ideological education in the Party. We must further heighten the class character and vanguard character of the Party, ceaselessly strengthen the Party's ties with the masses, and unite with all patriotic and progressive people in order to build socialism successfully and struggle for national reunification. We must strive to learn in a creative way from the experiences of the fraternal Parties. We must never fall into arrogance and conceit ; we must be modest, as Lenin taught us.

This Congress will elect a new Central Committee. We are confident that with the new Central Committee, our Party will be still more closely united and will mobilize the people throughout the country still more vigorously to fulfil the great immediate task now facing us : to build socialism in the North, to struggle for national reunification by peaceful means.

Long live great Marxism-Leninism !

Long live the heroic working class and people of Viet Nam !

Long live the Viet Nam Workers' Party !

Long live the solidarity and unity of mind of the fraternal Parties and of the great socialist family headed by the great Soviet Union !

Long live a peaceful, reunified, independent, democratic, and prosperous Viet Nam !

Long live world peace !

THE CHINESE REVOLUTION
AND THE VIETNAMESE REVOLUTION*

(July 1, 1961)

The triumph of the Russian October Revolution shook the whole world.

Marxism-Leninism began to propagate to China, one of the world's largest countries, which the imperialists contemptuously called "the sleeping lion".

On July 1, 1921, in a small room in the luxurious city of Shanghai, twelve revolutionaries (among whom was Comrade Mao Tse-tung) held a meeting and founded the Chinese Communist Party, which comprised 50 members (and which now has a membership of over 17 million). From then on, the destiny of China began to change.

After 28 years of extremely heroic struggle under the leadership of the Communist Party headed by Comrade Mao Tse-tung, the Liberation Army wiped out over eight million US-equipped Chiang Kai-shek troops and drove the US imperialists out of China; and the People's Republic of China was established (1949).

During twelve years of national construction, the Communist Party has led the 650 million Chinese people in selfless work emulation, turning China from a backward agricultural country, impoverished and illiterate, into a powerful socialist country.

Article written on the occasion of the 40th founding anniversary of the Chinese Communist Party *(Ed.)*

Forty years of glory — forty years of victory. Many comrades have written about the great history of the fraternal Chinese Communist Party. I shall here say only a few things :

— Viet Nam and China are two *neighbouring countries* which have had close relations with each other for many centuries. Naturally, the ties between the Chinese revolution and the Vietnamese revolution are also especially close. For instance :

— The influence of the Russian October Revolution and the Marxist-Leninist theory came to Viet Nam mostly through China.

— The Viet Nam Young Revolutionary Comrades' Association (1925), the conference to unify Vietnamese Communist groups into a Marxist-Leninist Party (1930), the first Congress of the Indochinese Communist Party (1935) were all organized in China and enjoyed the whole-hearted assistance of Chinese comrades.

— The Soviet crushing blow at the Japanese militarists in the Northeast helped China to win the war. China's victorious war of resistance created favourable conditions for the success of the Vietnamese August Revolution.

— From 1946 onward, the Chinese Communist Party had to carry on an unceasing fight against the US-supported troops of Chiang Kai-shek (as the civil war started, the 4,300,000-strong Chiang army was equipped with modern weapons supplied by the US, plus those taken from one million Japanese troops). In 1947, the Chiang clique attacked and seized Yenan. In such difficult conditions, the Communist Party and people of China continued their wholehearted support to our people's war of resistance till complete victory.

— Today, along with the Soviet Union and other brotherly countries, China gives us unreserved assistance in the building of socialism in the North, a solid foundation for the peaceful reunification of the country.

Thus, the relationship between the Chinese revolution and the Vietnamese revolution is made up of

A thousand ties of gratitude, attachment and love,

A glorious friendship that will last for ever!

As for myself, on two occasions I had the honour to work in the Chinese Communist Party.

During my stay in Canton in 1924-27, I kept a close watch on the revolutionary movement in our country while performing tasks entrusted by the Chinese Communist Party. The worker-peasant movement was surging up in China. From May 1925 onward, political strikes occurred in virtually all big cities. The biggest was the strike in protest against the British imperialists in Hongkong, in which more than 250,000 workers participated and which lasted 16 months. The peasant movement also began to spread, especially in Hunan (where it was led by Comrade Mao Tse-tung) and in Kwangtung (where it was led by Comrade Peng Bai). To push the peasant movement forward, Comrade Mao organized the Peasant Mobilization, Instruction and Training Office to train cadres for the peasant movement in 19 provinces.

I took part in the translation of materials for internal use and in "external propaganda", namely by contributing articles on the worker-peasant movement to an English-language newspaper.

The second time I came to China (late in 1938) was during the anti-Japanese war of resistance. As a private in the Eighth Route Army, I was club manager for a unit in Kwelin. Afterwards, I was elected secretary of the Party cell (and was entrusted with radio monitoring) of a unit in Hengyang.

(Thus I managed to acquire some experience in Party building when I was in the Soviet Union, some experience in the struggle against capitalism when in France, and some experience in fighting against colonialism and feudalism when in China). In the meantime, the Chinese comrades tried hard to help me get in touch with my comrades in our country. Our Party's Central Committee sent Comrade X. to Longzhou to look for me. Unfortunately X. was robbed of his purse by a "friend" and had to leave for home before I reached Longzhou.

Later on, however, the Chinese comrades managed to help me to communicate with home and return to the country.

In short : as they share a lofty aim, Communists all over the world unite closely on the basis of Marxism-Leninism and proletarian internationalism while showing mutual sympathy and love like brothers of the same family.

I take this opportunity to convey, on behalf of our Party, Government and people, to the great Chinese Communist Party headed by beloved Comrade Mao Tsetung, my most cordial and warmest congratulations.

ADDRESS TO THE FIFTH PLENUM OF THE VIET NAM WORKERS' PARTY CENTRAL COMMITTEE

(July 1961)

Comrades,

We can say that this Central Committee Plenum has achieved *good results*. This is because it has been guided by the Third Party Congress, because there has been an ideological remoulding drive, and because discussions have been extensive and centred on a single problem.

We must strive to advance rapidly, vigorously and steadily in the development of agriculture, because :

— "One must have enough to eat before one could practise the good doctrine," says the proverb; so we must gradually better the people's livelihood.

— Agriculture must supply enough food and materials for the development of industry, for socialist industrialization.

— If we do well in agriculture and industry, we shall do well in building socialism in the North, which provides a solid and strong foundation for the struggle for the peaceful reunification of the country.

We are all agreed that the co-operation movement is proceeding well in the main. At the same time we have found that it has shortcomings which should be overcome. These are shortcomings arising from the process of development. It is like the case of an over-grown child, whose clothes seem to shrink every month. The most widespread shortcoming is the weakness of many management committees, for the cadres' standards do not advance at the same rate as the progress of the co-operatives, and they are like squad leaders who have to command companies or battalions. We must help them to become level with their tasks.

In my opinion, we should stress the following points :

— The Party's line, guiding principles, policies, etc.. are all aimed at *improving the living conditions* of the people in general and of the peasants in particular. To achieve this aim, we must necessarily consolidate and develop the co-operatives in the best way possible, and *steadily raise the co-op members' income.*

This point we must stress, because at present some people still think that the Party encourages higher production only to get more food deliveries for the State, not in the interests of the peasants.

— We must strive to *strengthen Party cells* in the rural areas. Only with a good Party cell can one have a good management committee. With a good management committee, co-op members will unite and be eager to work, and the co-op will be well consolidated and developed.

At the same time the qualifications and powers of management cadres must be clearly defined. For example : the co-op congress elects management cadres and has the power to dismiss any incompetent ones ; management cadres should be of unquestionable integrity ; financial matters should be open to public control, etc.

— We must instil into every co-op member the *sense of being master and the qualities of diligence and thrift in building the co-op.*

— We must further increase control and supervision, so as to discover and propagate good experience, and in time correct the co-op's weaknesses and shortcomings.

— The Central Committee has unanimously agreed on the line, policy, targets and measures... We must *turn this unanimity into determination.* We must convey the Central Committee's unanimity and determination to every cadre, every co-op member, so that the whole Party and the entire people translate the Central Committee's resolution into a high tide of emulation to increase production and practise economy so as steadily to better the people's life.

— After this Plenum, the ministries and central departments should work out plans to serve agricultural production in a practical way. Provincial and district cadres must widely propagate the resolution and give clear explanations to every co-op cadre and member so that everyone will engage in enthusiastic emulation to carry it into effect and first of all to get a bumper autumn crop this year.

Our peasants have a tradition of working industriously and striving hard. Once they are imbued with the spirit of the Central Committee resolution, they are sure to feel greatly encouraged and a great change will result in agricultural production.

On behalf of the Central Committee I take this opportunity to praise the Dai Phong co-operative and the movement to emulate Dai Phong, and to remind co-op cadres and members that they should not grow complacent, but should endeavour to make ever greater progress.

ADDRESS TO THE SEVENTH PLENUM OF THE PARTY CENTRAL COMMITTEE

(April, 1962)

Comrades,

Our country is situated in the tropical zone, with a favourable climate.

It has rich forests, productive seas and fertile lands.

Our people are courageous, industrious and thrifty.

We enjoy considerable assistance from the brotherly countries.

Thus we have all the three favourable conditions — climatic, geographical and human — for the building of socialism, that is, to build a happy life for our people.

What our whole Party and our entire people must do is to strive to combine and make the most of those three conditions in economic construction in the Northern part of our country.

The Third Party Congress has adopted a resolution on the general line for economic development.

The Fifth Central Committee Plenum has adopted a resolution on agricultural development.

The Seventh Central Committee Plenum has adopted a resolution on industrial development.

Thus we have clearly-stated directions and concrete measures.

Here, I shall just make a few suggestions.

We Vietnamese have a saying, "One must have enough to eat before one could practise the good doctrine." The Chinese also have a saying, "To have enough to eat is a first priority for the people."

Those are two simple but very sound sayings.

To improve the people's life we must first of all solve the *problem of food* (then clothing and other problems). To solve the problem of food, we must manage to have enough *cereals*. And cereals are products of agriculture. Thus, *to develop agriculture is of the utmost importance.*

In colder countries with long frosty winters, they can only get one crop a year. Our warmer climate enables us to grow crops all the year round. Thus we have very favourable *climatic conditions*. The Northern delta has not enough land for its population, but we can double the cultivated acreage by growing additional and intercalary crops. The highlands have vast areas of fertile soil which we can reclaim at will. Thus the *geographical conditions* are very good.

At present, land belongs to the peasants, over 85 per cent of whom have joined co-operatives. Over 35 per cent of the co-ops cover whole villages. Soon practically all peasants will be co-op members. Well-organized, the ten-odd million peasants will be a tremendous force which can remove mountains and fill up seas. Thus the *human conditions* are very favourable too.

At present, the most important thing for agricultural development is to *improve the quality of co-op management committees*. If these committees are good, the co-ops will be good. And if the co-ops are good, agriculture is sure to develop well.

Industry and agriculture are the two legs of the economy.

Agriculture must develop strongly so as to supply enough food to the people, enough raw materials (such as cotton, sugar-cane, tea, etc.) to the factories, and enough farm produce (such as groundnuts, beans, jute, etc.) for exports in exchange for machinery.

Industry must develop strongly so as to supply enough consumer goods to the people, first of all the peasants; to supply water pumps, chemical fertilizers, insecticides, etc., for the development of agriculture, and gradually to supply farm co-ops with planting and harrowing machines. Agriculture can develop only when industry is developed. So industry and agriculture must help each other and develop together, as when both legs of a man walk briskly and regularly, his pace will be quick and he can quickly reach his goal. In this way we realize *the worker-peasant* alliance to build socialism, to build a happy life for the people.

Thanks to our own efforts and to wholehearted assistance from the brotherly countries, especially the Soviet Union and China, our industry has developed at a fairly quick rate. For example, of the total output value of industry and agriculture, industry only accounted for less than 17% in 1955. In 1961, it accounted for over 43%. However, our industry is still weak in relation to our needs. We have not enough electric power, steel, machinery, chemicals, etc., for our agriculture and other economic branches. What we have turned out is of poor quality and high cost.

To achieve the aim of socialist industrialization, our whole Party and our entire people must strive fully to carry out the resolution of the Seventh Plenum of the Central Committee.

In my view, the *key* to agricultural development is to improve the work of co-op management committees. The *key* to industrial development is to improve the management of enterprises and the technical standards of workers and cadres at the basic level ; while the leading bodies must serve production and keep in close touch with it.

In socialist construction, we certainly meet with *difficulties*. To transform an old society into a new one is not an easy task. But those are difficulties arising from growth. If the whole Party and the entire people are of one mind and join forces, any difficulty can be overcome.

On the other hand, we have very favourable conditions— climatic, geographical and human. The *patriotic emulation movement*, especially since 1961, has testified to this. Our workers, peasants and cadres have originated tens of thousands of innovations in order to overcome difficulties, increase production and practise economy.

In the patriotic emulation movement, there have emerged tens of labour heroes, thousands of emulation fighters, tens of thousands of front-rank workers, and hundreds of socialist-labour teams and brigades.

Those are very powerful driving forces. Led by the Party, combining the patriotic emulation movement with the campaign against embezzlement, waste and bureaucracy, instilling in all our people the sense of being masters of our country and the spirit of industry and thrift in building our motherland, we are sure to be successful in the socialist industrialization of the North, the solid base for the struggle for the peaceful reunification of the country.

I hope that all of you will carefully study, widely propagate and strictly carry out the two Central Committee resolutions, the 5th and the 7th, so as to turn the resolve of the Party into that of the masses. By so doing, we are sure to achieve success !

ADDRESS TO THE SIXTH SESSION OF THE SECOND NATIONAL ASSEMBLY OF THE DEMOCRATIC REPUBLIC OF VIET NAM

(May 8, 1963)

Comrade Deputies,

I am deeply moved and happy at the news I have just received that the National Assembly intends to award me the Gold Star Order, the highest decoration in our country. I wish to express my gratitude to the National Assembly.

But I should like to request the Assembly to allow me to put off accepting this decoration. The reason is that decorations are to be awarded to men of merit; for my part I don't think I deserve as yet this high award of the National Assembly.

Our Fatherland is temporarily divided in two. The US imperialists are intensifying their aggressive war in South Viet Nam. Our Southern compatriots are being trampled upon by the brutal US-Diem regime. Not a day passes without the US-Diemists terrorizing, mopping up, and killing people, burning down villages, spraying poisonous chemicals, destroying crops, forcing people into concentration camps, those hells on earth which they call "strategic hamlets".

In such conditions of blood and fire, our Southern compatriots are daily and hourly sacrificing their lives, struggling heroically, and resolutely opposing the aggressors and traitors, to win back freedom and the right to live.

Uniting closely around the South Viet Nam National Front for Liberation, our Southern compatriots — whether they are men or women, old or young, intellectuals, peasants, workers or tradesmen, whether they are majority people or highlanders — all are of one mind, resolved to overcome all difficulties and hardships, and to fight till final victory.

While the North is engaged in emulation to build socialism so as to support our Southern compatriots, the latter are heroically fighting to defend the peaceful construction in the North. That is why the Northern people think of their Southern compatriots every hour, every minute.

For nearly twenty long years struggling against the French colonialists then against the US-Diemists, our Southern compatriots are truly heroic sons and daughters of the heroic Vietnamese people. The South fully deserves the title "Brass Wall of the Fatherland" and the highest decoration.

For those reasons, I beg the Assembly to agree to this :

We shall wait till the day the South is completely liberated, the country peacefully reunified, North and South reunited into one family — then the National Assembly will allow our Southern compatriots to hand me this high decoration. Thus all our people will be happy and elated.

*
* *

I take this opportunity to dare President Kennedy to answer the following questions :

— Viet Nam is thousands of miles away from the United States. The Vietnamese and American peoples have no quarrel with each other. For what reason have you launched an aggressive war in South Viet Nam and wasted billions of dollars of the American people to support a corrupt and dictatorial administration, spat upon by the South Vietnamese people? What right do you have to force tens of thousands of young Americans to come and kill innocent South Vietnamese, then to get killed in this unjust, dirty war?

— In 1954, as a member of the US Congress, you criticized President Eisenhower in these words:

"To pour money, weapons and men into the Indochinese jungle without a remote hope of victory might be a dangerous and useless thing, an act of suicide. I am frankly of the belief that no amount of American military assistance in Indochina can conquer an enemy that seems to be everywhere and at the same time nowhere, an enemy... which has the sympathy and covert support of the people..."

So why has President Kennedy committed a blind act of suicide, against which Senator Kennedy had clearsightedly warned?

— The American people's just opinion, which American personalities pointed out in their letter to their President (March 1, 1963) is this: American military intervention in South Viet Nam must be ended, and an international conference must be convened to work out a peaceful solution. Will President Kennedy act upon this just opinion of the American people or will he not?

President Kennedy should know history. History has proved that when a people are of one mind and united in the struggle for independence and freedom (as his own forefathers were in the past and the South Vietnamese people are at present), they are bound to **win victory.** Therefore it is certain that :

Our Southern compatriots will win ;

North and South will be reunited in one family ; **and**

Our beloved Fatherland will be peacefully reunified.

Once again, I express my thanks to the National Assembly.

REPORT TO THE
SPECIAL   POLITICAL   CONFERENCE
(March 27, 1964)

Dear Elders and Comrades,

It is ten years since peace was restored in our country. During this time, there have been great changes in our country and the world. This Special Political Conference is a good occasion for us to review past events and discuss problems that lie ahead.

The past ten years have been a decade of struggle and construction during which our people have overcome many difficulties and won many victories.

Ten years ago, the Dien Bien Phu victory put a glorious conclusion to the long, arduous and heroic war of resistance of our entire people, waged against the French colonialists' aggression and the US imperialists' intervention. This was a great victory of our people, and also a common victory of all oppressed peoples in the world. The Dien Bien Phu victory is a brilliant illustration of this Marxist-Leninist truth 'in our time : imperialist aggressive wars are bound to be defeated, national-liberation revolutions are bound to be successful.

 The Dien Bien Phu victory led to the success of the 1954 Geneva Conference on Indochina. The Geneva Agreements solemnly recognize the independence, unity and territorial integrity of Viet Nam and of the brotherly countries of Laos and Cambodia. The Western countries which participated in that conference — the United States, Great Britain and France — also pledged to respect those inviolable national rights.

But immediately after the Geneva Conference, the imperialist powers instigated by the United States set up the so-called "South-East Asia Defence Organisation" which was in fact an aggressive bloc. Since then, the US imperialists have ever more openly intervened in the South of our country and in Laos, kindling fratricidal wars in those areas. They resort to every perfidious manoeuvre to jeopardize the peace and neutrality of Cambodia. They make use of Thailand as a springboard to commit aggression against the above countries. Recently, the US and British imperialists also rigged up "Malaysia" with a view to threatening the Republic of Indonesia.

They wrongly believe they can smash the newly-emerging nations and turn some Southeast Asian countries into military bases for attacks against socialist countries. But this perfidious scheme is being resolutely opposed by the peoples of Viet Nam, Laos, Cambodia and Indonesia and will be completely defeated.

After the Geneva Conference, the people in our whole country should have been able to enjoy a peaceful life and build up the country. But the US imperialists and their henchmen have undermined the Geneva Agreements, partitioned our country and launched an atrocious war in the South. They burn down villages and massacre people, imprison, rape, disembowel and behead old and young.

The whole civilized world seethes with indignation at their towering crimes. That is why our 14 million Southern compatriots have resolutely risen up and are resolved to fight them to the bitter end. Our Northern compatriots, feeling hurt in their own flesh and blood, never stop thinking of the heroic South and the struggle for national reunification.

Over the past ten years, under people's power, our 17 million countrymen in the North have been of one mind in striving to build up the country, shape a new life and increase our strength in all fields. The great achievements of the North have clearly proved the superiority of the socialist regime and are strongly inspiriting our Southern compatriots in their patriotic struggle.

The sight of the North undergoing constant change and growing ever more powerful is a source of pride and elation for our entire people from North to South. It is also a source of joy for our brothers and friends all over the world.

Only if we recall the situation in the North when peace was just restored can we clearly realize the progress made by our people.

The colonialist war of aggression had left our economy in a state of exhaustion.

One-seventh of the arable land was left waste, one-third was out of cultivation for want of water, irrigation works had been destroyed, one-fourth of our buffaloes and oxen had been killed by the enemy. Hundreds of thousands of houses, hundreds of localities, large and small, had been burnt to the ground. The few existing factories had also been ravaged by the enemy, most of their machines dismantled and taken away, and production was at a standstill. Most roads, bridges and vehicles were out of commission. In the cities, hundreds of thousands of workers were unemployed. Famine was looming everywhere.

In a word, it was a scene of ruin and desolation. But our people who had been heroic in the resistance to the enemy have been equally heroic in the arduous struggle to overcome all difficulties and rebuild their life.

Within three years, we succeeded in healing the war wounds, rehabilitating virtually all agricultural and industrial establishments. Farm production soon far surpassed the pre-war peak; industrial production again rose approximately to the level attained under French rule. During this period, we completed the *land reform,* distributing land and cattle to over 10 million working peasants. Thus our peasants have really become the masters of the countryside, masters of their own destiny.

During the subsequent three years, we scored another great victory, this time in *socialist transformation.* Eleven million working peasants voluntarily joined the farm co-ops, advancing steadily on the path of collective farming. Nearly all craftsmen were reorganized.

The whole sector of capitalist industry and trade has been peacefully transformed. The state-run socialist sector has been growing ever stronger, holding absolute superiority in the national economy.

The system of exploitation of man by man has been basically abolished. Socialist relations of production have been established, and all working people are brothers, united into a tremendous force for national construction.

Over the past three years, in the light of the Third Congress of our Party, our people have engaged in enthu-siastic emulation to fulfil the first Five-Year Plan, making the first steps in socialist industrialization, and laying the initial material and technical basis for socialism.

The results so far:

In *agriculture,* we have built many irrigation works, large and small, bringing water to over half a million hectares of land. We have reclaimed over 300,000 ha. and stepped up the production of fertilizers and improved farm tools. The State has given greater assistance to the peasants and striven to develop the sources of capital for the co-ops, so as to build the material and technical basis of agriculture; it has encouraged intensive farming so as to increase output. Though droughts, typhoons and floods have often occurred in the past three years, agricultural production has been developing in an all-round and steady way.

As compared with 1939, food output has more than doubled, animal husbandry has nearly doubled, while the output value of industrial crops is seven times larger. Our agriculture is advancing ever more vigorously, constituting a solid foundation for socialist industrialization.

In *industry*, we have built many new factories. Starting with 41 factories in 1954 (of which only twenty were large ones), we have now 1,000 factories (of which 217 are of large size). Important establishments of heavy industry : machine-building, electric power, metallurgy, chemical industry, mining, etc. have been gradually built. Light industry and handicrafts have turned out most of the consumer goods needed in the country.

Our present economy has in the main become a self-reliant economy in steady progress.

As regards *cultural and social affairs,* 95 per cent of the population have become literate while under French rule 95 per cent were illiterate. As compared with the day when peace was just restored, the number of general-education pupils has increased 3.5 times ; that of higher and vocational education students is 25 times greater. Alphabets have been designed for the languages of some minority peoples, and many young people from minority nationalities have graduated from our universities. Health work has recorded many achievements, many epidemics and old social diseases have been checked. the people's health has been improved. Children have been given ever better care.

The cultural life of the masses is in progress, as literature and art are developing vigorously with a socialist content and a national character.

Over the past ten years, the North has made big strides forward without precedent in our national history. The country, society and man have changed. Many large industrial areas have sprung up. Many cities which used to be just pleasure resorts have become centres of production. Many rural areas which used to get only one crop a year now harvest two or three crops as agriculture develops in an all-round way. Hundreds of thousands of people from the delta have gone to the formerly out-of-the-way midland and highland areas to join the highlanders in exploiting the abundant riches of the country.

The present society in the North is one of working people who are collective masters of the country and uphold the spirit of self-reliance, industry and thrift in order to build socialism and a new life for themselves and for all generations to come. The present society in the North is a great family formed by all strata of the population, all fraternal nationalities, closely united and helping each other, sharing weal and woe and working for the common interests of the Fatherland. Our regime is a new regime ; our people are cultivating new ethics, the socialist ethics of working people: "one for all and all for one." While building the new, we develop the fine qualities of our forefathers and learn from the good examples set by the people of brotherly countries.

We are proud to see many *old men and women* aged 70-80 and more working hard and studying eagerly, setting up "white-haired brigades'" to plant trees and afforest land as well as campaign for popular education, hygiene and disease prevention.

Our *women* have shown great merits in agricultural production ; many of them are heroines and emulation fighters, as well as outstanding factory team-leaders, co-op managers, militia commanders, doctors. teachers. etc.

Our *youth* are vigorous pace-setters in all activities — economic, cultural and national defence — who act upon the slogan: "Young people are present wherever they are needed and wherever difficulties arise."

Our *children* are well-behaved, studious and hard-working; many have shown bravery in rescuing their friends in danger; others have honestly return lost property to its owners; they love and help each other and emulate each other in doing "a thousand good deeds."

Our villages were places where people toiled and moiled all the year round and yet never got enough to eat. Our villages are now busy in all seasons with collective work Everywhere one can see schools, kindergartens, maternity homes, club-houses, co-op yards and stores, and new dwelling houses for co-op members. The people's material life is steadily improving while their spiritual life is getting ever richer.

At present, the *campaign for streamlining co-op management and improving techniques* is involving millions of peasants, who eagerly discuss production orientation and plans, as well as technical improvements. This has brought about a turning-point in agriculture and a new spirit in the rural areas.

In *industrial enterprises, construction sites and other economic undertakings,* our workers and cadres, conscious of being the collective masters, are enthusiastically emulating each other in their work, promoting innovations, and striving gradually to carry out the technical revolution, with a view to increasing labour productivity, stepping up production, improving the quality and reducing the costs of products. At present, preparations are being made everywhere for the *"three for and three against"* campaign: for a higher sense of responsibility, improved management, improved techniques; against embezzlement waste and bureaucracy. Those campaigns of revolutionary significance, aimed at producing more, quicker, better and at lower costs, in fulfilment of the State plan, are bound to create a dramatic change in the national economy, and bring an important contribution to the gradual realization of socialist industrialization and the further improvement of our people's life.

Intellectual workers are making great efforts in research, creation and invention, giving a great impulse to scientific, technical, educational, literary and artistic work, and have made numerous contributions to economic and cultural development, to the building of a rich and powerful fatherland, and to the training of cadres for the future.

The Army and *the people's armed forces* are enthusiastically advancing and becoming a regular and modern army. Constantly raising their revolutionary spirit and their socialist consciousness as well as their tactical and technical standards, they stand ready to fight, to defend the Fatherland, to keep peace and order and are resolved to smash all acts of sabotage by the US imperialists and their henchmen.

Vietnamese nationals living in foreign lands are always thinking of the Fatherland. Those who have returned home have eagerly contributed their talents and energies to national construction.

Chinese residents have actively joined our people in building socialism in the North, thus helping to strengthen the friendship between Viet Nam and China.

In all fields of activity in the North, the *patriotic emulation* movement is inspiring our people with ever greater revolutionary enthusiasm and creative working power in building up thousands of socialist-labour teams and brigades, recording outstanding achievements in every field, and striving to fulfil the 1964 State Plan and the first Five-Year Plan successfully.

*

*   *

The past ten years are ten years of arduous struggle and glorious successes. Those fine results are due to the correct leadership of the Party and the Government and the courageous endeavours of our people ; they are also due to the whole-hearted assistance of the brother socialist countries, especially of the Soviet Union and China. On behalf of our people, Party and Government, I take this opportunity to offer our sincere thanks to the brother socialist countries.

We rejoice at the great achievements that have been scored. We must, however, be fully aware of the *great difficulties* that face us on the path of revolutionary development and the *shortcomings and weaknesses* which we must strive to overcome. For example, the standard of economic management is still low, the sense of responsibility is not very high, the quality of manufac- tured products is not good enough, there are still many instances of bureaucracy, waste and embezzlement, etc.

But with the efforts of the whole Party and the entire people, who evince a strong sense of criticism and self- criticism as well as close unity and oneness of mind, and are advancing enthusiastically, we are sure to overcome all difficulties and win still greater successes.

All of us in the North should constantly bear in mind the fact that while we are living and working in peace, our Southern compatriots are heroically making sacrifices in the glorious fight against the US imperialists and their henchmen. Therefore, all of us should redouble our efforts to be worthy of our Southern kinsmen.

Dear Elders and Comrades,

We are deeply proud of our heroic South. The past ten years in the South are ten years of glorious fight and brilliant victories. For twenty long years, our Southern compatriots have ceaselessly struggled to defend the Fatherland. Fighting the French colonialists then the American imperialists, the Southern patriotic forces have overcome all difficulties and hardships, and are becoming ever stronger and winning ever more victories as they fight on. The South fully deserves to be called the "Brass Wall of the Fatherland."

At present, the world's people and even American public opinion have realized that the US war of aggression in South Viet Nam is doomed to defeat. Even among the US ruling circles, some have begun to realize that the US and its henchmen are in an impasse. The US imperialists have poured into South Viet Nam billions of dollars, tens of thousands of tons of weapons; they have sent there over 20,000 military advisers to command the over half a million troops of the Southern administration and wage an extremely brutal war against our Southern compatriots. The result is that they are sustaining ever more defeats and are getting ever more bogged down.

Why have they failed? They hold that this is because their henchmen are incapable. They think that if they change their puppets the situation will improve. But such changes have only worsened their predicament.

They blame the South Vietnamese army for being unwilling to fight, which is true. The South Vietnamese army is also made up of Vietnamese; there is no reason why they should obey American orders and kill their own countrymen. They have grown more and more conscious of this and more and more of them have been looking for opportunities to turn their guns against the aggressors and the traitors.

The US imperialists and their henchmen also slander-ously accuse the North of supplying the Southern patriotic forces with weapons. But everyone knows that the weapons used by the South Vietnamese patriots are American-made ones and that it is the Saigon regime's army itself which is their suppliers. American newspapers have admitted that over the past year, the South Viet-namese guerillas seized over 8,000 weapons to arm them-selves with. At present, the US warmongers and their new lackeys are again clamouring for a "march to the North"! But they must understand this : if they recklessly embark on a venture against the North, they will meet with ignominious defeat. Because the people of our whole country will resolutely fight them, because the socialist countries and progressive people all over the world will wholeheartedly support us, and because the people of the United States and its allies will also oppose them.

The present situation in the South is clear evidence of the inevitability of US failure in this "special war". The "special war" which the US imperialists are experi-menting in South Viet Nam has been defeated, and will fail in any other place. This is the international significance of the patriotic struggle of our Southern compatriots with reference to the national liberation movements in the world.

In face of such a situation, world opinion as well as American opinion are concerned about a settlement of the war in South Viet Nam.

For our part, we have all along consistently held that the only correct solution for the South Viet Nam problem is strictly to carry out the basic provisions of the 1954 Geneva Agreements on Indochina.

The participants in the Geneva Conference, including the United States, must honour their pledge : to respect the sovereignty, independence, unity, and territorial integrity of Viet Nam and to refrain from interfering in the internal affairs of Viet Nam.

Like the Government of the Democratic Republic of Viet Nam, the Saigon administration must strictly implement these very essential provisions of the agreements: not to enter into any military alliance with foreign countries, not to allow the establishment of any foreign military bases, not to admit any foreign military personnel into the country.

We fully support the very just demands of the South Viet Nam National Front for Liberation for an end to US imperialist intervention in the South, for the withdrawal of US troops and weapons from the South, that the internal affairs of the South should be left to the people of South Viet Nam who will settle them in the spirit of the Front's Programme.

On the question of the peaceful reunification of Viet Nam, our Government has repeatedly made clear its views and positions in conformity with the spirit of the Programme of the Viet Nam Fatherland Front and the Programme of the South Viet Nam National Front for Liberation.

We fully support Point 9 of the Programme of the South Viet Nam National Front for Liberation:

"The imperative demand of our compatriots in the whole country is to reunify the Fatherland peacefully. The South Viet nam National Front for Liberation stands for the gradual reunification of the country by peaceful means, on the principle of negotiations and discussions to be conducted by both zones on all forms and mesures that are in the interests of the nation, of the Vietnamese Fatherland.

"Pending reunification, the governments in both zones shall negotiate and pledge themselves not to conduct any propaganda likely to divide the nation and lead to war, and not to use military force against each other. Economic and cultural exchanges shall be conducted between the two zones. People in both zones shall be free to travel, carry out trade, visit and send letters to each other."

The Vietnamese people sincerely thank the people of the socialist countries and the world's people who have resolutely supported the just struggle of our Southern compatriots for self-liberation, and that of our whole people for the peaceful reunification of the country.

To the American people, I wish to say that the unjust war that the US government is carrying on in the South of our country has caused a great waste of lives and wealth for the American people, and has stained the honour of the United States. It is time the American people struggled even more resolutely for an end to this dirty war, to save the honour of the United States and to build friendship between the peoples of our two countries.

Dear Elders and Comrades,

Over the past ten years, *in the world,* great revolutionary changes have occurred, favourable to the cause of peace, national independence, democracy and socialism.

A century ago, Marx called on the proletariat of the whole world to unite and make revolution. Half a century later, Lenin called on the proletariat and oppressed peoples to unite to overthrow imperialism. Under the leadership of Lenin and the great Russian Communist Party, the October Revolution won brilliant triumph leading to the establishment of a powerful Soviet Union and ushering in a new era in human history, the era of victory of socialism. In the Second World War, the Soviet Union utterly defeated fascism, saving humanity from its brutal domination, and creating conditions for the success of the revolution in many countries.

19 SW.

The success of the Chinese Revolution and the establishment of the People's Republic of China tipped the balance of forces in the world definitely in favour of the revolutionary side, and strongly stimulated the struggle of the oppressed peoples and labouring people all over the world. The socialist camp came into being. It has grown ever more powerful and is becoming the decisive factor in the evolution of human society. It is the strong mainstay of the national liberation struggle in Asia, Africa and Latin America.

As imperialism is sustaining continual and heavy defeats, and is falling into decadence, it grows ever more brutal and reckless. Today, the world's people are fully aware of the wicked nature of US imperialism, aggressive and warlike, which is frantically carrying out extremely perfidious schemes against the socialist countries, against the sovereignty and independence of nations, against world peace and security. Everywhere, in Asia, Africa and Latin America, the peoples have risen up resolutely to fight the imperialists headed by the United States and have repeatedly scored brilliant victories.

The *foreign policy* of our Party and State is to strengthen solidarity with *the brother socialist countries* on the basis of Marxism-Leninism and proletarian internationalism; resolutely to oppose the aggressive and warlike policy of imperialism headed by US imperialism: to achieve peaceful coexistence between countries having differing political and social regimes; resolutely to support the movements for national liberation and safeguarding national independence; to support the struggle of the working class and the world's people for peace, national independence, democracy and socialism. Events over the past years have proved that this policy is fully correct and has brought about great successes. Our country's international status has been steadily raised. We have won the ever wider and stronger sympathy and support of the fraternal countries and of the world's people for the socialist construction in the North, for the liberation struggle of our Southern compatriots and for the struggle of the people of our whole country for peaceful national reunification.

As a country in Southeast Asia, we wholeheartedly support the just struggle of the peoples in this region against aggression and enslavement by imperialism, colonialism and neo-colonialism.

With regard to our neighbour, the *Kingdom of Laos,* we are always desirous and ready to develop friendly relations in all fields. We wholeheartedly support the just struggle of the Lao people against aggression by US imperialism; we support the efforts of the coalition government in Laos with Prince Souvanna Phouma as Prime Minister to carry out the 1962 Geneva Agreement on Laos and to safeguard the peace and neutrality of Laos. We sincerely wish that the Lao coalition government will soon achieve national concord and succeed in stabilizing the situation so as to build a prosperous Laos.

With regard to the *Kingdom of Cambodia,* we consistently stand for the establishment of good-neighbourly relations. We fully support the resolute stand of the Cambodian government against the provocation and threat of aggression by the US imperialists and their henchmen. We have repeatedly declared that we support, and are ready to participate in, an international conference, as proposed by Head of State Prince Norodom Sihanouk, which will guarantee the neutrality and territorial integrity of Cambodia.

We firmly believe that, with the strong support of the world's people, the Cambodian people will surely maintain their national independence and sovereignty, their neutrality and territorial integrity, thus making a worthy contribution to the defence of peace and security in this region.

We fully support the *Indonesian* people who, under the leadership of President Sukarno, are resolutely struggling against the "greater Malaya" bloc created by the imperialists with a view to retaining their privileges in Southeast Asia, and to be used by them as a springboard to attack the national liberation movement in this area. But surely the imperialists' scheme will meet with failure, and the just struggle of the Indonesian people is bound to be successful.

In the common interests of the world's revolutionary movement and the struggle against imperialism, we constantly strive to contribute our part to the safeguarding and strengthening of solidarity in the socialist camp and the international communist movement. Basing ourselves on the resolution of the 9th Plenum of the Viet Nam Workers' Party Central Committee, we pledge ourselves to persist in our efforts, along with the other fraternal Marxist-Leninist parties, to defend the purity of Marxism-Leninism and the revolutionary principles of the two Moscow Declarations. We fully believe that the differences in the international communist movement will be resolved. Marxism-Leninism will certainly be victorious, the socialist camp and the international communist movement will grow ever more united and powerful. By giving a strong impetus to the revolutionary struggle of the working class and the world's people they will win ever greater victories for peace, national independence, democracy and socialism.

Dear Elders and Comrades,

We have reviewed major events in our country and in the world over the past ten years. Our people have grown up; they have gained more strength and richer experience. We are advancing with firmer steps towards the completion of our nation's revolutionary tasks: to build socialism, to build a new life in the North, to support the patriotic struggle of our Southern compatriots, to achieve a peaceful, reunified, independent, democratic and prosperous Viet Nam, to contribute to the safeguarding of peace in Southeast Asia and the world.

To achieve those great aims, our *immediate tasks* are as follows :

1. Our entire Party, people and army should strengthen their unity even further. Let everyone heighten his mettle and revolutionary spirit and be fearless of difficulties and hardships ; let him develop his sense of collective masterhood ; let him dare to think and dare to act, strive to fulfil his tasks, and contribute to the successful completion of this year's State Plan and the first Five-Year Plan.

2. Let us successfully carry out the campaign for "streamlining management, improving techniques, and developing agriculture in an all-round, vigorous and steady way" ; and the campaign of the "three fors and three againsts" in industry and other branches of the national economy.

Let us step up the movement in which delta people go to the highlands to take part in economic and cultural development there.

Let us step up patriotic emulation, and develop socialist-labour teams and brigades and advanced farm co-ops.

3. Let us strengthen people's power unceasingly, and strictly observe this principle : democracy for the people, dictatorship toward the enemy. Let us strictly obey all State regulations and laws. Let us make a success of the forthcoming elections to the Third National Assembly.

Let us strengthen the national defence forces, maintain security and order, be always vigilant and stand ready to smash all acts of provocation and sabotage by the US imperialists and their henchmen.

4. Let us wholeheartedly support the patriotic struggle of our Southern compatriots. Let everyone work hard and make practical contribution to socialist construction in the North and the cause of peaceful national reunification.

5. Let us uphold the spirit of proletarian internationalism, safeguard and develop friendship with the brother socialist countries; let us wholeheartedly support the national liberation movements; unite with the world's working class and people in the struggle against imperialism headed by US imperialism, for peace, national independence, democracy and socialism.

The revolutionary struggle is a long and arduous process, but it is inevitably victorious. Everyone of us, whatever his work and position, must be a courageous fighter for this glorious cause.

Cadres of the Party, the State and people's organizations, Party members and Working Youth Union members must set good examples in their work, do their utmost to serve the people, and constantly cultivate revolutionary virtues: industry, thrift, integrity and uprightness.

Let us develop the fine traditions of our heroic people and stand ready for all necessary efforts and sacrifices in the supreme interests of the Fatherland, the people and the world revolution. Great and glorious victories are ahead!

Let our entire Party and people vigorously advance forward!

Dear Elders and Comrades,
Those are a few ideas which I hope you will discuss and complete.

SPEECH ON THE OCCASION OF THE 20th BIRTHDAY OF THE VIET NAM PEOPLE'S ARMY

(December 22, 1964)

Comrades,

On the occasion of the 20th anniversary of the founding of the Viet Nam People's Army, I wish to convey, on behalf of the Party Central Committee and the Government, my cordial congratulations to the regular army, the regional forces, the people's armed security forces and the militia and self-defence forces in the whole country, which have recorded many achievements and made great progress in fighting, study, work and productive labour.

I gladly welcome General Kim Tsang Bong and other comrades in the Military Delegation of the fraternal People's Democratic Republic of Korea and wish them good success in their friendly visit.

Ours is a heroic army of a heroic people. Right after its birth, armed with quarterstaffs and flintlocks, together with the entire people, it fought the French and the Japanese and won success for the August Revolution. It was ten years old when together with the people, it won the great victory of Dien Bien Phu, defeating the aggressive war of the French imperialists aided by the Americans.

Our army is heroic in war and in peace as well. It has successfully fulfilled its task of defending the North, smashing all acts of provocation and sabotage of the US imperialists and their henchmen. It vigorously hits back at the US imperialists as it recently did on the 5th of August this year.

Our army has also taken an active part in economic construction and cultural development, thus fulfilling the tasks of a revolutionary army.

Our army is loyal to the Party, faithful to the people, ready to fight for the Fatherland's independence and freedom, for socialism, ready to fulfil any task, overcome any difficulty, defeat any enemy.

Officers and men love each other like brothers and share weal and woe. The army and the people are like fish and water, united and of one mind. They learn from and help each other.

Our army is inspired by genuine patriotism and lofty proletarian internationalism; it is closely united with the people and armies of the brother socialist countries, with the people of countries in struggle for national liberation and peace-loving people in the world.

Our army is invincible, because it is a people's army built up, led and educated by our Party.

Officers and men should remain modest and make constant efforts. They must develop the army's revolutionary nature and tradition. They must learn from the determination to fight and win of the heroic people and armed forces of the South in the resistance for national salvation against the US imperialist aggressors and their henchmen.

The enemy still harbours perfidious designs. Our entire people and army should heighten their vigilance, stand ready to fight and eagerly take part in patriotic emulation with the spirit of "each man working for two" in order to build up and defend the socialist North, making it a solid base for liberating the South and achieving peaceful national reunification.

Victory will certainly be ours.

ADDRESS TO THE SECOND SESSION OF THE THIRD NATIONAL ASSEMBLY OF THE DRVN

(April 10, 1965)

Comrades,

Our National Assembly is holding its present session in a situation of great urgency, but also in an atmosphere of enthusiasm and confidence. The movement against US aggression, for national salvation is surging up everywhere. In both the North and the South, many great successes have been won.

Over the past ten years, the US imperialists and their henchmen have been waging an extremely cruel war, causing untold sufferings to our compatriots *in the South.* For the past few months, they have frenziedly extended the war to *the North* of our country. In defiance of the 1954 Geneva Agreements and internationl law, they have used hundreds of aircraft and dozens of warships to bomb and shell North Viet Nam continually. Showing their true colours as pirates, the US aggressors are brazenly encroaching upon our land. They are attempting to enslave our thirty million people by force of arms. But they are grossly mistaken. They are sure to meet with ignominious failure.

The Vietnamese people are a heroic people. For more than ten years now, our fourteen million Southern compatriots have been enduring hardships and sacrifices and fighting very valiantly. Starting with bare hands, they have seized weapons from the enemy to fight him, won victory after victory, and are now constantly on the offensive, inflicting ever bigger defeats on the US aggressors and the traitors, causing them to sink ever deeper in the quagmire. The heavier their defeats, the more cruel means they employ, such as napalm and noxious gases, to massacre our compatriots. It is precisely because they are bogged down in the South that they now furiously attack the North.

Like a thief crying "Stop thief", the US imperialist aggressors have impudently slandered North Viet Nam as "committing aggression" against South Viet Nam. Saboteurs of peace and of the Geneva Agreements, they brazenly claim that it is because they wish to "restore peace" and "defend the Geneva Agreements" that they are sending US troops to our country to kill and destroy. They are devastating our land and massacring our people, yet they hypocritically boast that they will grant one billion dollars to the people of Viet Nam and other Southeast Asian countries to "develop their economy and improve their livelihood".

US President Johnson has also loudly threatened to use force to subjugate our people. This is but foolish illusion. Our people will never submit.

The Taylor Plan has come to grief. The McNamara Plan has also gone bankrupt. The "escalation" plan which the US imperialists are now trying to carry out in North Viet Nam is also doomed to failure. Even though they may bring in hundreds of thousands more US troops, and strive to drag more troops of their satellites into this criminal war, our army and people are resolved to fight and defeat them.

The Statement of the South Viet Nam National Front for Liberation has highlighted this heroic spirit. The Appeal of the Viet Nam Fatherland Front has also stressed this iron resolve.

We love peace but we are not afraid of war. We are determined to drive away the US aggressors to defend the freedom, independence and territorial integrity of our fatherland.

Our people throughout the country are firmly confident that with their militant solidarity, courage and creative intelligence, and the sympathy and support of the world's people, they will certainly take this great war of resistance to complete victory.

Our people are very grateful to, and highly value the fraternal solidarity and devoted assistance of, the socialist countries — especially the Soviet Union and China — and the people on all continents who are actively supporting our struggle against the US imperialist aggressors— the most cruel enemy of mankind.

With regard to the Lao and Cambodian peoples who are valiantly struggling against the US imperialists and their henchmen, our people constantly strengthen our solidarity with them and wholeheartedly support them.

We warmly hail the youth of various countries who have expressed willingness to come to Viet Nam and join us in fighting the US aggressors.

The American people have been deceived by the propaganda of their government which has extorted billions of dollars from them to pour into the war. Thousands of their sons have been tragically killed or wounded on the Viet Nam battlefields thousands of miles away from the United States. At present, many organizations and personalities in the United States are urging their government to stop its unjust war at once and withdraw US troops from South Viet Nam immediately. Our people are determined to drive away the US imperialists, their sworn enemy. Yet we always express friendship toward progressive American people.

The Government of the Democratic Republic of Viet Nam once again solemnly declares that its unswerving stand is resolutely to defend Viet Nam's independence, sovereignty, unity and territorial integrity. Viet Nam is one country, the Vietnamese are one nation ; nobody is allowed to infringe this sacred right. The US imperialists must respect the Geneva Agreements, withdraw from South Viet Nam and immediately stop their attacks on North Viet Nam. That is the only way to settle the war in Viet Nam, to implement the 1954 Geneva Agreements, to safeguard peace in Indochina and Southeast Asia. There is no other solution. Such is the answer of our people and government to the US imperialists.

Comrades,

Our people are living a most glorious period of history. Our country has the great honour of being an outpost of the socialist camp and of the world's peoples fighting against imperialism, colonialism and neo-colonialism.

Our people are fighting and making sacrifices not only for their own freedom and independence, but also for the freedom and independence of other peoples and for world peace.

On the battlefront against the US imperialist aggressors, our people's task is very heavy but also very glorious.

At present, to oppose US aggression and save the country is the most sacred duty of every Vietnamese patriot. Under the leadership of the National Front for Liberation, the sole genuine representative of the South Vietnamese people, the heroic people and fighters of South Viet Nam are marching forward to achieve ever greater successes so as to liberate the South and defend the North.

Our armed forces and people in the North are eagerly engaged in emulation to build socialism while valiantly fighting to defend the North and giving wholehearted support to the South.

I propose that the National Assembly warmly support the Statement by the South Viet Nam National Front for Liberation and the Appeal of the Viet Nam Fatherland Front. Let us warmly hail our compatriots and fighters in the heroic South! Let us warmly congratulate our armed forces and people in North Viet Nam who are enthusiastically emulating one another in productive work and achieving new exploits in combat!

I call upon our compatriots and fighters constantly to heighten their revolutionary heroism, vigilance and combativeness. Let them promote the "Let each man work for two" emulation movement, resolutely overcome all difficulties, strive to build up and defend the socialist North, and wholeheartedly support the patriotic struggle of our compatriots in the South.

Let all of us unite and be of one mind, millions like one man, and be determined to defeat the US aggressors!

For the future of our Fatherland, for the happiness of our people, let all compatriots and fighters throughout the country valiantly march forward!

APPEAL
ON THE OCCASION OF JULY 20, 1965 *

Dear compatriots and fighters,

On the occasion of July 20, I cordially convey my warmest greetings to our compatriots and fighters in the whole country.

Our people deeply cherish independence and peace. That is why they were of one mind in their determination to wage the war of resistance against the French colonialists, and won great victory.

The 1954 Geneva Agreements solemnly recognize the sovereignty, independence, unity and territorial integrity of Viet Nam.

However, the US imperialists have tried their best to undermine the implementation of these Agreements. For over ten years now they have been waging an aggressive war in the South of our country, in an attempt to turn it into a new-type colony and military base of the United States with a view to perpetuating the partition of our country, attacking the socialist camp and jeopardizing the independence and peace of Asian and other countries in the world.

Over the past ten years, our Southern compatriots have been waging a heroic struggle and making innumerable sacrifices to liberate themselves from the cruel yoke of the US imperialists and their henchmen.

---

* Anniversary of the signing of the 1954 Geneva Agreements.

Under the glorious banner of the National Front for Liberation, our Southern compatriots and the Liberation Armed Forces, heroic and of one mind, have become ever stronger and recorded ever more successes; they are winning great victories on all battlefields. They have been fighting resolutely to liberate the South, defend the North, reunify the country, and also to contribute to the safeguarding of peace and the independence of other peoples.

In an attempt to retrieve their worsening situation, the US imperialists have of late introduced tens of thousands more American and satellite troops into South Viet Nam to intensify their aggressive war there and unleashed savage air-raids against North Viet Nam. They have committed towering crimes against our people. The whole world is seething with indignation and sternly condemning them.

The US imperialists are resorting to brute force in the hope of subjugating our people and intimidating other peoples in Indochina, Southeast Asia and the rest of the world. But they are grossly mistaken.

Ours is a heroic people. We have overthrown the Japanese fascists and defeated the French colonialists, and are now resolutely fighting to defeat the US imperialist aggressors.

We are determined to win complete independence for our Fatherland and complete freedom for our people.

In face of the danger created by US aggression, our people in the North and in the South are of one mind in their resolve to fight: even if the battle should last five, ten, twenty years or longer, we will resolutely fight on till complete victory.

The US imperialists are utterly barbarous and perfidious. On the one hand they clamour about "peace" and on the other they hasten to build more military bases, send more troops to South Viet Nam and intensify the bombing of North Viet Nam. Their deceitful talk about "peace negotiations" can certainly not fool our people and the world's people. As has been declared time and again by our Government, the most correct solution to the Viet Nam problem lies in the correct implementation of the 1954 Geneva Agreements by the US government and its acceptance of the four points put forward by the Government of the Democratic Republic of Viet Nam and the five points clearly stated by the South Viet Nam National Front for Liberation.

To fulfil our sacred duty of resisting the US aggressors to save the country, I call on our compatriots and fighters in the North to march forward valiantly, and enthusiastically emulate one another in productive work and fighting.

Let our *people's armed forces* fight bravely to win still greater victories, smashing all US air attacks.

Let our *workers and peasants* enthusiastically emulate one another in increasing production and practising economy, "each working for two". Let them stand ready to fight for the defence of the North and in support of the South.

Let our *intellectuals* do their utmost to serve the Fatherland, and contribute to our people's struggle for national salvation.

Let our *young people,* boys and girls, perform well in the "three readinesses" movement, and devote all their youthful energies, mental and physical, to the cause of national salvation, to the Fatherland, to socialism.

Let our *women* fulfil their "three responsibilities", and make effective contributions to defeating the US aggressors.

Let our countrymen of *all nationalities and all religions* unite closely like members of the same family in the resistance against US aggression, for national salvation.

The US imperialists are meeting with failures and are doomed to complete defeat. Our people are acting on the offensive and are sure to win glorious victory. But the enemy is still hatching vicious schemes and our people's patriotic struggle is still faced with hardships and difficulties. We must therefore constantly heighten our vigilance and combativeness, guard against self-complacency and refrain from underestimating the enemy. We shall neither be deterred by difficulties nor puffed up by successes.

Our entire people are turning towards our beloved South, the Brass Wall of the Fatherland.

Let our heroic Southern compatriots carry aloft the glorious national salvation banner of the National Front for Liberation, march towards still greater victories, resolutely defeat the brutal forces and foil all vicious schemes of the US imperialists and their henchmen, determined to win back independence and freedom for the people and advance toward peaceful national reunification.

Soldiers and officials of the Saigon administration! You are also descended from our Lac Hong ancestors. Why should you be resigned to serving the US aggressors and opposing your compatriots, thereby bringing eternal shame upon yourselves. Come to your senses and cross over to the people's side, join in the effort to liberate our native land and serve the country, and you will be welcomed by our people.

To the American people who are courageously opposing the aggressive war waged by the US government, I convey my greetings on behalf of the Vietnamese people.

Let them intensify their opposition to the US government's aggressive war in Viet Nam so as to prevent their sons and brothers from being used as cannon-fodder for the private interests of their oppressors and exploiters

Officers and soldiers of the United States and its satellites, who have been driven into this criminal war, listen

20 SW.

to reason! There is no enmity between you and the Vietnamese people. The US imperialists are forcing you to serve as cannon-fodder and die in their place. They are doomed to defeat. Demand your repatriation so that you can be re-united with your parents, wives and children! The Vietnamese people will support your struggle.

Viet Nam's resistance to US aggression, for national salvation, enjoys the warm sympathy and wholehearted support of the people of the brother socialist countries, and those of Asia, Africa, Latin America and other parts of the world.

On behalf of our entire people, I warmly thank the people of the Soviet Union, China and the other socialist countries, and progressive people on the five continents.

The Vietnamese people are determined to fulfil their sacred task of liberating their Fatherland, staying the hands of the US imperialist aggressors, firmly defending the outpost of the socialist camp in Southeast Asia and making an active contribution to the movement for national independence and the safeguarding of world peace.

Dear compatriots and fighters,

It is because we cherish independence and peace that we resolutely fight against the US aggressors.

Our struggle against the US imperialists, for national salvation, is a just one. The people all over the world sternly condemn the American aggressors and warmly support us.

Let our compatriots throughout the country have firm confidence in final victory and the bright future of the Fatherland. Let everyone be resolved to overcome all hardships and difficulties and defeat the US aggressors.

For the Fatherland, for independence and peace, let our entire people march forward valiantly!

The enemy is sure to be defeated! We are bound to win!

APPEAL TO COMPATRIOTS AND FIGHTERS THROUGHOUT THE COUNTRY

(July 17, 1966)

The barbarous US imperialists have unleashed a war of aggression in an attempt to conquer our country, but they are sustaining heavy defeats.

They have rushed an expeditionary force of nearly 300,000 men into the South of our country. They have fostered a puppet administration and puppet troops as instruments of their aggressive policy. They have resorted to extremely savage means of warfare — toxic chemicals, napalm bombs, etc. — and applied a "burn all, kill all and destroy all" policy. By committing such crimes, they hope to subdue our Southern compatriots.

But under the resolute and skilful leadership of the National Front for Liberation, the South Vietnamese armed forces and people, closely united and fighting heroically, have scored splendid victories, and are determined to fight on until complete victory in order to liberate the South, defend the North, and proceed towards national reunification.

The US aggressors have cynically launched air attacks on the North of our country in the hope of getting out of their disastrous situation in the South and compelling us to "negotiate" on their terms.

However, North Viet Nam has not flinched in the least. Our army and people have eagerly emulated one another in production and fighting. So far, we have downed over 1,200 enemy aircraft. We are determined to frustrate the enemy's war of destruction and at the same time extend all-out support to our kinsfolk in the South.

Of late, the frenzied US aggressors have taken a very serious step in their escalation by starting air strikes on the suburbs of Hanoi and Haiphong. That is a desperate act, the death throes of a mortally wounded wild beast.

Johnson and his clique should realize this : they may bring in half a million, a million or even more troops to step up their war of aggression in South Viet Nam. They may use thousands of aircraft for intensified attacks against North Viet Nam. But never will they be able to break the iron will of the heroic Vietnamese people, their determination to fight against American aggression, for national salvation. The more truculent they grow, the more serious their crimes. The war may last five, ten, twenty or more years ; Hanoi, Haiphong and other cities and enterprises may be destroyed ; but the Vietnamese people will not be intimidated ! *Nothing is more precious than independence and freedom.* Once victory is won, our people will rebuild their country and make it even more prosperous and beautiful.

It is common knowledge that each time they are about to step up their criminal war, the US aggressors will resort to their " peace talks " humbug in an attempt to fool world opinion and lay the blame on Viet Nam for unwillingness to engage in "peace negotiations."

President Johnson. answer these questions publicly, before the American people and the peoples of the world : Who has sabotaged the Geneva Agreements which guarantee the sovereignty, independence, unity and territorial integrity of Viet Nam ? Have Vietnamese troops invaded the United States and massacred Americans ? Or isn't it.

the US government which on the contrary, has sent US troops to invade Viet Nam and massacre the Vietnamese people ?

Let the United States end its war of aggression in Viet Nam, withdraw all American and satellite troops from this country and peace will be restored immediately. The stand taken by Viet Nam is clear: it is the four points[22] of the Government of the Democratic Republic of Viet Nam and the five points[23] of the South Viet Nam National Front for Liberation. There is no other alternative.

The Vietnamese people cherish peace, genuine peace, peace in independence and freedom, not sham peace, not "American peace".

To safeguard the independence of our fatherland, to fulfil our duties to all peoples struggling against US imperialism, our people and army, united as one man and fearless of sacrifices and hardships, will resolutely fight on until they gain complete victory. In the past we defeated the Japanese fascists and the French colonialists in much more difficult circumstances. Now that conditions at home and abroad are more favourable, our people's struggle against US aggression, for national salvation, will all the more certainly end in complete victory.

*

* *

Dear compatriots and fighters,

Our cause is just ; our people are united from North to South ; we have a tradition of undaunted struggle and the great sympathy and support of the fraternal socialist countries and progressive people all over world. We shall win !

At this new juncture, we are one in our determination to go through all hardships and sacrifices to accomplish the glorious historic task of our people : to defeat the US aggressors.

On behalf of the Vietnamese people, I take this opportunity to express heartfelt thanks to the peoples of the socialist countries and progressive people in the world, including the American people, for their wholehearted support and assistance. In face of the US imperialists' new criminal scheme I am firmly confident that the peoples and governments of the fraternal socialist countries and of peace- and justice-loving countries in the world will support and help the Vietnamese people still more vigorously until they win complete victory in their struggle against US aggression, for national salvation.

The Vietnamese people will surely win !

The US aggressors will surely be defeated !

Long live a peaceful, re-unified, independent, democratic, and prosperous Viet Nam !

Compatriots and fighters throughout the country, march valiantly forward !

TALK TO DISTRICT CADRES ATTENDING A
TRAINING CLASS
(January 18, 1967)

Dear Comrades,
    I am very glad today, for seldom have I had an occasion to meet such a large number of district cadres.
    How many people are attending this course ?
    ("Uncle, we are 288 in all, and 131 of us are working at district level.")
    And how many women ?
    ("Sixteen, Uncle.")
    The women are too few and this is a shortcoming. The comrades in charge of this course have not paid enough attention to the training of women cadres. This is also a common shortcoming in our Party. Many still underestimate the women's abilities, because of their prejudices and narrow-mindedness. This is utterly wrong. At present, many women are holding responsible posts at basic level. Many are doing a very good job. There are women managers of large farming co-ops who are not only zealous but also efficient. Women co-op members generally have many good qualities : they are less liable to commit embezzlement and waste, indulge in revelry and display domineering behaviour than some of their male counterparts. Am I right ? If what I say is not true, please correct me.
    ("You're right, Uncle.")

I hope that you will seriously correct your biased and narrow-minded attitude toward women. And the women, especially you who work at district level, must fight hard against this attitude. For if you don't fight, the men who hold prejudices against women will not readily mend their ways.

*

*   *

This course is designed to help you understand better the Party lines in our anti-US resistance for national salvation, in the building of socialism in the North, the people's war, the course of agricultural development, Party work and work among the masses in the present situation, so that when you are back home you can do better in fighting and productive work, in organizing the people's life, and in building organizations at basic level, thus turning your district committees into "four-good" ones.

The aims and contents of this course are very practical in the present situation. Members of the Party Central Committee have given you lectures. Did you understand ? Did you really grasp what they said ?

("Yes, we did")

Speaking of study, I should like to tell you a favourite story of mine.

During the anti-French resistance, I once met several comrades who were having a rest in the shade of a large banian. I asked them, "Where have you been ?"—"We are back from a political class," they answered. "What did you study ?" — "We studied Karl Marx" — "Was it interesting ?"—"Very interesting !"—"Did you understand ?" — Now they answered falteringly, "Uncle, there were so many difficult points we could not understand."

Such studies were not practical.

Let me tell you another story. Before the August Revolution, a house of culture was set up in the Tan Trao liberated area. One day, two cadres, one man and one woman, came and gave lectures. They spoke with great enthusiasm. I was there. I turned to my neighbour and asked him whether he understood anything of what was being said. He shook his head, saying he did not understand a whit. This was easy to explain. The cadres were talking about too many things and using too many scholarly words. The general educational level was quite low then, so people could not understand such words as "subjective", "objective", "positive", "negative", etc.

Those stories are for your entertainment and also to remind you that now we must learn things that are practical and will help you to do your work better. And when you go back home and organize training courses for Party members and cadres in the villages, you should try to do it in the same spirit.

Now your course is drawing to an end. I want to give you a few recommendations :

1. You must firmly grasp the Party's lines and policies and keep close contact with the base and the co-ops so as to be well informed of the state of affairs in production, the people's life, Party cells and mass organizations. This will allow you to take correct and timely steps.

This point you probably know already. But I want to stress the necessity to keep in close touch with the basic level, to live among the masses in order to lead them. You should not get into touch with the base the way dragon-flies skim over the water. This seems quite easy, but it is still not being done well. At present, a number of district committee members have not really been in close touch with the grassroots; they flinch from difficulties and hardships and don't know the real state of affairs in the area in their charge.

At present, each district committee is made up of 15 to 20 members. You must divide the job among yourselves, each watching one commune or two. You must be fully informed not only about the co-ops, but also about the individual families, their living conditions, housing, education and health problems, etc. If you fail to do so, how can you correctly apply the Party's lines and policies and the provincial directives to your districts?

2. You must devote your energies to building the co-ops, Party cells, youth and women's organizations into truly good ones.

The cells are the basic units of the Party. If they are good, everything will go well. Therefore you must strive to build the cells into "four-good" ones. You must get practical results, avoid formalism and abstain from sending misleading reports to higher authorities.

To build a good cell, Party members must first of all set good examples in carrying out Party policies; they must truly *respect the people's right to be the collective master* and listen to the masses. Only then will the people trust, respect and love them. And if they do, any difficulties can be overcome.

Members of the Working Youth Union and young volunteers' brigades should act as an arm to the Party cell, taking the lead in productive work and fighting. *The co-op management committees should practise democracy and oppose embezzlement and waste.* Embezzlement is still prevalent in some co-ops. Who are responsible for this state of affairs? Should the district committee be held responsible? Are any district cadres guilty of corruption and commandism? You must check up and conduct severe control.

3. Party members and cadres must unite closely, practise democracy and observe discipline within the Party. All Party members, whether of long standing or newly admitted, old and young, men and women, must love and help each other so as to advance together.

At present, there are both veterans and young cadres in the Party. The veterans are a valuable asset to the Party ; they have gained experience in leadership and have been tempered and tested in actual struggle. But there are some veteran cadres who stop at a certain point and cannot make any further progress. They cling to the old and are not sensible of the new. On the other hand, the young cadres, though they haven't yet acquired some of the qualities of the old cadres, are zealous, aware of the new and eager to learn. As a result, they can make rapid progress.

Our Party should closely associate veteran and young cadres.

Young cadres should not be looked down upon. Some veteran cadres are puffed-up and have too high an opinion of their past records. They are haughty toward young cadres and Party members, and often ignore their suggestions, reproaching them for trying to "teach Grandma to suck eggs." Ours is a seething epoch. Society and the world are making great strides. So it is wrong for veterans to look down their noses at young cadres. On the other hand, the young cadres must not be pretentious ; they must humbly learn from their older and more experienced comrades.

All cadres and members of the Party must zealously work for the Party and the people. They must painstakingly study politics, economics, science and technique so as to improve their abilities and help develop the economy, win victories in fighting and better the people's life.

When I speak of studying science and technique, some people think that these goals are too remote. But viewed from a popular and simple angle, they are by no means out of reach. For example, how to grow azolla for green manure, or to ferment compost is a problem of science and technique. That's what science and technique are about. You should study them if you are to provide guidance to production work and raise the yields of the crops.

4. You must rely on the masses to promote all movements, either in-production or fighting. You must inspire the masses with enthusiasm and confidence.

In everything you must get the participation of the masses. Nothing can be done without the masses. Recently the *Nhan Dan* newspaper carried a story about air defence. Some village officials were discussing the question of air raid defence. This meant digging trenches and building air-raid shelters, which would necessitate tens of thousands of bricks, thousands of bamboos and hundreds of *dong*. The costs were quite great. How to meet them? A young woman engineer suggested that the issue be put before the masses. People were invited to a meeting and were told about the wanton bombing by enemy aircraft and the need for air-raid shelters. They were quite cooperative: some offered wooden planks, others bricks or bamboos, etc. The shelters were completed within two days. In Quang Binh and Vinh Linh, it is thanks to the mass line that thousands of kilometres of trenches and tens of thousands of shelters have been dug. It follows that with the participation of the masses, the most difficult tasks become easier and can be successfully undertaken. The comrades in Quang Binh have aptly put it this way:

Even an easy task cannot be done without the people,
While the most difficult ones can be fulfilled with their help.

In Thai Binh, Quang Binh and some other places, a campaign is being conducted on "reporting and rating one's services ". Thanks to this campaign, everyone knows what is being well done, not done or poorly done. This is real democracy, a very good form of criticism and self-criticism. By so doing, the masses educate themselves and also help educate the cadres, for while there are good cadres who work hard and match their words with deeds, there are others who only like to give orders. So the campaign is also a good way of selecting people, educating them, bringing them into the Party and making cadres of them. In this way we shall never lack cadres. This is a very good way of building the Party.

Do you think this a good way to act ?

("Yes, we do, Uncle.")

Can you do it ?

("Yes, we can, Uncle.")

But some comrades have not acted this way. In some places, the people have not spoken, or have not dared to speak, their mind, fearing "reprisals" or "labels" stuck on them by the cadres. Cadres who have committed mistakes often fear that the people will speak out. But if they are sincere in admitting their mistakes and apologize to the people, the latter will be pleased and will forgive them. Our people are very kind, they love the Party and love the cadres. If we frankly admit our mistakes, the people far from showing dislike or contempt, will feel even greater love, respect and confidence in us.

5. The winter-spring production drive is an urgent and immediate task. Cultivation must be done in time. Buffaloes and oxen must be well looked after. They must be well fed and given good shelter; they should not be left out in the cold. People should be urged to practise economy. Don't indulge in revelry. Illicit distillation of rice wine,

slaughter of pigs and oxen and wasteful feasts are forbidden. District officials must go to the villages to have a look and check up everything. They must not indulge in a bureaucratic style of work and be content with forwarding provincial circulars to the villages. Circulars cannot protect buffaloes and oxen from the cold. And if buffaloes and oxen grow thin and weak from hunger and cold, production will be very badly affected.

Buffaloes and oxen should be well tended with a view to production work, not feasts and revelry ! The New Year is drawing near, so economy should be emphasized. The central administration often reminds everyone that we must strive to promote production and practise economy. This has been correctly carried out in many places. But in others, the letters in the circulars seem to have blurred and *"tiet kiem"** has somehow been read as meaning *"tiet canh" !***

I can give you ample evidence of this. Let me read this passage from the *Hai Phong* newspaper : "As the cadres fail to set good examples, illegal slaughter of pigs still often occurs in My Phuc commune. Two pigs were killed to inaugurate the pumping-station. Four pigs were killed to greet the annual assembly of the co-op. Then the collective feast of a production team entailed the slaughter of one more." And so on, and so forth.

Listen to this : Doan Ket and Ngo Quyen communes in Thanh Mien district have illegally killed many pigs and buffaloes for their feasts.

Cadres and Party members who did those things were setting bad examples.

This has happened because of the lack of democracy. The Party's rank-and-file dare not speak out, the people dare not speak out. How can the co-op members not feel

* *Tiet kiem :* thrift, economy.
** *Tiet canh :* a dish.

irritated ? How can the co-op progress in such conditions ? While the people work day and night, a few seize upon the least occasion to eat and drink, and, believe me, they don't do things by halves.

The above are a few bad examples, but we have also many good examples.

D. commune in Thai Nguyen has a large population but only little land. There are many difficulties in farm production. For over a year now, US planes have repeatedly attacked various hamlets in the commune. But the people have courageously carried on their work, reorganized their life to meet war-time conditions, stepped up production to serve the anti-US resistance for national salvation and socialist construction. The 1965 autumn crop was not good, and the co-op members' income decreased. But the people encouraged each other to carry on production and achieved self-sufficiency in food. They didn't have to ask for help from the State. The villagers overcame all difficulties and for the last summer rice crop they achieved the highest-ever acreage under cultivation, average yield and total output. Vegetables and subsidiary crops increased by half or twofold. Every household has a patch of kitchen garden. The co-op management controls the crops to help needy families in pre-harvest periods People no longer indulge in wasteful revelry on the occasion of weddings or religious ceremonies. They carefully calculate the food ration in every family and consume subsidiary cereals so as to economize rice and have enough food supplies for the whole season.

Thanks to the practice of economy and the judicious expansion of production, the D. people not only have enough food for the whole village but have also delivered more than their quota of grain to the State, while other villages have had to ask for relief from the State in the period between two crops.

So although that commune has suffered from both natural calamities and enemy destruction, its people have managed not only to be self-sufficient in food but also to discharge their duty to the State.

The 1966 autumn crop at D. was marked by repeated attacks by enemy planes in addition to serious drought and ravages by insects. Yet the D. people recorded an unprecedented success. The average rice yield rose by 400-700 kilograms per hectare in comparison with the previous years. Good rice, carefully selected and winnowed and dried, was immediately sent to the State stores. After calculating the food rations for the co-op members, five hundred kilograms more of rice were sold to the State at the incentive price. Old people in Minh Hoa and Thong Nhat co-ops sold to the State all the rice they got from the extra land they had reclaimed. Everyone acts upon the slogan : "To economize a grain of rice is to supply our soldiers with an extra bullet to fire at the US aggressors."

As a result of ten air-raids by enemy planes, great damage was caused to the people's property. But, thanks to good organization of civil air defence, no one was killed or wounded in the whole village. People said : "So long as we live, we can create wealth." They shared with each other food, clothes, pots and pans, etc., and not a *dong* of relief was asked from the State.

Over the past two years, D. commune has taken the lead in depositing savings in Thai Nguyen. In 1965, the average savings deposited by each villager were 13.2 *dong*. In 1966, by late November, the total was already 42,000 *dong*, not including the sums earmarked for production. The per capita average was then 31 *dong*. Almost all Party committee members, Party members and cadres set good examples in depositing money in their savings accounts. Many of them after selling their pigs or poultry only retained a small sum for their daily spendings and deposited the rest in the credit fund of the village. The village schoolmasters also deposited close to 1,000 *dong* in the credit fund, thus contributing some more capital to farm production in the village. Many other villagers, like Mrs. Le Thi Thu, have saved up to 2,000 *dong* each.

Thanks to those savings, the farm co-ops have had more capital for expanding production and improving the living conditions of their members. This year, the village credit co-op has granted loans totalling 2,000 *dong* to the farm co-ops for the purchase of production means such as husking machines and 120 piglets for breeding ; it has also helped victims of air raids.

This commune is an example of good work in air defence, farm production, economy, solidarity and mutual assistance among members. Other communes should imitate it.

We should learn from good examples and avoid following bad ones.

6. We must be active in air defence and dig more trenches and shelters. Help should be given to evacuees, especially old folk and children, to victims of air raids, to families of disabled armymen, war martyrs and soldiers at the front.

Finally, I ask you to convey my greetings and those of the Central Committee and the Government to our countrymen, cadres, soldiers, militiamen, young people and children. I hope you will work hard and turn your districts into "four-good" ones.

Tet* is drawing near. This is a Tet of resistance for national salvation. It must be a joyful but economical festival. Do you all promise that this will be so ?

(All present answered : *"Yes, we do, Uncle."*)

* Lunar New Year.

LETTER TO LAWYER NGUYEN HUU THO
(March 6, 1967)

To Lawyer Nguyen Huu Tho,
President of the Presidium, and
Members of the
Central Committee of the South Viet Nam National
Front for Liberation.

Dear Comrade President and Central Committee Members,
Dear compatriots, fighters and cadres in the South,
The South Viet Nam National Front for Liberation has
issued its Political Programme at a time when the people
and armed forces in both zones of our country are winning
glorious victories in the struggle against the US
aggressors, for national salvation. It is a *Programme of
broad union of the whole people,* a Programme showing
firm determination to win complete victory over the US
aggressors and the traitors.

Over the past seven years, under the clearsighted
leadership of the Front, the heroic people and fighters of
the South, closely united and fighting valiantly, have
smashed all aggressive schemes of the enemy. Over a
million US, puppet and satellite troops have been dealt
heavy blows. The US aggressors have suffered setbacks
and have been driven into an impasse. Encouraged by
their successes, the people and armed forces in the South
are launching repeated attacks against the enemy on all
sides and everywhere. Those glorious victories have

helped strengthen and enhance, both in the country and in the world, the prestige of the South Viet Nam National Front for Liberation, the only genuine representative of the South Vietnamese people. Our nation, our fatherland is very proud of the heroic South, the Brass Wall of the Fatherland.

Bogged down in the South, the US aggressors have frenziedly widened the war there while "escalating" the air war against the North. At the same time they loudly proclaim hypocritical proposals for peace. But their bombs and shells can never intimidate our compatriots, nor can their deceitful talk hoodwink them. The Vietnamese people will resolutely fight on till there remains not one single US aggressor in their beloved land.

Unity accounts for our invincible force. The Front's Political Programme is the banner of *great unity* which brings the entire people of the South together to resist the US aggressors till final victory. Let our united people strive for still broader and closer unity. Let us achieve still broader and closer solidarity with our brothers and friends all over the world, including progressive Americans, who are actively supporting us. However truculent the US aggressors may be, the immense force of our unity will surely overcome them.

Our compatriots, fighters and cadres in the South have won tremendous victories on account of their close unity and great heroism. At present, the entire people of the South, to a man, are strengthening their unity, faithfully carrying out the correct Political Programme of the Front, and displaying great valour. They will certainly bring to a successful end the struggle for liberating the South, defending the North and advancing toward peaceful national reunification.

Determined to defeat the US aggressors, our 17 million compatriots in the North pledge to do their utmost in production and fighting and to fulfil their sacred duty toward their kinsmen in the South.

Thanks to the invincible strength of our great unity, we are sure to win!

When the country is reunified, and North and South are reunited, how happy we shall be!

I take this opportunity to send my affectionate kisses to the old folk, combatants' mothers, cadres and soldiers, heroes and outstanding fighters against the US aggressors, and my nephews and nieces, the young people and children.

I send my cordial greetings to you, Comrade President and Members of the Central Committee of the South Viet Nam National Front for Liberation. We shall win!

THE GREAT
OCTOBER REVOLUTION OPENED THE
ROAD TO LIBERATION TO ALL PEOPLES*
(October 1967)

Together with the Soviet people and the working people all over the world, the Vietnamese people are jubilantly celebrating the 50th anniversary of the Great Russian October Revolution.

At the height of their anti-US resistance for national salvation, determined to defeat the US aggressors and successfully build socialism in their land, the Vietnamese people, grateful and confident, turn their thoughts to the Soviet Union, the home of the great Lenin and the glorious October Revolution.

Like the shining sun, the October Revolution illuminated the five continents, and awakened millions and millions of oppressed and exploited people. In human history, there had never been a revolution with such great and profound significance.

The October Revolution was the first triumph of Marxism and Leninism in a large country, the Soviet Union, which covers one-sixth of the world. It was the greatest victory ever recorded by the working class, the labouring people and oppressed peoples led by the working class and their vanguard, the Bolshevik Party.

* Written for *Pravda* on the occasion of the 50th anniversary of the Great October Socialist Revolution. *(Ed.).*

The October Revolution made use of revolutionary violence to overthrow the bourgeoisie and the land-owning feudal class, established the power of the working people, and built a completely new society, in which there is no exploitation of man by man.

The October Revolution opened the road to liberation to the peoples and to all mankind and ushered in a new era in history, the era of transition from capitalism to socialism on a world scale.

On the historic significance of the October Revolution, Lenin said:

"We have the right to be proud, and indeed we are proud of having had the honour to *start* building a Soviet State and thereby *open* a new era in the world's history, the era of domination by a *new* class, oppressed in all capitalist countries and now advancing everywhere toward a new life, toward victory over the bourgeoisie, toward the dictatorship of the proletariat, toward the liberation of mankind from the capitalist yoke and from imperialist wars."*

The world situation in the past fifty years has eloquently testified to the truth of this brilliant statement by Lenin. Indeed, since the October Revolution, there have happened tremendous revolutionary changes in the world.

The Soviet Union, the first state to have a dictatorship of the proletariat, has displayed extraordinary strength. Right after its foundation, it not only smashed the counter-revolutionaries at home but also defeated armed intervention by 14 imperialist countries. Less than 30 years later, through its complete defeat of the German, Italian and Japanese fascists, it not only safeguarded the

---

* Lenin : *Complete Works*, Vol. 33, French version, *Editions Sociales,* Paris and *Editions en Langues Etrangères,* Moscow, 1961, p. 47.

Soviet State but also greatly contributed to the liberation of other countries and to saving mankind from enslavement by fascism.

In spite of the heavy ravages of war and innumerable hardships and sacrifices (20 million dead, 1,710 cities destroyed and over 30,000 enterprises damaged), thanks to the correct leadership of the Party and the extraordinary efforts of the people, within a few years, the Soviet Union succeeded by dint of heroic struggle in healing the war wounds and successfully building socialism and has proceeded to the building of the material and technical basis of communism. The Soviet Union has become a great industrial power with a science and technology that ranks among the most modern in the world and was the first nation to embark on the conquest of outer space.

After the Russian October Revolution, the success of the Chinese Revolution also assumed tremendous international significance. It was another great victory of Marxism-Leninism in a semi-colonial and semi-feudal country with a population of 700 million, under the leadership of the Communist Party of China. Within less than twenty years, China, formerly a backward agricultural country heavily oppressed and exploited by foreign imperialists and internal bureaucratic bourgeoisie and feudal landlords, has risen up, wrested back and strengthened national independence, built socialism and become a great power with modern industry, developed agriculture, advanced science and technology.

The successes of the national liberation revolutions and socialist revolutions in Poland, the German Democratic Republic, Hungary, Rumania, Czechoslovakia, Albania, Mongolia, Korea, Cuba and Viet Nam also have very great historical significance.

Thanks to the above-mentioned successes, a world socialist system has come into being, stretching from Central Europe to Southeast Asia and the first outpost of socialism in Latin America has been set up. The socialist camp has been growing more and more powerful. It is the decisive factor for the development of world revolution and a brilliant future for mankind.

Inspired and supported by the Russian October Revolution and the socialist countries the revolutionary movement of the working class in capitalist countries and the national liberation movement in colonial countries are surging up vigorously and are developing on an unprecedented scale. All over Asia, Africa, and Latin America, the national liberation movement is rising like a tempest, disintegrating the colonial system of imperialism piecemeal, and allowing hundreds of millions of people to break free from enslavement and advance toward independence and freedom.

The strength of the socialist camp, the struggle of the working class in capitalist countries and the national liberation revolutionary movement — those three great revolutionary forces with a tremendous aggregate strength continuously assault the strongholds of imperialism headed by US imperialism. The general situation in the world today is marked by the fact that the revolutionary and peace-loving forces have grown stronger than the imperialist, reactionary and warmongering forces. Generally speaking, the world revolution is on the offensive; it is growing more powerful and winning more victories. On the contrary, imperialism and other reactionary forces are on the defensive; they are weakening and suffering setbacks and are doomed to destruction.

Socialism and communism, which was only a lofty dream of humanity in the past, has since the October Revolution become a social reality, which has displayed tremendous power and involved thousands of millions of people in revolutionary action, for the sake of peace, national independence, democracy and social progress.

*

* *

The great triumph of the October Revolution has taught the working class, the toiling people and oppressed peoples throughout the world many invaluable lessons, which are a guarantee for the complete emancipation of the working class and the whole of mankind. The Vietnamese working class and people are more and more deeply imbued with the teachings of Lenin and the great lessons of the October Revolution :

— It is essential to have the leadership of a *genuine revolutionary party of the working class, wholeheartedly devoted to the service of the people.* Only the leadership of a party which knows how to apply Marxism-Leninism creatively to the specific conditions of its country can take the national liberation revolution to victory and the socialist revolution to success.

— *The worker-peasant alliance* must be realized, for it is the surest guarantee for the successes of the revolution Only the worker-peasant alliance led by the working class can resolutely and thoroughly overthrow the counter-revolutionary forces, seize and consolidate power for the toiling people, fulfil the historical mission of the national democratic revolution and advance to socialism.

— Under the leadership of the working class and on the basis of an increasingly firmer worker-peasant alliance in each revolutionary stage, a *broad front* should rally all revolutionary and progressive forces for united action in various forms against the common enemy.

— In the arduous struggle against the enemy of the class and the nation, *revolutionary violence should be used to oppose counter-revolutionary violence, seize power and defend it.*

According to concrete conditions, one should adopt appropriate forms of revolutionary struggle and skilfully use and judiciously combine various forms of armed struggle and political struggle so as to achieve victory for the revolution.

— *Proletarian dictatorship should be constantly strengthened and consolidated.* After seizing power, the working class has the primary task of strengthening the dictatorship of the proletariat in order to fulfil the historical tasks of the revolution, thoroughly abolish the system of exploitation of man by man, build socialist relations of production, build socialism and advance toward communism.

— In the life-and-death struggle between the working class, the toiling people and oppressed peoples on one side and the imperialists and their henchmen, the feudal landlords and reactionary bourgeois on the other, the people must display a radically revolutionary spirit, and constantly hold high the banner of revolutionary heroism. They should be fearless of hardships and sacrifices and determined to fight to the bitter end for national independence and socialism.

— *There should be close association of patriotism and proletarian internationalism* in both the national liberation revolution and the socialist revolution. In our time, the national liberation revolution is an inseparable part of the world proletarian revolution ; the national liberation revolution must develop into the socialist revolution if it is to achieve complete victory. The success of the struggle for independence and freedom of the peoples is inseparable from the active support and assistance of the socialist camp and the workers' movement in the capitalist countries.

" Workers of all lands and oppressed peoples, unite ! " This sacred appeal by Lenin is still echoing in our ears, reminding us constantly to safeguard and strengthen the great solidarity among the revolutionary forces in the common interest of the working class and of mankind.

The above is a summary of the practical experiences of the Vietnamese revolution.

*
* *

We Vietnamese have a saying, " When you drink, think of the source." The more they recall the days of humiliation under foreign rule and the revolutionary struggles marked by sacrifices and hardships and also by glorious victories, the more the working class and people of Viet Nam are grateful to Lenin and the October Revolution.

Before the October Revolution, the Vietnamese people, kept in the dark by the colonialists, knew nothing about Marxism and had never heard of Lenin. With the success of the earth-shaking Great October Revolution, Marxism-Leninism was gradually propagated in Viet Nam. In early 1930, the Indochinese Communist Party (now the Viet Nam Workers' Party) was founded, holding high the banner of revolutionary leadership. A seething national liberation movement surged up, culminating in the Nghe-Tinh Soviets (1930-1931). Since then, the Vietnamese working class have found the road to self-liberation. In spite of bloody terror by the colonialists, the Vietnamese people resolutely marched forward. In August 1945, a favourable opportunity presented itself when the

heroic Soviet Army defeated the German and Japanese
fascists. The Indochinese Communist Party led the entire
people in an uprising, seized power in the whole country,
overthrew the Japanese fascists and their henchmen, and
founded the Democratic Republic of Viet Nam. The Vietnamese August Revolution was the first successful national and people's democratic revolution in Southeast Asia.
Less than one month after seizing power, without having
time to organize and consolidate their forces, the Vietnamese people, armed only with pointed bamboo sticks,
had to start a long and heroic war of resistance against the
French colonialist aggressors aided by the US imperialists.
Eventually they won a great victory at Dien Bien Phu
and completely liberated the North. The Geneva Agreements signed in 1954 officially recognize the sacred
national rights of the Vietnamese people : independence,
sovereignty, unity and territorial integrity. Since 1954, the
Vietnamese people have been carrying out two strategic
revolutionary tasks : socialist transformation and socialist
construction in the North, and, at the same time, patriotic
struggle for the liberation of the South from the rule of
the US imperialists and their henchmen and for ultimate
national reunification.

The socialist revolution in the North has recorded great
successes. After the completion of land reform, the Viet
Nam Workers' Party led the people in the socialist
transformation of agriculture, handicrafts, capitalist trade
and industry and small trade, thereby building new
relations of production and abolishing the system of
exploitation of man by man. The material and technical
basis of socialism has been gradually built, agricultural
and industrial production has ceaselessly developed, and
the material living conditions of the people have been
steadily improved. In the cultural field, illiteracy has been
done away with and education work has been expanded.

During those years, *in the South,* in spite of barbarous terror and massacre by the US imperialists and the traitors, our Southern compatriots have never submitted. On the contrary they have carried on an extremely valiant armed and political struggle. The South Viet Nam people have defeated the US "special war" and are defeating the US "limited war", a very brutal war of aggression, waged with over one million troops including nearly 500,000 US troops and over half a million puppet and satellite troops, thousands of aircraft, hundreds of warships, millions of tons of modern weapons and the most cruel means of war : noxious chemicals, gases, napalm, pellet bombs, etc... Even more barbarous than the Hitlerite fascists, the aggressors have carried out everywhere a "burn all, destroy all, kill all" policy. In an attempt to escape from the quagmire in South Viet Nam, the US imperialists have launched an increasingly more brutal air and naval war of destruction against North Viet Nam. They attack our communication lines, industrial centres, populous areas in both the cities and the countryside, hospitals, schools, churches, pagodas, dams and dykes, etc. They wrongly assume that with bombs and shells they can damp the patriotism and destroy the sacred militant solidarity of the Vietnamese people in both zones. But, for the sake of their Fatherland's independence and freedom, the 31 million Vietnamese people, united and of one mind, *are determined to fight and defeat the US aggressors to save the country.*

The Vietnamese people's resistance against US aggression, for national salvation, has won great victories. On the Southern battlefield, taking into account only the last two dry seasons *, the number of enemy troops put out of action amounted to 290,000 of whom 128,000 were US and satellite troops. During the previous dry season

* The dry season lasts 7 months, from October to April.

(1965-1966), out of a total of 700,000 US, puppet and satellite troops, 114,000 were put out of action by the South Viet Nam Liberation Army and guerillas. During the 1966-1967 dry season, out of a total of 1,200,000 enemy troops, 175,000 were put out of action.

In the North, from August 1964 to September 1967, more than 2,300 US aircraft were downed. Obviously, the more troops the US imperialists brought in, the heavier their failures. Though still facing further hardships and sacrifices, the Vietnamese people grow stronger as they fight on and will certainly achieve complete victory.

Why has the Vietnamese revolution achieved such great successes ? Why are the Vietnamese people bound to defeat the much more powerfully equipped US aggressors ?

This is due to *the correct leadership of the Viet Nam Workers' Party* and the South Viet Nam National Front for Liberation. The Viet Nam Workers' Party, when defining its political line, constantly tries to combine the universal truths of Marxism-Leninism with the realities of the Vietnamese revolution, while modestly learning from the valuable experiences of the fraternal parties. Our Party always sets great store by the education of cadres, Party members and the people at large so as to enhance their radically revolutionary spirit, their heroism and readiness to face sacrifices in the interest of the class and the nation. Our Party always maintains close ties with the masses. For this reason, it enjoys the people's confidence, love and support, and its line and policies are eagerly carried out by the people. Our Party has succeeded in building up a national united front against imperialism on the basis of the worker-peasant alliance. This front includes democratic parties, mass organizations, religious bodies, and various nationalities, who work together under the leadership of the Viet Nam Workers' Party to carry out the Front's common programme, build a peaceful, reunified, independent, democratic and prosperous Viet Nam.

Our Party knows how to make use of various forms of revolutionary struggle according to the concrete situations facing the movement, especially the *combination of armed struggle with political struggle, in a long, arduous and heroic people's war to defeat the aggressors.*

Our Party constantly educates cadres, Party members and the masses in *genuine patriotism and proletarian internationalism* and ceaselessly strengthens solidarity and friendship with the Soviet Union, the People's Republic of China and the other brotherly countries. Our Party advocates relying mainly on our own forces, while at the same time winning active support and assistance from the brother socialist countries and peace- and justice-loving people in the world, including progressive people in the United States.

On the strength of their own experience, the Vietnamese people are firmly confident that in the present conditions, which are favourable to the revolutionary movement, any nation, even a small one, which is closely united and resolutely fighting according to a correct political and military line, and is furthermore enjoying active support and assistance from the socialist camp and revolutionary peoples in the world, such a nation will certainly be able to defeat any imperialist aggressor, including the ring-leader, US imperialism.

*
* *

Following the path charted by the great Lenin, the path of the October Revolution, the Vietnamese people have won very great victories. That is why their attachment and gratitude to the Soviet people are most profound.

The Vietnamese people always bear in mind that their victories are inseparable from the considerable assistance of the Soviet Union, the People's Republic of China and the other brother socialist countries, inseparable from the active support of progressive people all over the world.

On the occasion of the 50th anniversary of the glorious October Revolution, on behalf on the Vietnamese people, I wish to express my profound gratitude to the Party of Lenin and to the brotherly Soviet people, who have wholeheartedly assisted our people in their resistance to US aggression, for national salvation.

Sharing the common jubilation of the working class, toiling people and oppressed peoples in the world on the occasion of the 50th anniversary of the Great October Revolution, the Vietnamese people wish the brotherly Soviet people still more brilliant achievements in the building of the material and technical basis of communism and hope that they will play an increasingly more considerable role in the struggle of the world's people against imperialism, for peace, national independence, democracy and socialism.

Long live Marxism-Leninism !

Long live the brotherly solidarity between the Vietnamese people and the Soviet people !

Long live the brotherly solidarity in the great family of socialist countries and the international communist movement·!

NEW YEAR'S GREETINGS

(Spring 1968)

Dear compatriots and fighters,

Since 1965, the US imperialists have sent in hundreds of thousands of troops to commit direct aggression against the South of our country and unleashed a war of destruction against the North. Our people, united and of one mind, are determined to fight the US aggressors and save the country, and have won many glorious victories.

By the end of 1967, the heroic armed forces and people of South Viet Nam had killed, wounded or disbanded hundreds of thousands of US, puppet and satellite troops.

The heroic armed forces and people of the North have shot down over 2,680 US aircraft.

This year, the US aggressors have been driven further into passivity and confusion, while our armed forces and people, carried forward by the impetus of their successes, are sure to win still greater victories.

On the occasion of the New Year, on behalf of our countrymen and fighters, I wish to send my greetings to the brother socialist countries, friendly countries and the people of the whole world, including American progressive people, who have wholeheartedly supported our people's just struggle.

I hope that Vietnamese nationals living abroad will make new efforts and achieve new progress in the new year.

To the people and fighters in the whole country, I send
these New Year's greetings:

> *This spring outshines the previous ones,*
> *News of victory rejoices the whole country.*
> *South and North emulate each other in fighting*
>   *the US aggressors,*

> *Forward!*
> *Complete victory will be ours!*

APPEAL ON THE OCCASION OF JULY 20, 1968

Dear compatriots and fighters throughout the country,

Fourteen years ago, following our great victory at Dien Bien Phu, the Geneva Agreements were signed, recognizing the independence, sovereignty, unity and territorial integrity of the Vietnamese nation. Our people should have had general elections in July 1956. Our country should have been completely independent, free, peaceful and reunified. North and South should have been reunited.

Yet the warlike US imperialists, breaking their own pledge, have openly sabotaged the Geneva Agreements. They rigged up the traitorous puppet administration and launched a war of aggression in the South of our country. But they have run into the extremely heroic resistance of our compatriots and fighters in the South and have suffered heavy setbacks. In an attempt to get out of their passive posture in the quagmire of South Viet Nam, for over three years now, they have frantically bombed and shelled the North. They undermine the independence, peace, neutrality of Laos and continually use threats and provocations against the Kingdom of Cambodia.

The US war of aggression in our country is a most cruel war in human history. The US aggressors wrongly believe that with over one million troops, including over half a million US troops, and with the use of modern weapons, they can subdue our people. But the truth is quite the opposite. Our heroic compatriots and fighters in the South and the heroic Vietnamese people as a whole have resolutely risen up, millions to a man, and fought with the utmost bravery, defeating all enemy military and political plans and winning ever greater victories.

Since early 1968, the war of resistance in the South has reached a new stage: our compatriots and fighters in the South have launched a general offensive and concerted uprisings in the cities and achieved glorious exploits which have shaken the United States itself and the whole world. The founding of the *Alliance of National, Democratic and Peace Forces* is a great success of the policy of uniting all the people against the US aggressors for national salvation. It helps expose the true face of the US aggressors and the traitors and isolate them even further. In the North, over three thousand US aircraft have been shot down. Thus, "both South and North are fighting well." The US imperialists are sustaining bigger and bigger defeats, and are doomed to complete failure.

However, "the leopard does not change his spots"; the US aggressors are still very stubborn. In the South, they go on intensifying the war, savagely bomb the cities and destroy whole areas in the countryside, while carrying out frantic raids against the southern provinces of the North.

At the Paris talks, in face of our serious attitude and just stand, they still brazenly demand "reciprocity" in a most absurd manner. It is obvious that the US imperialists have not given up their criminal war of aggression, and still try to cling to the South of our country with a view to perpetuating the division of our fatherland.

Confronted with such a grave situation, the people of our whole country must all the more persevere in and step up the resistance to US aggression, for national salvation. For the sake of independence and freedom, our 31 million people are resolved to overcome all hardships and sacrifices, determined to fight and win. The US aggressors are driven further into passivity and are facing more failures. They find themselves in a tight corner. The armed forces and people of our whole country are holding the initiative and acting on the offensive; the more they fight, the greater their victories.

Our compatriots and fighters in the South, closely and broadly united under the glorious banner of the National Front for Liberation, will certainly fight even harder and win even greater victories.

Our compatriots and fighters in the North must constantly heighten their vigilance, fight · valiantly, emulate one another in production work, defeat the enemy's war of destruction, be ready to smash all their new schemes of escalation, and give wholehearted assistance to our Southern kinsmen, thus fulfilling the task of the great rear area toward the great fighting front.

North and South are of one mind. Our entire people will resolutely resist and defeat the US aggressors so as to liberate the South, defend the North, and advance toward peaceful national reunification.

Our people cherish peace, but genuine peace only comes with real independence and freedom. Our position is very just and clear : the day the US imperialists end their war of aggression against our country, end the bombing of the North, withdraw all US and satellite troops from South Viet Nam and let our people freely settle our internal affairs, that day peace will be restored. This is the desire of our people and also of progressive people in America and peace- and justice-loving people in the world. The only way to restore peace is to achieve the total withdrawal of US and satellite troops. Viet Nam for the Vietnamese !

Dear compatriots and fighters,

The Vietnamese people are waging the greatest war of resistance in their history. For the sake of the independence and freedom of the Fatherland, in the interest of the socialist camp, the oppressed peoples and progressive mankind, we are fighting and defeating the most cruel enemy of humanity. In our land a fierce struggle is taking place between justice and injustice, between civilization and barbarity. The people of the brother socialist countries and progressive people all over the world are turning their eyes toward Viet Nam and warmly congratulating our compatriots and fighters. On behalf of the Vietnamese people, I take this opportunity to extend our sincere thanks to the brother socialist countries and all our friends on the five continents who have given wholehearted assistance to our people in our sacred resistance against US aggression, for national salvation.

Our people are very heroic. Our line is most correct. We have justice on our side. We are inspired by an unbending will and determination to fight and win. We have the invincible force of the unity of our entire people and enjoy the sympathy and support of all progressive mankind.

The US imperialists are sure to be defeated !

Our people are sure to be victorious !

Compatriots and fighters in the whole country,
                              march forward !

ON THE
OCCASION OF THE NEW SCHOOL YEAR
(October 1968)

My dear friends and children,

At the beginning of this fourth school year of the war of resistance against US aggression, for national salvation, I wish to convey my greetings to all of you.

Although our whole country is at war, our educational work is developing more rapidly and more vigorously than ever before.

I am glad to hear that in spite of difficult circumstances, there are now in the North of our country about 12,000 general-education schools, each village having a primary school, many villages having junior secondary ones, and every district having at least one senior secondary school. The number of school-goers has risen to over six million, including over one million cadres, workers and peasants attending spare-time classes. The number of those admitted to universities and secondary vocational schools has nearly trebled compared with the figure before the anti-US war began. Over thirty higher-education establishments and 200 secondary vocational schools have worked in close co-ordination with various branches and local authorities for the rapid training of cadres, in regular schools as well as in spare-time classes.

All the schools have made great efforts in the emulation movement to teach well and learn well, ensure safety for teachers and pupils, and gradually improve their material and spiritual life.

In spite of furious US air attacks against the North we have defeated the aggressors not only on the political and military fronts, but also on the front of education and cadre training.

This is because our Party has a correct line, because our armed forces and people are very heroic, and also because all of you in the schools have striven together to overcome many difficulties and fulfil your tasks well.

I take this opportunity to congratulate all of you on your efforts and the results you have achieved.

However, the US imperialists are very stubborn. Our revolution still has to overcome many difficulties and hardships before achieving complete victory. At present, the Party and the people are entrusting you with even greater tasks. So I should like to remind you of the following things:

— Teachers and pupils should constantly heighten their love of the Fatherland and socialism, foster revolutionary feelings toward workers and peasants, show absolute loyalty to the revolutionary cause, have full confidence in the leadership of the Party, be ready to fulfil any tasks given by the Party and the people, and make ceaseless efforts to be worthy of our heroic compatriots in the South.

— The emulation movement to teach well and learn well should be continued even in the most difficult circumstances. On the basis of good political and ideological education, you should try to raise the standards of cultural and technical education so as to help provide practical solutions to the problems posed by our revolution and, in a not-too-distant future, scale the high peaks of science and technology.

— All of you should work jointly to improve the organization and management of the material and spiritual life in the schools and ensure better health and security for everyone.

The tasks of the teachers are very important and very glorious.

Education is the work of the masses. Socialist democracy should be fully developed. Truly good relations and close unity should be achieved among teachers, between teachers and pupils, among pupils, among cadres of various levels and between the school and the people, in order to fulfil this task successfully.

Education is aimed at training continuators for the great revolutionary cause of our Party and people. Therefore all branches and all Party and administrative authorities should show more interest in this work. They should look after the schools in every respect, and push our educational work forward.

I look forward to hearing of new achievements from you.

We shall win!

APPEAL TO THE NATION

(November 3, 1968)

Fellow-countrymen and fighters all over the country,
Under the impact of the great victories won by our
armed forces and people in both zones, especially in the
South since early spring this year, the United States
government was forced on Nov. 1st, 1968 to end unconditionally its bombing and shelling on the whole territory
of the Democratic Republic of Viet Nam.

Indeed, four years of incredibly heroic fighting of our
armed forces and people have yielded tremendous results:
more than 3,200 aircraft shot down, hundreds of war
vessels, big and small, set on fire, the US war of destruction
against the North of our country brought to nothing.

This is a victory of momentous significance for our
people's great resistance against American aggression, for
national salvation.

The American imperialists had mistakenly expected
that the savage destructive power of their bombs and
shells would weaken the North, prevent the flow of
support from the great rear area to the great fighting
front and impair the fighting strength of the South. In
fact, in the course of the fight against the American
aggressors, the all-round strength of the North has never
ceased growing, and its wholehearted assistance to the
liberation struggle of our valiant Southern fellow-countrymen has been maintained. Similarly, our Southern

compatriots' unity, force, and successes have been increasing as their struggle against US aggression grows in intensity.

Our victory can be ascribed to our Party's sound revolutionary line, our people's fervent patriotism, the strength of their oneness of mind and determination to win, and our fine socialist regime. It goes to the common credit of our armed forces and people in both zones, South and North. It is also a victory won by the people of the fraternal socialist countries and our friends on the five continents.

On this occasion, on behalf of the Party and the Government, I warmly praise our fellow-countrymen and fighters all over the country, and sincerely thank the fraternal socialist countries, friendly countries far and near, and the world peoples, including the progressives in the USA, for their great help and for their sympathy and support.

Dear fellow-countrymen and fighters,

We have defeated the war of destruction of the American imperialists in the North. But this is only an initial victory. The American imperialists are very obdurate and perfidious. They talk of "peace" and "negotiation" but still harbour dark aggressive designs. More than a million American, puppet and satellite troops are still daily committing untold crimes against our Southern compatriots.

Therefore, the sacred duty of our entire people at present is to stiffen our determination to fight and win, our resolve to liberate the South, defend the North and ultimately achieve peaceful national reunification.

So long as a single aggressor remains on our soil, we must continue our fight and wipe him out.

Let our gallant Southern people and fighters, under the glorious banner of the South Viet Nam National Front for

Liberation, stage uninterrupted offensives and uprisings and resolutely advance towards complete victory.

Let the Northern armed forces and people bend all their efforts in patriotic emulation to build socialism and fulfil their duty towards their Southern kinsmen, constantly sharpen their watchfulness, practise self-reliance, increase their strength and preparedness, and frustrate all new schemes of the enemy.

We are confident that our people's resistance to American aggression, for national salvation, will enlist ever growing sympathy, support and help from the peoples of the fraternal countries and all over the world, including progressive Americans.

After nearly a hundred years under the yoke of colonial servitude and more than twenty years of resistance against imperialist aggressive wars, our people, more than any other people hold peace which is so badly needed for national construction deep in their hearts. But this must be genuine peace in independence and freedom.

That is why we firmly insist that:

— The United States government put an end to its war of aggression against Viet Nam and definitively abstain from all encroachments on the sovereignty and security of the Democratic Republic of Viet Nam;

— All American and satellite troops be withdrawn from South Viet Nam;

— The internal affairs of the South be settled by the Southern people themselves in accordance with the Political Programme of the South Viet Nam National Front for Liberation, without foreign interference;

— The question of the reunification of Viet Nam be settled by the people of the two zones, South and North, free from foreign intervention.

Dear fellow-countrymen and fighters,

Many hardships and sacrifices still lie ahead, but our people's great resistance against American aggression and for national salvation, is progressing at a brisk pace toward victory. The Fatherland is calling on us to march vigorously forward to defeat the American aggressors completely!

The American imperialists will certainly be defeated!

Our people will undoubtedly win!

NEW YEAR'S GREETINGS
(Spring 1969)

Dear compatriots and fighters,

1968 was a year of glorious victories for our armed forces and people in the whole country. The US imperialists have been forced to end unconditionally the war of destruction against the North.

Since the early spring of 1968, the heroic people and fighters in the South have carried out continual attacks and uprisings and have won many brilliant successes.

It is certain that the US aggressors will be completely defeated. Our armed forces and people in the whole country, carried forward by the momentum of their successes, will certainly win complete victory.

On the occasion of the new year, 1969, on behalf of the people of our whole country, I wish to send my warm greetings and thanks to the brother socialist countries, friendly countries and peace- and justice-loving people in the world, including progressive people in America, who have wholeheartedly supported and aided the Vietnamese people in their resistance to the US aggressors, for national salvation.

I cordially wish my compatriots, fighters, cadres, the Chinese residents living in both zones, South and North, of our country, and Vietnamese nationals living abroad, a new year of *unity, struggle and victory*. And here are a few lines to greet the new spring :

Last year we won brilliant successes.
This year still greater victories will surely be
ours on the front.
For the sake of Independence and Freedom,
Let us fight till the Americans quit and the
puppets topple.
Forward! Fighters and compatriots,
North and South reunited, can it be a happier
spring?

ELEVATE REVOLUTIONARY ETHICS, MAKE A CLEAN SWEEP OF INDIVIDUALISM*

(Feb. 3, 1969)

Our people usually say : The Party members go in front, the people follow behind. This is a sincere praise for Party members and cadres.

After 39 years of glorious struggle, having brought the August Revolution to triumph and the first war of resistance to victory, and at present fighting against the US aggressors to save the country while building social-ism in the North, our people are confident that our Party's leadership is very clearsighted and has led our nation continually from victory to victory. In the Party's history of struggle and in its daily activities, especially on the fighting and production fronts, numerous cadres and Party members have displayed great valour and exemplary conduct. They are always the first to face hardships and the last to claim rewards, and have been credited with great achievements.

Our Party has brought up a revolutionary young generation of boys and girls full of zeal and courage in fulfilling every task.

Those are beautiful flowers of revolutionary heroism. Our people and our Party are very proud of such merito-rious sons and daughters.

* Written on the 39th founding anniversary of the Viet Nam Workers' Party — Feb. 3, 1969. *(Ed.)*

However, besides those good comrades, there are still a few cadres and Party members whose morality and quality are still low.

They are burdened with *individualism* and always think of their own interests first. Their motto is not "each for all" but "all for me."

Because of their individualism, they flinch from hardships and difficulties and sink into corruption, depravation, waste and luxury. They crave for fame and profits, positions and power. They are proud and conceited, look down on the collective, hold the masses in contempt, act arbitrarily and tyrannically. They are cut off from the masses and from realities, and are affected by bureaucratism and commandism. They make no efforts to improve themselves and don't seek to improve their ability through study.

Because of their *individualism,* too, they provoke disunity, and lack a sense of organization, discipline, and responsibility. They do not carry out correctly the line and policies of the Party and the State, and harm the interests of the revolution and the people.

In short, *individualism* is the source of many wrongdoings.

In order to turn all our cadres and Party members into meritorious revolutionary fighters, our Party should strive to imbue them with the ideals of Communism, the Party's line and policies, the tasks and morals of Party members. Criticism and self-criticism should be seriously practised in the Party. Frank criticism of cadres and Party members by the people should be welcomed and encouraged. The life of the Party cell should follow the rules. Party discipline should be just and strict. Party control should be rigorous.

Every cadre and Party member should place the interests of the revolution, the Party and the people above everything. They must resolutely make a clean sweep of *individualism*, elevate *revolutionary* morals, foster the collective spirit, and the sense of solidarity, organization and discipline. They must keep in constant touch with realities and in close contact with the masses. They must truly respect and develop the collective sovereignty of the people. They must study and train hard, and seek to improve their knowledge so as to fulfil their tasks well.

The above is a practical way to observe the anniversary of the founding of our Party, the great Party of our heroic working class and people. It is also a necessary thing to do in order to help all cadres and Party members advance and make greater contributions to the complete victory of the resistance against US aggression, for national salvation, and the successful building of socialism.

APPEAL
ON THE OCCASION OF JULY 20, 1969

Dear fighters and compatriots throughout the country !

Fifteen years ago, after the glorious victory of Dien Bien Phu, the Geneva Agreements on Viet Nam recognized our people's fundamental rights — independence, sovereignty, unity and territorial integrity. These agreements provided for the holding of free general elections in July 1956 to reunify the whole of Viet Nam.

But the US imperialists have impudently sabotaged the Geneva Agreements, carried out aggression against our country, and unleashed the most atrocious colonial war in human history.

Throughout the past fifteen years, our armed forces and people in the whole country, united as one man, braving all sacrifices and hardships, have fought with sublime heroism against US aggression to save the country. The US imperialists' aggressive plans have gone bankrupt one after another, they have suffered heavier and heavier setbacks ; our people have gone from success to success, and are sure to win total victory.

The armed forces and people in the North have defeated the US aggressors' war of destruction.

The armed forces and people in the South are defeating the US "limited war"

Since the spring of the year Mau Than, the situation has radically changed in our favour, to the disadvantage of the enemy. Four-fifths of South Viet Nam's territory with three-quarters of its population have been liberated. In these conditions of victory, the South Viet Nam Congress of People's Representatives met and unanimously elected the Provisional Revolutionary Government of the Republic of South Viet Nam and the Advisory Council. This Government has been promptly recognized by over twenty fraternal and friendly countries, and warmly hailed by the people of the world.

Betraying the American people's interests, President Nixon has continued to step up the war of aggression in the southern part of our country, intensified attacks by B. 52's and toxic chemicals, launched frenzied air bombings to destroy our villages and cities and massacre our compatriots, perpetrating new crimes of utmost barbarity.

Nixon is carrying out a scheme for "de-Americanization" of the war in an attempt to use puppet troops to fight the South Vietnamese people.

At the Paris Conference, the US imperialists have stubbornly put forward extremely absurd demands, and refused to discuss seriously the reasonable and logical 10-point overall solution advocated by the National Front for Liberation and the Provisional Revolutionary Government of the Republic of South Viet Nam.

Nixon plans to withdraw 25,000 US troops in an attempt to appease American and world public opinion. This is a trick.

The Vietnamese people firmly demand the withdrawal of all US and satellite troops; not the withdrawal of 25,000 or 250,000 or 500,000 men, but a total, complete, unconditional withdrawal. Only in this way will it be possible to retrieve the honour of the United States, and to avoid a useless death in South Viet Nam for hundreds of thousands of young Americans, and suffering and mourning for hundreds of thousands of American families.

After the total withdrawal of the US and satellite troops and the complete liberation of South Viet Nam from foreign invasion, the Provisional Coalition Government, as provided for in the 10-point overall solution, will organize free and democratic general elections to enable the South Vietnamese people to determine themselves their own political regime, elect a Constituent Assembly, work out a Constitution, and set up the official Coalition Government of South Viet Nam without any foreign country being allowed to interfere. So long as US troops and the puppet administration remain in existence in South Viet Nam, really free and democratic general elections will be absolutely impossible.

The defeat of the US imperialists is already evident, yet they have not given up their evil design of clinging to the southern part of our country. Our armed forces and people throughout the country, millions as one man, upholding revolutionary heroism and fearless of sacrifices and hardships, are determined to carry on and step up the war of resistance, with the firm resolve to fight and win, till the complete withdrawal of US troops and the total collapse of the puppet army and administration, in order to liberate the South, defend the North and ultimately achieve peaceful reunification of the country.

I take this opportunity to express, on behalf of the Vietnamese armed forces and people, our sincere thanks for the great support and assistance we have received from the world. I am confident that the fraternal socialist countries, all the peace- and justice-loving governments and peoples, including progressive people in the United

States, will extend increased support and assistance to the Vietnamese people's struggle against US aggression, for national salvation, till total victory is gained.

Fighters and compatriots in the whole country, march forward resolutely!

The US imperialist aggressors are doomed to defeat!

The Vietnamese people are sure to win total victory!

TESTAMENT

Even though our people's struggle against US aggression, for national salvation, may have to go through more hardships and sacrifices, we are bound to win total victory.

This is a certainty.

I intend, when that comes, to tour both South and North to congratulate our heroic fellow-countrymen, cadres and combatants, and visit old people and our beloved youth and children.

Then, on behalf of our people, I will go to the fraternal countries of the socialist camp and friendly countries in the whole world and thank them for their wholehearted support and assistance to our people's patriotic struggle against US aggression.

*
* *

Tu Fu, the famous poet of the Tang period in China, wrote : "In all times, few are those who reach the age of seventy."

This year, being seventy-nine, I can already count myself among those "few"; still, my mind has remained perfectly lucid, though my health has somewhat declined in comparison with the last few years. When one has seen more than seventy Springs, health deteriorates with one's growing age. This is no wonder.

But who can say how much longer I shall be able to serve the revolution, the Fatherland and the people ?

I therefore leave these few lines in anticipation of the day when I shall go and join Karl Marx, Lenin and other revolutionary elders ; this way, our people throughout the country, our comrades in the Party, and our friends in the world will not be taken by surprise.

First about the Party: Thanks to its close unity and total dedication to the working class, the people and the Fatherland, our Party has been able, since its founding, to unite, organize and lead our people from success to success in a resolute struggle.

Unity is an extremely precious tradition of our Party and people. All comrades, from the Central Committee down to the cell, must preserve the unity and oneness of mind in the Party like the apple of their eye.

Within the Party, to establish broad democracy and to practise *self-criticism and criticism* regularly and seriously is the best way to consolidate and develop solidarity and unity. Comradely affection should prevail.

Ours is a Party in power. Each Party member, each cadre must be deeply imbued with *revolutionary morality,* and show industry, thrift, integrity, uprightness, total dedication to the public interest and complete selflessness. Our Party should preserve absolute purity and prove worthy of its role as the leader and very loyal servant of the people.

The Working Youth Union members and our young people in general are good; they are always ready to come forward, fearless of difficulties, and eager for progress. The Party must foster their *revolutionary* *virtues* and train them to be our successors, both "red" and "expert", in the building of socialism.

The training and education of future revolutionary generations is of great importance and necessity.

Our labouring people, in the plains as in the mountains, have for generation after generation endured hardships, feudal and colonial oppression and exploitation; they have in addition experienced many years of **war.**

Yet, our people have shown great heroism, courage, enthusiasm, and industriousness. They have always followed the Party since it came into being, with unqualified loyalty.

The Party must work out effective *plans* for economic and cultural development so as constantly to *improve the life of our people.*

The war of resistance against US aggression may drag on. Our people may have to face new sacrifices of life and property. Whatever happens, we must keep firm our resolve to fight the US aggressors till total victory.

Our mountains will always be, our rivers will always
be, our people will always be;
The American invaders defeated, we will rebuild our
land ten times more beautiful.

No matter what difficulties and hardships lie ahead, our people are sure of total victory. The US imperialists will certainly have to quit. Our Fatherland will certainly be reunified. Our fellow-countrymen in the South and in the North will certainly be re-united under the same roof. We, a small nation, will have earned the signal honour of defeating, through heroic struggle, two big imperialisms — the French and the American — and of making a worthy contribution to the world national liberation movement.

About the world communist movement: Being a man who has devoted his whole life to the revolution, the more proud I am of the growth of the international communist and workers' movement, the more pained I am by the current discord among the fraternal parties.

I hope that our Party will do its best to contribute effectively to the restoration of unity among the fraternal parties on the basis of Marxism-Leninism and proletarian internationalism, in a way which conforms to both reason and sentiment.

I am firmly confident that the fraternal parties and countries will have to unite again.

About personal matters: All my life, I have served the Fatherland, the revolution and the people with all my heart and strength. If I should now depart from this world, I would have nothing to regret, except not being able to serve longer and more.

When I am gone, a grand funeral should be avoided in order not to waste the people's time and money.

*

* *

Finally, to the whole people, the whole Party, the whole army, to my nephews and nieces, the youth and children, I leave my boundless love.

I also convey my cordial greetings to our comrades and friends, and to the youth and children throughout the world.

My ultimate wish is that our entire Party and people, closely joining their efforts, will build a peaceful, reunified, independent, democratic and prosperous Viet Nam, and make a worthy contribution to the world revolution.

Hanoi, May 10, 1969
HO CHI MINH

NOTES

1. *Tours Congress :* National Congress of the French Socialist Party held in Tours (France) from December 25 to 30, 1920. Splitting of the French Socialist Party : the majority aligned themselves with the Third International (French Communist Party) and the remainder with the Second International (French Socialist Party). At this Congress, Nguyen Ai Quoc favoured the founding of the French Communist Party, the "only party struggling resolutely for the liberation of the colonial peoples". Thus, Nguyen Ai Quoc participated in the founding of the French Communist Party. He was also the first Vietnamese Communist. (P. 15).

2. *Jean Longuet :* One of the leaders of the right wing of the French Socialist Party. (P. 16).

3. *Intercolonial Union :* Organization set up in Paris in 1921 by Nguyen Ai Quoc and revolutionaries from various French colonies with the help of the French Communist Party. (P. 20).

4. *Wilson's Declaration :* Early in 1918, US President Wilson put forward a 14-point "peace" program, using alluring words, like the right to self-determination, in an attempt to deceive the peoples and diverting them from revolutionary struggle.

After the First World War, the victor countries : USA, Britain, France and a number of other countries met in Versailles (France) beginning January 18, 1919. Several delegations from oppressed peoples came to this Conference to present their claims on the strength of Wilson's Declaration.

On behalf of "a group of Vietnamese patriots" residing in France Nguyen Ai Quoc sent a *List of Claims by the Vietnamese People* to the French Parliament and to all delegations to the Versailles Conference. (P. 22).

5. *Fifth Congress of the Communist International :* held in Moscow from June 17 to July 8, 1924. It reviewed the class

struggle from 1918 to 1923 and set great store by the bolshe-vization of Communist parties. As a representative of the French Communist Party and the French colonies, Nguyen Ai Quoc attended the Congress to which he made a speech. (P. 24).

6. *Manuilski* (1883-1959) : a Presidium member of the Communist International's Executive Committee. He presented a report on the national and colonial questions before the Fifth Congress. (P. 24).

7. *Lyons Congress :* Third National Congress of the French Communist Party held in Lyons in January 1924. Main item on the agenda : struggle to consolidate the Party organizationally and ideologically. (P. 27).

8. *Incidents of 1917 in Russian barracks in France :* During the First World War, the Czarist government sent to France a Russian expeditionary corps to fight against the Germans. In 1917, these troops refused to fight for the interests of the bourgeoisie, set up Soviets, and demanded their repatriation. Fearing the spread of revolutionary ideas among its troops, the French government withdrew the Russian troops from their positions and penned them up in a concentration camp surrounded with barbed wire and guarded by colonial troops. (P. 28).

9. *United Confederation of Labour (Confédération générale des Travailleurs unitaires :* a federation of French trade-unions found-ed by revolutionary trade-unions and active in France from 1922 to 1936. The CGTU energetically worked for the restoration of trade-union unity and the defence of the vital interests of the proletariat, and sided with the French Communist Party in the struggle against fascism and war. (P. 29).

10. *Democratic Front :* In face of the danger caused by the German, Italian and Japanese fascists who were preparing for a new world war and an assault on the Soviet Union, the Com-munist parties changed their program of action and set about establishing a broad popular front against fascism and war. In Viet Nam, in July 1936, the Central Committee of the Indochinese Communist Party decided temporarily to shelf the watchwords : "Overthrow French imperialism" and "Confiscate landlords' estates for distribution to the peasants", and to set up the Indo-chinese Front against Imperialism (later renamed Indochinese Democratic Front). Comrade Nguyen Ai Quoc was then in China.

He closely followed the situation in the country and gave constant help to the Party's Central Committee in leading the movement. (P. 42).

11. *Propaganda Brigade of the Liberation Army :* founded by decision of Comrade Ho Chi Minh on December 22, 1944, from small guerilla groups operating in Cao Bang, Bac Can and Lang Son. At the start, it comprised only 34 men equipped with rudimentary weapons. It aroused in many places a movement of armed struggle which was to culminate in the August 1945 general insurrection. It was the embryo of the present Viet Nam People's Army. (P. 47).

12. *National Congress :* Convened at Tan Trao (Son Duong district, Tuyen Quang province) on August 16, 1945, by the Viet Minh National Committee, it gathered 60 delegates of political parties, mass organizations and nationalities.

The Congress adopted the Viet Minh's Ten-point Political Program and its Order for General Insurrection. It elected the National Liberation Committee which was to become the Provisional Government of the Democratic Republic of Viet Nam, with Comrade Ho Chi Minh at its head. (P. 49).

13. *Teheran Conference :* A conference of Soviet, American and British delegations held in Teheran, the capital of Iran, from November 28 to December 1, 1943. It adopted a plan to crush the Nazi armed forces, a resolution to open a second front in Europe before May 1, 1944, a resolution to ensure lasting peace in the world after the war, etc. However, the ruling circles in the USA and Britain evaded their responsibilities instead of carrying these principles into effect. (P. 56).

14. *San Francisco Conference :* 50 countries met in San Francisco from April 25 to June 26, 1945, at the convocation of the Soviet Union, the USA, Britain and Chiang Kai-shek's China. The conference set up the United Nations Organization. (P. 56).

15. *To Our Fellow-countrymen in Nam Bo before Going to France for Negotiations :* On May 31, 1946, President Ho Chi Minh went to France as an honoured guest of the French government. A delegation of the DRVN led by Comrade Pham Van Dong also went to Fontainebleau for negotiations with the French government. As these talks failed owing to the ill will of the French side, President Ho Chi Minh signed with the French government a *modus vivendi* before returning to Viet Nam (September 14, 1946) so as to create favourable conditions to prepare for the resistance. (P. 66).

16. *Lien Viet :* (Viet Nam National League) : founded on May 29, 1946, by decision of the Party and Comrade Ho Chi Minh to broaden the unity of the whole people and assemble the patriots who were not members of the Viet Minh. In 1951, it merged with the Viet Minh into the Lien Viet Front. (P. 82).

17. *Truman Doctrine :* aimed at achieving US hegemony in the world. Point Four of its program promised "aid" to the under-developed countries but was in fact meant for economic and political intervention in the internal affairs of these countries, and for turning them into US colonies. The Truman doctrine was adopted by the US Congress on June 3, 1950. (P. 121).

18. **Marshall Plan :** a plan for economic invasion put forward by US State Secretary Marshall on June 5, 1947, in the form of economic "aid" to European countries after the Second World War. A number of West European countries accepted this plan, which compelled them to give the USA the economic preroga-tives it demanded, and to cut off all trade relations with the Soviet Union and the people's democracies. The USA used the Marshall Plan to intervene in the internal affairs of the West European countries. (P. 121).

19. *Atlantic Pact :* or North Atlantic Treaty Organization (NATO). Signed on April 4, 1949, in Washington between the USA, Belgium, Canada, Denmark, France, England, Iceland, Italy, Luxemburg, Norway, the Netherlands and Portugal. In 1952, Greece and Turkey also joined in. This Pact is a military alliance led by the USA, allegedly to defend the contracting countries, but in fact to carry out the arms race, kindle a new world war, encircle and attack the Soviet Union and the socialist countries. (P. 121).

20. *Congress of the Viet Nam National United Front :* held in Hanoi from September 5 to 10, 1955. It set up the Viet Nam Fatherland Front, adopted its program and rules. The setting up of the Fatherland Front has broadened and strengthened national unity. (P. 188).

21. *Special Political Conference :* convened by President Ho Chi Minh on March 27, 1964, at the Ba Dinh Meeting Hall (Hanoi). Attending the Conference were President Ho Chi Minh, Vice-President Ton Duc Thang, Comrades Le Duan, Truong Chinh, Prime Minister Pham Van Dong, General Vo Nguyen Giap and over 300 representatives (veteran revolutionaries, public figures,

representatives of various strata of the people and branches of
activity, heroes and emulation fighters, progressive intellectuals,
patriotic personalities. (P. 277).

22. *Four-point position of the DRVN government.*

1. Recognition of the fundamental national rights of the Vietnamese people : peace, independence, sovereignty, unity and territorial integrity. According to the Geneva Agreements, the US
government must withdraw from South Viet Nam all US troops,
military personnel and weapons of all kinds, dismantle all US
military bases there, cancel its "military alliance" with Saigon.
It must end its policy of intervention and aggression in South
Viet Nam. According to the Geneva Agreements, the US government must end its war acts against the North, definitively end all
encroachments on the territory and sovereignty of the Democratic
Republic of Viet Nam.

2. Pending the peaceful reunification of Viet Nam, while Viet
Nam is still temporarily divided into two zones, the military
provisions of the 1954 Geneva Agreements on Viet Nam must
be strictly respected : the two zones must refrain from joining any
military alliance with foreign countries and there must be no
foreign military bases, troops, and military personnel on their
respective territories.

3. The affairs of South Viet Nam are to be settled by the South
Vietnamese people themselves, in accordance with the programme
of the South Viet Nam National Front for Liberation, without
any foreign interference.

4. The peaceful reunification of Viet Nam is to be settled by
the Vietnamese people in both zones, without any foreign
interference. (P. 309).

23.*Five-point position of the South Viet Nam National Front
for Liberation.*

1. The US imperialists are the saboteurs of the Geneva Agreements, the most brazen warmongers and aggressors, and the
sworn enemy of the Vietnamese people.

2. The heroic South Vietnamese people are resolved to drive
out the US imperialists in order to liberate South Viet Nam,
build an independent, democratic, peaceful and neutral South
Viet Nam and ultimately achieve national reunification.

3. The valiant South Vietnamese people and the South Viet Nam
Liberation Army are resolved to fulfil their sacred duty, which

is to drive out the US imperialists so as to liberate the South and defend the North.

4. The South Vietnamese people express their profound gratitude to the peace- and justice-loving people all over the world for their wholehearted support and declare their readiness to receive all assistance, including weapons and all other war materials, from their friends in the five continents.

5. Let our entire people unite, take up arms, continue to march forward heroically, and be resolved to fight and defeat the US aggressors and Vietnamese traitors. (P. 309).

Lightning Source UK Ltd.
Milton Keynes UK
26 August 2010
159056UK00001B/4/A